Nick Williams is a Trustee Director of the Alternatives Organization based at St James's Church, Piccadilly, a premier venue for major authors and seminar leaders. He is founder of the Heart At Work project, a consultant and trainer for a number of major public and private businesses, and is the author of the critically acclaimed *The Work We Were Born To Do* and *Unconditional Success*. He lives in London.

POWERFUL BEYOND MEASURE

POWERFUL BEYOND MEASURE

AN INSPIRING GUIDE TO PERSONAL FREEDOM

NICK WILLIAMS

BANTAM PRESS

LONDON · NEW YORK · TORONTO · SYDNEY · AUCKLAND

TRANSWORLD PUBLISHERS
61–63 Uxbridge Road, London W5 5SA
a division of The Random House Group Ltd

RANDOM HOUSE AUSTRALIA (PTY) LTD
20 Alfred Street, Milsons Point, Sydney,
New South Wales 2061, Australia

RANDOM HOUSE NEW ZEALAND LTD
18 Poland Road, Glenfield, Auckland 10, New Zealand

RANDOM HOUSE SOUTH AFRICA (PTY) LTD
Endulini, 5a Jubilee Road, Parktown 2193, South Africa

Published 2003 by Bantam Press
a division of Transworld Publishers

A catalogue record for this book is available from the British Library.
ISBN 0593 048989

Permissions granted
© Juan Ramón Jiménez, 'I am not I' (p.24)
© Diane Berke, story of the African village, from Love Always Answers, 1995 edition, The Crossroad Publishing Co. (p.28)
© Christopher Fry, A Sleep of Prisoners, first published 1951 by Oxford University Press, first issued 1971 as an Oxford
University Press paperback (p.129)
© Chuck Spezzano, 'The Snow Falls', from Psychology of Vision Light Bytes, 2003 (p.211)
© Dawna Markova, 'I Will Not Die An Unlived Life', Conari Press, 2000 (p.30)
© Robert Bly, 'Every breath taken in by the man' from The Rag and Bone Shop of the Heart,
Harper Collins, reprinted by Perennial 1993 (p.187)

Typeset in 11/16pt Sabon by
Falcon Oast Graphic Art Ltd

Printed in Great Britain by
Clays Ltd, Bungay, Suffolk

1 3 5 7 9 10 8 6 4 2

Our deepest fear is not that we are inadequate. Our deepest fear is that we are powerful beyond measure.

MARIANNE WILLIAMSON, *A Return to Love*

CONTENTS

PREFACE

Like so many people, I have always been fascinated by power. The kind of power the world worships is the power of force. I have been fascinated by the power of love, inspiration and creativity. I am fascinated by our power to transform and undo the fear, guilt and pain that is within us. I know that within myself, and I believe within everybody, is this alchemical power to gradually transform myself and my consciousness. In my favourite spiritual text, *A Course in Miracles*, this power is referred to as the *Holy Spirit* and it is the power to undo everything that isn't love. The course teaches that only the love is real. The world we see with our eyes is not the *real* world. The *real* world, it teaches, is the world of love, and the world we see is actually an illusion, based on the belief that we could be separate from the source of love, from God. In this state of separation we are asleep, and our dreams are of pain and suffering. The answer is not to try and change the dream, but to wake up. It is a very challenging thing to say, but this world is not the problem: our thinking about this world is the problem. This world is the effect of our thoughts of separation, not the cause of our pain. All power is within us to undo this illusion, and with that our pain and suffering. Every solution to every problem does exist – not as some external divine intervention, but as an internal divine expression. Whatever power any spiritual teacher has ever had is available to each of us. This is not blasphemy, but truth. I hope this book will give you some clue to this incredible power and to how to express it in your own life.

ACKNOWLEDGEMENTS

As ever, I am deeply grateful to my partner Helen for being such
fun, for her silliness and for being a fabulous partner and support
to me. To my parents Pam and Harold, for all their love and
support, and my sister Amanda. Thanks to Maurice Simons, who
sadly died as I finished this book. To my family of friends at
Alternatives, especially Steve Nobel, Tom Cook, Karen Shah and
Richard Dunkerley, also Niki Hignet and Steve Jakob. Thanks to
all in the church at St James's. Thanks to everyone at Psychology
of Vision and the transformative work they do, and especially to
David Peat for helping me through some difficult times, and Pam
Carruthers, Serenna Davies and Jaki Harris for friendship.
Continuing thanks to Juliette Pollitzer, Jan, Peter, Linda and
Catherine. Thanks to all the Dreambuilders I have met in London
and around the world. Thanks to Brian Mills for being such an
inspiration to me, and Natalie for her support. Thanks to Julia
McCutchen for our growing friendship and creative partnership.

Thanks to my editor, Brenda Kimber, and to Sadie Mayne at Transworld for the astonishing amount of time, care and energy they put into supporting me and editing the manuscript. Thanks yet again to Adam Stern, Matt Ingrams and Martin Wenner for their presence in my life over the last 10 years. Thanks to Bill Pitcher and Phyllis Holmes for friendship.

Thanks to Barbara Winter for being a wonderful friend, a great teacher and an inspiring presence in the world. Thanks to Helen Burton for all she does in South Africa, and Paul Coughlin for his support and for being a teacher to me. To Kathy Doyle and Jane Norbury. Thanks to Gill Edwards for support in surprising ways, to Karen Byrne for the wonderful acupuncture, and Irenie Barbari for great massages. Thanks again to Hergist and our family.

And finally once again for the source of and the book that is *A Course in Miracles*. It is stunning in its beauty and truth, and I hope I keep catching more glimpses of the beauty it contains.

THE NEW POWER ETHIC

One way of telling the story of human history is as the ego-based story of domination and control, of wars, winning and losing. Power has been a scarce resource, and an external commodity, and those with it have used it to subjugate those who haven't. *Dominate or be dominated* has been a theme. Yet there have always been those who have known that the greatest power is within themselves, and that if they exercise their power, nobody loses. This power is not sourced in our ego sense of our self, but from the spirit within us, which is the same spirit that is within everyone. There is enough room for us all to be powerful, indeed the world needs more *truly* powerful people. Spiritual power comes from our very being and is our capacity to influence others and knows no position and is evident in both the poor and the wealthy, in people in high and low positions.

This is power *with*, not power *over*, and is available to each of us, because of our essential spiritual nature. We exercise it with humility and compassion, not force. It is the power to educate and transform, not fight and judge, to love and inspire rather than despise and destroy. Whilst political and economic power are usually fuelled by ambition, spiritual power results from giving up ambition and surrendering oneself. Paradoxically, only by giving up ambition can we truly achieve any lasting power, but once we have spiritual power, we can exercise any other given power with greater wisdom, justice and love, and for the good of all, not the few. We realize that the true source of the power comes from a higher source, not from ourselves.

INTRODUCTION

*The secret is that love isn't about someone else loving you. It is
about your ability to love yourself and the people around you,
regardless of what the world does or doesn't give you. Love isn't
about outside proof.*

RHONDA BRITTEN, author of *Fearless Living*

YOU ARE POWERFUL, NOW

All the power, the love and prosperity we could ever want or need
has already been created, and is sitting in an incredibly safe place,
right now – inside each and every one of us. We have the richest
inheritance of all – being the loved children of a loving creator. Our
job is simply to remember this and reveal it in our lives and in the
world. We are infinitely powerful, and in complete denial of this
fact. It is our connection to the source of love that makes us powerful beyond measure, right now. Did you have lessons in love at

school or home? Most of us haven't had somebody telling us each day when we were growing up, 'Hey, you are amazing. There is such incredible power within you. We are going to teach you how to be very powerful, but not in an overwhelming way but in a loving and creative way. Your life is going to evolve wonderfully for you.' How do you think we'd have grown up if we did? Mostly we have been told that power is outside us, and that someone else has it, not us. And mostly we have been taught that power is domination, it is power over something or someone else. One way of telling the story of human history is the drive for power and domination. We have been taught that power is control, and that is how the world functions.

This book is about a different kind of power. Inside us is a stirring, a remembering of a different kind of power that doesn't involve loss or domination. We are remembering our spiritual power, the power of love. It is a power that has been equally distributed, and doesn't create winners and losers. It is about beginning to *relinquish* control in order to be truly powerful. This spiritual power comes from our very being, the essence of who we are and our capacity to influence others. It is evident in both the poor and the wealthy, in people in 'high' and in 'low' positions. It knows nothing of class, age, race or sex. It is truly available to everyone. Those who recognize it do not feel arrogant, separate or self-satisfied, but rather gain a greater humility. They feel more connected, less judgemental, they realize that the true source of the power is a higher power, not their egoistic selves. They know they are channels and vehicles. They know they have accessed something precious and special and that everyone can have access to this power. This understanding ensures their humility; they feel no superiority.

POWERFUL BEYOND MEASURE

*At the heart of each of us is a power beyond measure –
the power of love and the power of creation. This is
our true identity, it is who we are and how we were
created. We can awaken from our dream of littleness
into the truth of our spiritual greatness.*

I

OUR POWER OF TRUE IDENTITY

Everything in the universe is within you. Ask all from yourself.
Jalaluddin Rumi, 12th-century Persian mystic and poet

THE NATURE OF FEAR AND LOVE

We are here to prove that love is real, and that fear is not. Love is the only thing worth living for. We all long for something that we will love so much that we want to celebrate it. The world needs our spiritual gifts, and now is the time for us to give them. Our gifts are the expression of the love within us. Our ego is a creation of fear while our true nature is a creation of love: there are only two forces operating in life – love and fear. Each of us is incredibly powerful, and we are terrified of our power. In this book I want to help you to undo that fear, and as you do, your authentic power will naturally follow. When we take away our fear and our guilt, love is all that is left.

3

The one constant in this world is the miracle of the creator's love for us and its reflection in our human hearts. When we tap into this love, we start to live from the highest place that lies within us. We all know it is there, but we don't always know how to get and stay there. This book is about the incredible evolution that happens when we find and put this mystical power of divine love at the centre of our life, in relationships, work and friendships.

Whilst the mortal mind focuses only on the physical, the divine mind within us focuses on the spiritual. Together we will explore how we can, in practical ways, bring this power to the centre of our lives for we are here to *be* power not *get* power. We are most alive and fulfilled when we are extending and sharing ourselves, and we put ourselves on an upward spiral.

Only our fear stops us from sharing and extending the love within us. Our fear arises from the belief that we are separate and alone, that we live in a finite world, and that what we extend we will lose. There is no such thing as fear *out there*, there are only fearful thoughts and responses within our minds. This world is made of thoughts – thoughts of either the loving mind or of the fearful mind within us. Our power is in knowing that we can transform the source of thinking, from fear to love. Fear believes in danger and limits, whereas the divine mind knows only safety and limitlessness. Love stems from the knowledge and experience that we are all part of the divine mind of creation. Personally and collectively we are now being called to cross a threshold, from living in a consciousness of fear to one of love; love in our relationships, love in our work, love in our families, and love for people we don't even know. The only way we can make that transition is with divine illumination. It is as if we are in labour, giving birth to our own souls, dissolving what is unworthy in us in order for something new and higher to emerge.

FROM FEAR TO POWER

Many years ago I attended a workshop called 'The Mastery' organized by the Actors' Institute in London. One of the first exercises was to identify the physiology, the actual physical experience, of fear. Most of us agreed that it involved blood rushing around the body, the heart beating faster, flushed cheeks, etc. Then we were asked to describe sexual arousal, and guess what – it involved blood rushing around the body, the heart beating faster, and flushed cheeks! Finally we were asked to describe the experience of excitement and, amazingly, it was similar to the other two. From that I learned that the only difference between fear, excitement and arousal is a judgement, a label, and the meaning we give the experience.

Within the arena of fear is also a form of attraction. What we are afraid of, we are also drawn towards. What we are afraid of shows us where our hidden power lies. In my workshops I get people to identify what they are afraid of, and invite them to retell that story, but instead of saying, 'I am afraid of . . .' they tell each other, 'I am excited by . . .' Remarkably, as they shift their story from fear to excitement, a whole new energy opens up for them. They tell each other, 'I am really excited by starting my own business,' 'I am excited by the changes I am making!' 'I am excited about trusting my creativity more fully,' 'I am excited about leaving my job.'

EXERCISE

Do you have permission to get excited about yourself and your life, or do you think that it would be unrealistic, even childish?

Take your journal and write a list of the things you are telling yourself you are afraid of. Now rewrite that list, but in front of each one write:

I am excited by . . .

I am excited by . . .
I am excited by . . .
I am excited by . . .
I am excited by . . .
I am excited by . . .

See how you feel about this. Does it make you smile? Does it help you to feel differently, even empowered?

THE SIX TRUTHS OF LOVE

When we contact our Higher Self, the source of the power within, we tap into a reservoir of infinite power.

DEEPAK CHOPRA

* Love is the ultimate reality behind all appearances, behind all our senses. Whatever stories we tell to the contrary, love is what is always and eternally present. Love is the glue that keeps things from falling apart, even when they seem to be falling apart. This world hides the truth of love.

* Love is the heart of creation and the creator. God is only love. Love is the energy field of unconditional acceptance that we live within, and that we can never be apart from. We are always held in love despite the appearances of our life.

* We are the extension of love. We are what love is made of. Like the rays of light extending from the sun that cannot be separate from the sun, we cannot be separated from our source, even though we may believe we can be. We are profoundly sacred and precious. We are an essential creation of the universe, not a spare part.

* The ultimate and sole purpose of our life is the awakening to the love within us, to face everything unlike love in order to let it drop away, to

reveal the truth of love within us. Like a lantern in a dark tunnel, we take hold of the light to face the dark.

* We are qualified to teach love, because it is how we were created and who we are. We are not here to be more comfortable in a fearful world, but to undo fear – the thought of separation – completely. We are blessed and graced in ways that we barely comprehend.

* Love knows nothing of pain and is not the cause of pain. Love is the unlimited undoing of all pain. Pain is caused by *need* not by love, and need is of our ego, our separated sense of self. Love is full and complete within itself and lacks nothing. In essence, we are complete.

This earth is a place of forgetting, a physical place where we seem limited by bodies, shortages, conflicts, death, hatred and loneliness. This earth is a place where we are in collective amnesia and trance. We have succumbed to lack and scarcity thinking, we have fallen into the belief in separation. We have traded our birthright of grandeur and true power for paltry trinkets. We get by, we compete and survive. Yet this is a place where we have come to remember who we really are. We are not here to live in darkness, but to awaken to our nature. Love is not simply an emotion, but the ever present Presence of the divine, and is our *own* presence. We can *feel* distant and removed, but in truth we are never truly isolated. We are held safely even when we don't know it. We are all gods and goddesses in embryo, and when we awaken to the truth of us, we begin a truly heroic journey. Each of us has come with the bold goal of bringing a piece of heaven to earth. When we grow in awareness we let go of the past, of old conditioning, and begin being in the present moment. We begin to realize that the best thing that can ever happen to us is happening to us now.

WHAT IS LOVE?

Many of us have experienced love as an emotion, or a preference. Our love can range from 'I love this dress or this football team' to 'I love sex', 'I love my partner' or 'I love God'. A preference is not love. Real love is firstly fostering our own growth, and as we do so we want to foster the growth of others too. Love naturally overflows and wants to extend itself. Love is what helps us give birth to ourselves, to discover what we can be and become. Through love we explore the mysterious depths of our own being, and discover our own soul.

One of the most powerful ways we love is by accepting, which is not the same as condoning. True acceptance is the release of judgements, and the acceptance of what love is. Love is not trying to change anyone or anything: it is accepting them as they are. Although this may make us feel like we are being trapped with much that we don't want, in essence it is merely a move towards growth and maturity, and learning to accept with compassion and without judgement.

MOTIVATED BY LOVE, MOTIVATED BY FEAR

There is no greater illusion than fear, no greater wrong than preparing to defend yourself, no greater misfortune than having an enemy. Whoever can see through all fear will always be safe.
Tao Te Ching

Love is the ever present power of creation within all of us right now, and it is only fear that tells us to stay where we are in order to be safe, encouraging us not to change. Fear tells us that to be safe, we need to build new and bigger defences against the dangers of life. In fact, we may feel safer behind our barricades, but may feel dead. Indeed, the thing that causes us most pain is resistance to change, not change itself. Beyond our fear is the miracle of mystery, of new beginnings, new life, unexpected creativity and exciting uncharted territories. We can discover that we are under universal laws not earthly ones.

Often when we choose to be a force for love in our life, we encounter resistance within ourselves. We may hesitate, or rationalize why we shouldn't. We may get into a fight with someone, or get involved in some other distraction that hinders our progress. These are our unconscious fears rising, our hidden resistance. Playing a bigger game for love means loving ourselves more. Our power comes from connecting with others, not being distant from them. We have the leverage to lift a great weight when we are close to it, while it gets harder to lift the further back we get. The same with people – the closer we get, the more powerful we become.

WE ARE ALL MYSTICS

Evolution is healing until we realize our wholeness . . . Every problem set before us is a lesson we are called upon to learn in order to step forward. The courageous, the visionaries leap forward. Where we read pages, they read chapters. Where visionaries read chapters, masters read books, while the enlightened are living bridges between Heaven and Earth.

DR CHUCK SPEZZANO, author and teacher

Love is teaching us all the time, it is our inner teacher on the journey of learning to trust ourselves in freedom, creativity and joy. It shows us where we are stuck, where we are caught in fear, in guilt, in holding on. It is the endless undoing of all our mistaken thinking. Love calls us to release ourselves from the small sense of ourselves and step into a greater sense. We are the ocean pretending to be a drop. Little by little by little we learn to listen to, follow and trust that inner voice of love, the unshakeable guide within us, which the mystic poet Rumi calls 'The Beloved' and the poet Kabir calls 'The Friend'.

MOMENTS OF INSIGHT

Often we have moments or periods of time when we awaken, when our awareness shifts, times of initiation when we open up to a new level of consciousness. Back in my computer salesman days I won a four-day skiing trip to Saalbach in Austria with a group of my work colleagues. We had a great time, playing and drinking hard, but this trip coincided with the beginning of my work in psycho-therapy back in London, and I was on a real growth path, so I had a split personality. I was the tough computer salesman to them, and the soft spiritual person with myself. I had taken away with me a copy of *Out on a Limb* by Shirley MacLaine, and was enjoying it. As I was reading a particular chapter, I suddenly had the thought 'I've been here before! My problems are not just of this lifetime. This life of mine is a snapshot of a bigger picture!' That insight was the start of my spiritual journey and my real interest began to shift from externals alone to inner worlds.

LOVE IS INSPIRATION

What we love inspires us, and to be inspired is to be infused with love. To be inspired means to be infused with the divine. When we are inspired, we transcend our limited sense of identity and stand on the higher ground of spiritual consciousness. When we are inspired we are no longer *us*, we are taken beyond ourselves. *Who are you when you are inspired?* When we are inspired, ideas, having set off from another place, bubble up within us and rise to the surface of our consciousness. We are blessed by our own inner universe.

Inspiration awakens the secret life of our soul; awakening our sleeping greatness, creating a new shoreline where our invisible and visible worlds meet. We are carried forward to the higher ground of awareness and understanding. We are called to bring to life faculties, talents and gifts that have lain dormant within us. In essence, inspiration is as necessary for our emotional and spiritual health as food and drink are for our physical well-being.

Through inspiration, our limits and the prison we have created inside become the thresholds of new life. We are courageous when we are willing to dwell at these thresholds. Old hardened thinking gives way to tender new shoots. What may have seemed like a place of death can become a place of birth of new mystery, potential and promise. Our imagination thaws and our world renews and begins to flow. Inside every prison we have made for ourselves, inspiration is longing to lead us to immeasurable blessings. Where our mortal mind only sees problems and difficulties in the world, our soul only sees opportunity and new worlds waiting to be born. Here is a poem I wrote about this:

Behind every conflict is a peace waiting to be born
Behind every law is Truth waiting to be born
Behind every scarcity is an abundance waiting to be born
Behind every loneliness is a love waiting to be born
Behind every guilt is an innocence waiting to be born
Behind every boredom is creativity waiting to be born
Behind every harshness is a tenderness waiting to be born
Behind every pain is a comfort waiting to be born
Behind every sadness is a joy waiting to be born
Behind every misunderstanding is a gift waiting to be born
Behind every hatred is forgiveness waiting to be born
Behind every insult is a blessing waiting to be born
Behind every darkness is the light of heaven waiting to be born
When we are willing

WE SHOULDN'T BE ASHAMED TO IMMERSE OURSELVES IN INSPIRATION

A recent article in the journal of the Chartered Management Institute gave the results of some research into leadership qualities. It reported, 'The most striking absence is that of inspiration. While over half the managers reported see this as one of the most important qualities in a leader, only a tiny proportion (11%) experience this in their daily working lives.' We no longer want remote leaders, but leaders who engage. *We* want to be engaged more fully in our own lives. Our inspiration is what engages us. Often we can be harsh on ourselves, wondering why we can't just be content with a secure job and material things. We can never be deeply fulfilled by those alone. We must have our soul engaged somewhere in our life.

Sometimes we need to start to immerse ourselves in the inspiration of others in order to awaken, nurture and discover our own sense of inspiration. I spent eight years immersing myself in the teaching of others before I felt I was ready to find my own voice, my own wisdom. We all have wisdom in us, and our unique ways of expressing universal truths.

We all have an imprint in our soul, the instructions for what would make us happy and would lead us to our deepest fulfilment. The instruction manual is the intuition within us, the signpost is our joy and inspiration. Sometimes the blueprint is close to the surface, sometimes it lies buried deep within us.

Inspiration can make everything new. With inspiration, when we make love it can feel like the first time; we see a lover with new eyes; a talk we've given dozens of times can excite us as much as ever. With inspiration, even chores can become joys and we know that there are greater forces at work in our life, unseen hands that are guiding and orchestrating our lives in beautiful ways, weaving delicate plans for us to enjoy.

FROM GETTING LOVE TO BEING LOVE

In this world of ego and separation, we struggle to find the love, approval and acceptance which we think we need. We are taught how to be attractive to employers, to the opposite sex, how to manipulate and distort to buy love and get love. When our ego gets hold of power, someone must lose. But we need to recognize a new, truer starting point. What we aren't taught is that *we are love, it is how we were created*. Within our own depths is already wholeness, fullness and divine love. The great Vedic texts of India, the Upanishads, remind us: 'In bliss and love, these creatures are born. In bliss and love, they are sustained. In bliss, they return.' Behind the world we experience with our body's senses is a silent and invisible backdrop of love. Love has dominion over everything. In our blind attempts to find love, we may fail to recognize the love that is around us and in our life right now. The universe operates through dynamic exchange. Giving and receiving are different aspects of the flow of energy in the universe. And in our willingness to give that which we seek, we open the doors to the abundance of the universe circulating in our lives. The universal principle is 'To have all, give all to all.'

Each of us is love in essence, and this is the source of our true power. Through putting love at the centre of our lives, ordinary people can experience extraordinary lives. Love is the play of the divine. It transforms our awareness from separation to unity. This book is about finding that love within us, and as we do, allowing and supporting our natural desire to extend that love. It reflects the deepest longing of the human heart as it searches for the divine. As we move towards the love and light within us, it is inevitable that this will lead to a longing for meaningful relationships and creative work. All our exploring is our attempt to discover the love that we are. As Deepak Chopra tells us, 'Love is the experience of unity consciousness; the animating force that sustains me is the same force that sustains you.'

LOVE IS OUR POWER OF PRESENCE

We have an immense presence, which is rooted in unseen worlds. We are not accidents: we have been created for a purpose and our existence in the universe is planned and needed. Our existence is significant. Whole universes are hidden within us, new frontiers and unbelievable gifts and energies. Our presence mirrors other worlds. There is something deeply sacred in each of us, mysteries abound within us and our presence holds the secret code of our past and our future potential. We have an unconditional value that goes beyond usefulness and when we exercise power without reverence we easily create violence and imbalance. Reverence is the appreciation of the sacred. It is holy perception, seeing through appearances and the shell into the essence.

Our functioning mind sees us and others in terms of usefulness and has become expert in using people and nature efficiently for our own ends. This eats into the respect we need for each other and for life. Our obsession with efficiency and functionalism needs to be balanced with reverence for all things and all people. We lament the loss of soul and the divine in modern life, but they haven't gone away; we have simply become numbed and have desensitized ourselves to the awareness of their presence. We are asleep to enchantment and need to be awoken to the living presence of life.

We are asleep to the incredible power of our own divine nature, and we must wake up. This book will give you ideas and simple strategies to reawaken this enormous power in all areas of your life. In doing so we need a great sense of humour. As well as being so powerful within our very being, we are, in our humanness, fragile, vulnerable and funny. I remember seeing a cartoon of two

Daleks from *Dr Who* at the bottom of some stairs, and the balloon above one read, 'There goes our plan to conquer the universe!' I still feel so powerless when I have trouble getting my laptop repaired and fly into a rage of powerlessness when I deal with my local government authority about council tax! But part of the amazing journey of being a spiritual being on a human journey is to live with the paradoxes of life. Often we feel so weak and vulnerable: we can have such visions for our life and the world, and can trip at the bottom of the stairs! Most of us have had a pretty thorough training in victimhood and powerlessness, so part of the journey into our authentic power is recognizing all the broken, hurt and disempowered parts of us, of which there are many. Love can embrace all.

OUR FEAR OF OUR OWN POWER

We are unaware of how powerful we are, and I think we are often terrified of how powerful we are. Jesus told us 'These things and more you shall do too.' *A Course in Miracles* teaches us, 'Miracles enable you to heal the sick and raise the dead because you made sickness and death yourself, and can therefore abolish both. You are a miracle, capable of creating in the likeness of your Creator.' The Buddha taught us that Buddha nature is within us. One great fear we have about reclaiming our own true power is that we fear we will fall into some trap within it. We fear being grandiose, claiming power for ourselves that is actually delusional. Below is a list of fears that our ego creates to stop us reclaiming our true power. See which ones you can relate to and add your own:

EXERCISE

If I am more powerful I will:

* *be rejected*
* *become a tyrant*
* *delude myself*
* *go on an ego trip*
* *go mad*
* *destroy everything*
* *become corrupt*
* *be unlovable*
* *trust no-one*
* *become distant*

Add your own thoughts to this list.

Instead of seeing our power as a blessing, we have created great fear around it, and it almost seems that we have been deliberately educated to believe we are not powerful. We have the unlimited power of the universe within us, and so does everyone else, so it is actually no big deal at all! It's nothing to take personal credit for, or feel guilty about or afraid of, because our real power emanates from a force that is in us but not of us.

POWER THAT CREATES CLOSENESS

The traditional pattern of power is to establish some dominance over people, directing their behaviour and having control over the rewards and punishments for their behaviour. Power is something we operate at a distance, not close up and personal. So one of the great myths that our ego creates is that when we are powerful and successful we will be separated from others, and will become distant. Part of us may want to be special and set apart. But it is important to recognize that the greatest power we have is the power to connect with others.

A popular image of a leader is a godlike figure who is feared or revered, or both – the commander. We see this in world leaders, who carry burdens of responsibility and are somewhat distant. They appear to lead from the front. However, the most powerful leaders often lead from behind, and although it might sound contradictory, we can't lead people unless they are willing to follow. So we must inspire them to trust us with their well-being. This trust comes about when we bring to the surface their own sense of self-worth and creativity. We need to get *beneath* them, to understand them and become familiar with their strengths and weaknesses, not to exploit them but to support and encourage them. This requires contact, not distance. To be a servant leader requires a lot more courage because it means risking knowing and being known. This requires true humility, not a quality in which most managers are trained. No-one feels oppressed. On the contrary, people feel you really understand them. One of the greatest powers is the ability to create true rapport and resonance with people. We can have a resonance with someone on the other side of the world, whom we have never met, when we know the story and experience of their life.

Too often we only see a skewed picture because we are too far away from the real action. We can let go of the ego myth idea of the leader and truly join with people, serving, following and leading all at the same time. When we can be humble enough and powerful enough to let others take credit, yet still know the contribution we have made, we are truly powerful. We become almost invisible leaders when people are aware of their effort, not ours. This is not manipulation, but mastery. We are resources for our people, not vice versa. We can accept a leadership role without the limelight if we can trust people, get them the resources they need, be a resource ourselves.

POWER WITH EASE, NOT FORCE

I read an interview with British athlete Roger Bannister, the first man to run the mile in less than four minutes. We are taught that to achieve things of value we have to push and force ourselves beyond limits, yet as he described it, breaking that record was actually *easy*. 'No longer conscious of my movement, I discovered a new unity with nature. I had found a new source of power and beauty, a source I never dreamed existed before.' He moved from force to true and authentic power. Within himself he found a new energy source that had always been there but that he hadn't connected to before. His success was less reliant on physical effort, and was achieved through reaching a new level of consciousness. In essence, he got out of his own conscious way and let a greater force, power and intelligence work within him. He forgot the 2,000 years of human limitation and the belief that what he was doing was impossible, and just did it! What was even more amazing was the ripple effect that his triumph had. Having been impossible for 2,000 years, this feat was achieved within months by many people. Once one man had shown his power, thousands of others were inspired to do the same and find their power.

Recently I shared a speaking platform with Penny Mallory, rally car champion and TV presenter. She described how she and her navigator were marooned in deep mud in one rally, miles from anywhere and with no-one available to help. On the verge of giving up, she explained how she decided to have one last go at lifting the three-ton rally car out of the mud. She was quite embarrassed to explain that she actually did it: she managed to lift a car that was physically impossible for her to lift. She had no rational explanation for how she did it, but she did it, accessing a power that was 'impossible'.

There is something within us more than our limited ego sense of ourselves. Rudolf Steiner, pioneer of new educational methods, said, 'If we do not develop within ourselves this deeply rooted feeling that there is something higher than ourselves, we shall never find the strength to evolve to something higher.' But this power is not higher than ourselves, it is our true self and is within us right now. We are simply in a state of forgetting. Our job is not to curse the darkness, but turn on the light – our own light.

SO MUCH EVIDENCE

Quantum physicists are now telling us that subatomic particles only come into being *as and when we look for them*. Our attention and focus literally brings physical reality into existence. In the Bible we are told that the Kingdom of Heaven is within us. We are literally miracle workers. Evidence shows that people who meditate have an impact on the people in the city in which they meditate. The founder of the Transcendental Meditation movement, Maharishi Mahesh Yogi, said that if a mere 1 per cent of the world's population meditated at a certain level then this would be powerful enough to transform the whole world's consciousness away from fear. Study after study on prayer shows that ill people who are prayed for recover more quickly and require fewer drugs, even if they don't know they are being prayed for! *A Course in Miracles* reminds us that this whole is *our* creation. The Buddha taught us that everything springs up from within us. The evidence is all there: the only thing that hasn't really changed is *our thinking*. We are still mainly educated to believe we live in a material universe, not a universe of consciousness.

Just a few years ago I had an amazing experience in my own life. On his way to an ex-servicemen's parade in central London, Maurice, my partner Helen's father, suddenly had a massive coronary, collapsed and was taken to hospital. We were on our way back from Ireland and didn't hear this until we landed at Stansted airport. We raced back into London and went to visit him and talk to the doctors, who informed us that the prognosis was not good. Even if he recovered, he would probably have brain damage, and at his age, 78 at the time, it was very likely that he would have another coronary soon. They gave us little hope. Maurice wouldn't be able to leave hospital for at least 10 days, and would need full-time care. When we went to see him he was barely conscious, and had lost his memory. Helen just held his head and I held his feet and we both gave him some Reiki healing, which we had just been taught by our friend Mari Hall. When we got home I contacted Mari, who is a Reiki master and lives in the Czech republic. I asked her to put Maurice on her healing list and she said she would, and would also ask her colleagues to pray and put him on their healing lists. To cut a long story short, within a week he was sent home, was pretty much fully functioning, and lived well for nearly four years.

Notice that with all these examples of power there is no great effort or struggle. This power comes from our very being, from who we are in essence. It comes from our spirit, which is love. Each of us has this power, none more than anyone else. Yet in this world we tend not to value ease, we value what we have to sacrifice and struggle for. When was the last time you received an award or qualification for being, ease, naturalness and grace? We value difficulty so much.

A GREATER POWER AND INTELLIGENCE WITHIN US

There is such incredible intelligence and power within us right now that we hardly ever think about. How do we digest our food and turn it into the chemicals and nutrients we need to sustain our physical life? How do we turn an egg and sperm into another human being? How do we make our hair grow? How do we make our nails grow? How do we carry out the billions of chemical reactions that take place within our body every second? How does an invisible thought get translated into a physical movement? In truth we don't know. We live with such mystery every moment of our lives. Science can answer many of the questions on a physical and chemical level, but it doesn't allow insights into the *greater intelligence* that is the orchestrating force beyond the physical plane.

WE HAVE FORGOTTEN WHO WE ARE

Imagine going to see a wonderful film, with a cast who have tremendous acting abilities. There is a great bad guy, a hero, a sinner, lovers, victims, persecutors, a saviour and many other characters. You are very lucky to be invited to the after-screening party and to meet the actors. You are enjoying yourself when suddenly you begin to realize that the actors are still in character. They seem to have gone into collective amnesia and forgotten that they are actors playing the roles they have chosen, they imagine they *have become* the role. What will you do? Will you blame the actors, the director, the scriptwriter or the projectionist? How can you wake them from their sleeping awareness and remind them who they really are? How can you get them to remember that they are multi-talented and many-faceted, bigger than any role they have ever played?

In our life we have forgotten who we really are and have taken on roles, believing the roles we play are who we really are. Throughout history, mystics have reminded us that who we are is much greater than one body in one lifetime. We are eternal souls having human experiences, imagining we are separate beings, apart from our creator and each other. We imagine ourselves as small and powerless, when the whole power of creation is sleeping within us. And our imagining feels pretty real to us. We try and change the world of our imagining rather than wake up to the truth of who we really are. Our power beyond measure lies not in any of the roles we play, but in our true nature. We are not of *this* world. This is *not* our home. This world is 'One grand fantasy, not to be valued, but to be enjoyed, to be played with, with laughter and a chuckle, nothing more,' writes Jesus through Brent Haskell in *Journey beyond Words*. All our problems stem from the belief that we are separate and that this world reflects who we are.

WE ARE EVERYTHING

To understand our true power we need to have a larger view of ourselves and of life, to see the bigger picture. We contain all that there is within the universe. The mystics have always taught us this, but now it is the time in human history when we are called to realize what is within us. This is a challenging and puzzling idea for many of us. Modern science has enlightened us to the idea of holography, which teaches us that each of us is a microcosm of the macrocosm. Each of us contains all the knowledge and information of the whole universe. How empowering an idea is that?

Did you know that it is literally true that every time we breathe in and out, we exchange 100, 000, 000, 000, 000, 000, 000, 000, 000, 000 atoms with everyone and everything on the planet? Is it literally true that we are made up of what has made up Saddam Hussein, Jesus, George Bush, Osama Bin Laden, Mother Teresa, Buddha and Princess Diana? We are made of stars, of animals, of dinosaurs, squirrels and dolphins. It is as if there is a raw material of the universe – a quantum soup it has been described as – and we are all made of it. The thought that we are separate is literally that, a thought, what Albert Einstein called 'an aberration of consciousness, a prison from which we must free ourselves'. We live in a unified and completely connected universe, and love is what glues it together.

The hologram idea is this. If you cut up a holographic picture into a million pieces, and shine a laser beam onto one piece, you will see the whole picture. In the same way, if we examine one human being we will find a hologram of the universe. The universal blueprint is within the DNA of every living being. Every strand of my DNA carries the entire evolutionary history of all life: the whole is contained in every part. So every aspect of the universe is contained within each of us. This is not just a poetic idea, but may be literally true.

If it *is* true, our mind contains the potential of every thought that ever was or will be expressed. Understanding this opens the door to freedom, and experiencing it is the basis of wisdom. It is the beginning of the realization that although we appear to be separate in mind and body, we actually aren't. We are all billions of expressions of one whole mind. Our sense of isolation and separation is like a trick of the light, an apparent fragmentation of what is whole and complete.

> *To see a world in a grain of sand*
> *And a heaven in a wild flower,*
> *Hold infinity in the palm of your hand,*
> *And eternity in an hour.*

WILLIAM BLAKE, from *Auguries of Innocence*

Within every one of us is every human and divine trait, and its polar opposite; every emotion and impulse is within us. That is what wholeness means. The human soul is its own universe: it was so at the beginning of creation and still is now. But we have been taught to disown and cut off aspects of ourselves that we believe are unlovable, unacceptable, or that we have judged as bad. So we end up feeling severely diminished. The poet Robert Bly says that at birth we contain everything, naturally and without judgement. Light, creativity, vitality, joy and beauty are within us, as are the dark, competitive, the evil and the nasty. As we grow we are encouraged by family, friends, teachers, partners, bosses, colleagues and leaders as to what is acceptable and unacceptable. Those traits we come to judge as unacceptable are relegated to our shadow, meaning that they are disowned but still exist, buried deeper in our mind. We lose conscious contact with them, and now can only see them in other people.

REMEMBERING OUR TRUE IDENTITY

If you have read the first book about Harry Potter, you will remember that moment when Hagrid says to him, 'Harry, you're a wizard.' Suddenly his whole life begins to make sense. I wonder if that is one of the reasons why these books have been so successful. They deeply resonate with us – we are not who we think we are; we've been told untruths about ourselves. Remembering our true identity is the major goal of our life. Most of us think we are the separate sense of identity we have grown up with. We think we are our name, our sex, our qualifications, our experiences, our address, the clubs we belong to, the work we do, the possessions we have. We are none of them. We are another self, the *other* self. We are the experiencer of our life, not the experiences, we are the thinker of our thoughts, not the thoughts themselves. We are what in Buddhism is called the witness.

The founder of psychoanalysis, Sigmund Freud, said that wherever he went in the human psyche, he found a poet had been there before him. Sometimes logic can't express what we experience. The Nobel Prize Laureate in Literature, Spanish poet Juan Ramón Jiménez, expresses this other sense of self beautifully:

I am not I.
I am this one
Walking beside me whom I do not see,

Whom at times I manage to visit,
And at times I forget.
The one who remains silent when I talk,
The one who forgives, sweet, when I hate,
The one who takes a walk when I am indoors,
The one who will remain standing when I die.

We are not who we think we are, and our lifetime is a journey of remembering and rediscovering this other 'I'. As we search and find the real us, we are naturally drawn towards our true place in life.

FINDING OUR TRUE PLACE IN LIFE

The universe doesn't have spare parts: there is a divine plan waiting to unfold within all of us, and this plan contains happiness, fulfilment and prosperity on every level. Each of us arrives here with this plan wrapped up within our soul. Plato called it *the divine design*. This plan calls to us constantly, longs to be released and manifested in our life. Often signals to our plan manifest as inclinations, passions and interests in our childhood, but without someone who *sees* those things in us, it is easy for us to lose hold of the plan and bury it away. If we are lucky we will reawaken the plan later in life; if not it may remain buried for our whole life.

Our divine plan is not to suffer, but to be released from the suffering. We have a purpose for being here, and we are perfect for that purpose. We discover that by focusing on and loving what we are, not berating ourselves for what we aren't. We are not here to play roles and try to be who we aren't, although so much of our education encourages just that. Instead of feeling small and trapped, we are here to awaken to the power within us. We are being called to awaken to our spiritual nature, and as we do so our life takes on wondrous dimensions. Instead of work being a place to lose ourselves, we are called to embrace massive love, happiness, joy, abundance, inspiration and power in our work. The path we are going along is truly beautiful, when we realize what is happening. We are called to stand on new and solid ground. But when we don't understand what is happening we can feel scared, resistant, anxious and inadequate. We are called to shed skin after skin, limit after limit, so that our heart can shine through, and our willingness is the greatest power we have. We want to belong within ourselves. A beacon is calling us home, not to a physical place, but to a place deep within us, a place where our wholeness resides.

We awaken to our own divine plan by listening to that intuitive voice within, by trusting and acting on it. We can affirm to ourselves

> There is a divine plan for my life. I am now attuned to the divine plan for my life, co-operate fully and welcome its unfolding through me, step by step. I release what is no longer a true part of my life and welcome what is truly part of my life. Help me know it and live it.

When we do this daily we *will* be shown. Sometimes we listen with our fingers in our ears, we only half want to hear or are even scared to hear the answers and direction. However old we are, however off track we may feel, however many mistakes we think we've made, we are always offered fresh beginnings, when we are willing to take them. Sometimes, out of fear of loss or uncertainty, we cling to what isn't really ours. We may settle for crumbs, or the starter, not knowing that we are invited to the banquet. Also we may sense that following our divine plan will involve change and transition, so we cling to what is familiar but uncomfortable out of our fear of the unknown.

A GREATER POWER WITHIN US

Our power, however, is not of us. It is God's spirit inside of us that enlightens and enlivens our lives. Of ourselves we're really no big deal. This thought has helped me in my career. I walk onto a stage and sometimes speak to more than a thousand people at a time. I can't imagine dealing with the pressure of having to convince myself that I have something special to offer. I don't try. I don't have to impress anyone, and if I'm not thinking that I have to there's nothing to do but relax. I walk out on stage without feeling the need to make people think I'm special, because I know I am not. I just talk to friends, casually and with enthusiasm. That's it. There isn't anything else. Everything else is just an illusion. The Son of God doesn't need to embellish who he is.

MARIANNE WILLIAMSON, author of *A Return to Love*

A great example of the power of identity is the poet David Whyte, an Englishman who now lives in the USA. He reminds business leaders of the importance of soul and creativity in the modern workplace. He is immensely successful. What fascinated me about him was *how, as a poet, does he create success in the corporate world?* When I met him, I realized that one important pillar of his success was that *he knew who he was!* He was very clear in his sense of identity. He was a poet, and made no pretence to be anything other than a poet. When someone asked him how he adapted and marketed his message for the corporate market, he responded, 'I don't, I am simply myself!' The concept of moulding his message didn't enter his consciousness. His message is integrity, and he *is* his message. Because he knew and lived from his own sense of identity, he was very powerful. He had very little to prove and everything to be. In a world of test marketing, market research and soundbites, David is his authentic self and people love him.

EXERCISE

* *When do you feel most yourself?*
* *When are you in your element?*

There is something immensely attractive about finding our own inner and solid ground of identity. When we find it, we are able to venture more into other territories without losing ourselves. Through knowing our own identity, we access an energy source within us, which doesn't run out. Indeed, as we evolve we delve deeper into our own being.

OUR STORY ABOUT WHO WE ARE

What negative story or stories do you tell about yourself, that you use either to define yourself to others or to yourself? For example:

- *I am not good enough*
- *I am a loser*
- *I never get it together*
- *I am the angry one*
- *I give too much*
- *I am hard done by*
- *I am the worst*

We only make up stories about who we are when we have forgotten our true identity. I have always loved the following story, told in Diane Berke's book *Love Always Answers*, that reminds us of our true identity.

I felt very lost and confused about who I was, where I was going, and what I was doing. And I was crying out in weariness and pain to be reminded, to be shown the way to healing and to peace. That same day I attended a workshop with meditation teacher Jack Kornfield. During the workshop, Dr Kornfield shared a story that stirred something, a memory, a longing, deep in my heart. There is a village somewhere in Africa, he told us, that counts the birthday of a child, not from the day the child is born into physical existence, not even from the day the child is conceived in the womb, but from the day the child is born as a thought in his mother's mind. One day a woman in the village has the thought, 'I will have a child with my mate.' She then goes apart from the village and sits under a tree. She sits, listening, until inside herself she hears the song that is the song of this child who would come into being through her. Once she has heard the song, she sings it to herself again and again until she knows it. Then she returns to her home and teaches the song to her mate. They sing it together while making love, inviting the child to be born of their union.

Later the song is taught to the midwives, who sing it to the child during and immediately after the birth process, to welcome him to life. And the song is taught to all the people of the village. Then if the child is playing and falls down, whoever is nearby can pick him up and comfort him by singing his song to him. This song is sung throughout his life, at all rites of passage, and is sung finally as his earthly life comes to its end.

When Dr Kornfield finished telling this story, there was a profound silence and stillness in the room. Everyone felt touched by a nameless sense of recollection and longing and by the recognition that we all shared this same response. What touches the heart so deeply about this story, I believe, is that we all know, on some level, that we too have a song of our creation, a song we long to sing and to hear sung. How wonderful it must be, Dr Kornfield reflected, to be a part of a community in which everyone knows your song and sings it to you, in affirmation and celebration of your truth and your being. An ancient song in our hearts, nearly forgotten, calls us to remembrance of the deepest truth in us, to the Self who is born and reborn and lives eternally as a Thought in the Mind of God.

WHO WE ARE IS SIGNIFICANT

Love is about living fully, and sharing our life fully, giving ourselves fully; it is the only thing that will fulfil us, that will make us happy and give our life true meaning. Love is without question life's greatest experience. It brings us into communion with infinite intelligence. In truth, it is the only thing we want and our only real need. One of the best ways I have heard this expressed is by Dawna Markova in her poem 'I Will Not Die An Unlived Life'.

I will not die an unlived life
I will not live in fear of falling
Or of catching fire
I choose to inhabit my days
To allow my living to open me
Making me less afraid
More accessible
To loosen my heart
So that it becomes a wing, a torch, a promise
I choose to risk my significance
To live so that that which comes to me as seed
Goes to the next as blossom
And that which comes to me as blossom
Goes on as fruit.

DON'T DELAY – THIS IS THE RIGHT MOMENT, YOU ARE THE RIGHT PERSON

Don't delay in moving forward to act from love in your life. If you are still trying to figure out what your purpose is, realize that there are calls for your love, inspiration and your kindness right now. Are you noticing them? There are so many ways that your presence and actions can make a difference right now. Anything and everything that comes from our heart is helpful. Don't try to change the whole world: just your sphere of influence will be more than enough. We have no idea how powerful even the tiniest acts of kindness can be. Pray or meditate for daily assignments and you will receive them. You are the right person, today is the right day. When the doors open, don't doubt your ability: walk through the doors and open your heart.

GIVING UP THE ROLE OF HELPER

My friend Tina, a consultant, called me, saying, 'I am a bit bored. I've done lots of great work with clients recently, but I feel like something is coming to an end. I am bit scared.' 'So, what would you do next?' I asked. 'Dance, sing and have fun with people!' she replied as quick as a flash. 'But that doesn't seem like it is going to help much,' she went on. I asked, 'Don't you think that making people feel alive and happy is helpful?' She thought for a moment and responded, 'I suppose it is, but I hadn't thought of it that way before.'

Tina, like many of us, had got caught in the *role* of being a helper, an ego trap that many of us fall into. She was bored with 'helping' and wanted to be more alive. Some of the people who have most helped and inspired me never set out to, and would never have called themselves helpers. Many people simply live their purpose, do what they love, are alive and passionate, and in the process inspire and touch thousands. The way we can most help is to be our true self. We should not be asking so much what the world needs, but asking our self what would make us come most alive, and then go out and be and do that.

31

The world needs more people who have come alive.

Most of us want to help our fellow humans and we think that the best way to help is to sacrifice ourselves. Our ego takes hold of our natural desire to serve and spins it around into a role. Being ourselves and being human is our greatest gift to the world. We need to find the courage to give up the role of helper and let our essential goodness out. Everything flows from the finding of our simple but essential humanity. Within each of us is a tender and pure heart, which may have got lost, forgotten or hidden. It takes enormous courage to be *that* innocent, *that* open, love ourselves *that* much and give ourselves *that* fully, holding nothing back. Our fulfilment comes from giving all we are to those around us, from withholding nothing. That is how love is with us, it cannot help but extend itself. Only by giving all we can receive all. Dr Chuck Spezzano asks: 'Would you be willing to be that pure? Would you be willing to be that beautiful? Would you give yourself to those around you in such a way as to inspire everyone? Would you be a friend to everyone on that level, including yourself? Would you be a friend to the earth, that they could look at you and see this is the way to go forward, this is the human being I want to become?'

THE POWER OF LOVE

Leslie Kenton, the health guru, said, 'Love keeps you young.' From so many points of view, love is seen and known to be the most powerful force there is. Here are some quotes from extremely wide and varied perspectives. From a metaphysical perspective, a beautiful articulation of the power of love is this:

> *There is no difficulty that enough love will not conquer;*
> *No disease that enough love will not heal;*
> *No door that enough love will not open;*
> *No gulf that enough love will not bridge;*
> *No wall that enough love will not throw down;*

No sin that enough love will not redeem . . .
It makes no difference how deeply seated may be the trouble;
How hopeless the outlook, how muddled the tangle;
A sufficient realization of love will dissolve it all.
If only you could love enough you would be the happiest and most
powerful being in the world.
EMMET FOX (1886–1951), one of the most influential New Thought movement
authors of the 20th century

Love stimulates the immune system and activates our inner pharmacy, creating wonder drugs and healing chemicals. When Deepak Chopra was a medical doctor, he noticed that 'Patients with serious illnesses, who felt they were loved, sometimes made astonishing recoveries against all odds, while patients with relatively mild illness who felt they were not loved, could languish and wither away to death. Love can make us younger biologically.'

From a medical and scientific perspective, the power of love was expressed wonderfully by Dean Ornish, in *Love and Survival*, written after his prolonged studies into the role love and connection play in the healing process:

> Love and intimacy are at the root of what makes us sick and what makes us well, what causes us sadness and what brings happiness, what makes us suffer and what leads to healing . . . If a new drug had the same impact [as love] virtually every doctor in the country would be recommending it for their patients. It would be malpractice *not* to prescribe it – yet, with few exceptions, we doctors do not learn much about the healing power of love, intimacy and transformation in our medical training. Rather these ideas are often ignored or even denigrated.

And the spiritual teacher Jerry Jampolsky describes it well in *Love is Letting Go of Fear*:

The world's distorted concept is that you have to get other people's Love before you can feel Love within. The law of Love is different from the world's view. The law of Love is that you *are* Love, and that as you give Love to others you teach yourself what you are.

And finally from the world of business, Tim Sanders, a senior executive in Yahoo.com, writes in his pioneering book, *Love is the Killer App*:

> The most powerful force in business isn't greed, fear, or even the raw energy of unbridled competition. The most powerful force in business is love. It's what will help your company grow and become stronger. It's what will propel your career forward. It's what will give you a sense of meaning and satisfaction in your work, which will help you do your best work.

GOD AND LOVE

Throughout this book I will largely use the word 'love' instead of 'God' because the word 'God' tends to create resistance and division, which are of the ego, but for me they are interchangeable. I like Gandhi's idea that in Heaven there is probably no religion! Love is the power that unifies, not separates. The love I am writing about is the love that God created and the unchanging reality behind all of physical reality. It is the love that everything comes from, and all returns to, and that sustains all life. It is the womb of creation. Love never changes; it cannot change. Only appearances change.

Look at the universality of this, as expressed in various religions:

- **Christianity:** *God is love; you are God's and children of the most high.*
- *A Course in Miracles: You were made in love. You are as God created you.*

- **Shinto:** *Love is the receptacle of the Lord.*
- **Zoroastrianism:** *Man is the beloved of the Lord and you should love him in return.*
- **Sikhism:** *God will regenerate those in whose hands there is love.*
- **Buddhism:** *Let man cultivate, for the benefit of others, a heart of love.*
- **Taoism:** *Heaven arms with love those it would not see destroyed.*
- **Islam:** *Love is this, that thou should'st account thyself very little, and God very great.*
- **Baha'i:** *If thou lovest me not, my love can no wise reach thee.*
- **Confucianism:** *To love all men is the greatest benevolence.*
- **Hinduism:** *One can best worship the Lord through love.*

UNDERSTANDING LOVE'S TRUE NATURE

We need a true understanding of God and therefore of divine love. It is the principle of giving all to all. From our egoistic personality perspective so much of what we think to be love isn't actually love at all; it is need, it is attachments, it is seeking approval out of fear. In short, it is conditional love. We live in a world where most things are conditional. So we compete, and we mould and distort ourselves in order to be worthy to receive these conditional rewards. We try to earn and deserve love, affection, power and success. Love is conditionally given, freedom is conditionally granted. We may find it hard even to imagine what unconditional love is really about, or to conceive that it really exists.

Instead of an image of a creator who wishes her creations to have every good thing, every blessing, every healing, every form of love, we can think of God as capricious, unpredictable and usually angry and seeking approval. We create a God in our own image. We imagine a God who has blessings but withholds them; who could offer happiness but denies us it; who punishes us; who can manipulate and play favourites; who has enemies; who has gifts but keeps them from us for some future date; who loves, but not now. We think if we pray hard enough, do enough good deeds, live virtuous enough lives or obey all the rules, we can influence God in order to get some of our own needs met and fill up some of the blank holes we feel in our own life. We believe we can buy God's approval.

Perhaps one of the toughest, and yet most liberating, ideas we need to understand is that *we can't influence God*. In the best possible way, God's mind is made up about all of us. This does not leave us helpless, but powerful beyond measure. We are all loved unconditionally and eternally, and there is nothing we can do about it. Yes, whatever behaviour we exhibit, good or bad, can't make us more or less acceptable to God. God's unconditional love is the one thing we are *truly* a victim to. It is not God's mind we need to change, but our own! The truth about us remains eternally safe and unchangeable. It is our story about ourselves, our perceptions of ourselves and each other that we need to change.

OUR POWER OF PERCEPTION

Among the gifts we have is our power over choice of perception, and within that is the power to recognize and acknowledge new meanings in our experiences. Jo called me full of fear. A very successful management consultant, she had recently had some bad and painful experiences with a couple of big clients. Although she loved her work, and loved leading big projects and helping people develop, these experiences had badly shaken her confidence in herself. She felt burnt out and was exhausted.

As she was someone who totally threw herself into whatever she was involved in, she decided to restore some balance. She had taken time out and spent 10 weeks on an art course, something she hadn't done much since she was 14, and she missed it a lot. She absolutely loved the art, and found that she was actually very talented and gifted at it. Surrounded by other artists, she felt affirmed, and they encouraged her to continue. It was easy and natural for her. 'But it feels like self-indulgence to paint,' she explained. 'It doesn't help anyone else. I feel torn apart, thinking that I should be marketing myself to get more consultancy to pay my mortgage, but wanting to do more art. I am confused and terrified. I feel like disaster is around the corner, and that I am going to implode. I feel like I am at a brick wall.'

As we talked further it emerged that Jo was the oldest of five children and that her role was to take care of her younger siblings. 'I never really had my own childhood, I didn't get to play myself and always needed to be in charge and in control. I needed to be responsible for the whole family.' As we continued talking it became clear that the reasons why she had experienced conflict with her clients was that she was trying too hard to be the expert, the one with all the answers, feeling overly responsible, which led her into conflicts and fights with some of the senior people she was working with, who felt disempowered by her need to control too much. She was being challenged in her need to be in control; this seemed like a survival issue when she was a child – if she wasn't in control, she was in trouble.

One of our greatest blocks to our power is a feeling of being overly responsible, of having to carry people, like a burden. We don't want to get too close to anyone, because we think we have to sacrifice ourselves to them, and yet our distance from them makes our life harder.

This happens whenever we have negatively judged people. You may have heard the story about a young and an old monk. Walking along, they reach a river. At the riverside is a woman trying to get across but unable to as the water is too high. Having taken vows, they are not supposed to have contact with women, but the older monk offers to carry her across. She accepts, they cross the river and he puts her down. She thanks him and they go their separate ways. The monks continue walking for an hour in silence, but the younger one is angry and fuming at the older one. Eventually he erupts. 'You broke your vows, you carried that woman!' 'Yes, I know,' he responds peacefully. 'I put her down at the riverbank, but you are still carrying her.'

Often we carry people years after we should have put them down. Usually through our judgement of them we carry resentment and grievances, and inside we are arguing years after actual events. We can carry people through not being able to let go of the love we experienced with them. Either way, holding on blocks our power by keeping us in the past, not the present. Learning to let go opens the door to our power again, which is to take the gifts from the past and bring them into the present, and release ourselves from our judgements so that we can be present now. Byron Katie, author of *Loving What Is*, suggests that there are three types of business – my business, your business and God's business. When we know whose business is whose we can have a good life; all our stress and pain comes from confusing the different types of business.

This feeling of responsibility is often sourced out of a feeling of not being needed, out of a need for control. By feeling responsible we find an untrue sense of purpose that masks our deep fear of not being needed. We are called to a new way of relating to people that is not based on mutual need, but on mutual want. We are all responsible for ourselves. Obviously the ideal is for parents to be responsible for children and then children learn to be responsible for themselves and how to be healthily interdependent.

Every place where we are fighting, or in a power struggle, with someone else is a place where *we* are frightened to move forward in greater partnership, creativity and intimacy. Our ego is invested in keeping this person in the wrong, but a part of us is delighted that we are in conflict because we are *even more scared to get closer to this person, or group*. Our ego doesn't like equality with anyone else, it loves being distant: above or below, but rarely equal. By its difference it thinks it can extract something of value from someone else.

In our struggle for power, we too often cut ourselves off from the greater source of our energy and so feel weak and insecure. We tend to manipulate or force others to give us attention, and thus energy. When we successfully dominate others in this way, we feel more powerful, but they are weakened and often fight back. Competition for apparently scarce human energy is the cause of all conflict between people.

The gift in Jo's crisis was that she was being called to find another level of power, to trade some control for power with her clients. She could learn to share power with them, not keep it from them. She was also being called to discover more of her creative and spiritual side, which she had neglected since her teens. She began to see that the choice wasn't between being creative or being a consultant, but maybe being a more creative consultant. She had neglected her feminine side in the belief that she had to in order to survive and be successful. She began to see that by reclaiming that side of her she could probably be *even more* successful, but this time with balance, perhaps even greater ease, more fun and more connection with the people she worked with. She wasn't a great example to her clients when she herself was modelling being out of balance. She was being called to make her own needs important too, not only the needs of others, as had been her family scripting.

By the end of our conversation, Jo was laughing. Suddenly she could see that what had felt like an end was really a beginning; she could see a way forward. What our ego tells us to think is death and disaster, our soul knows to be a new birth, a shedding of a skin, with the possibility of a whole new level of success, when we have the eyes to see it, and when we are willing to see it, and willing to let go of outdated ways of being. It's all about perception. What seemed a major problem for Jo was an opportunity being offered to her, an opportunity that her ego was trying to keep from her.

WHAT OBSTRUCTIONS HAVE WE CREATED?

In *A Course in Miracles* we are told, 'Your job is not to search for love, but for the barriers you have erected to the awareness of Love's presence.' Within us is the power to deconstruct all these barriers. We have built so many defences *against* love. If God stopped loving, she would lose her God licence! The universe would literally fall apart and disintegrate. It is hard for us to realize that it is *we* who have erected barriers to love, not love erecting barriers to us. How do we block our awareness of this everlasting love? To answer this question, we need to understand the nature of our ego, and the basis of this world. This world is built on the belief in separation from the source of love. It is built on and out of fear and guilt. We seek the comfort of real love, and real love is comforting but not always at first. Not enough of us have been told and experienced that love *will* challenge every defence. It can be horrible and painful as love dismantles the defences we have built. Marianne Williamson expresses it beautifully: 'Those who allow those tears, even honour those tears, are not failures at love but rather love's true initiates. First pain, and then the power. First the heart breaks and then it soars.' Only through facing the illusions can we discover the truth behind them.

So the ego does all it can to keep this sense of separation and difference going. Here are some of its major strategies:

- **Conflict** – *our ego loves conflict, battles and wars, either outright or hidden, so will do everything it can to keep these going. We see this everywhere.*
- **Grievance** – *our ego cherishes the way it has been hurt, abused, attacked and victimized. The ego doesn't want to let go, forgive and join. We only have to look at Ireland, the Middle East or the Balkans to see this going on today.*
- **Judgement and condemnation** – *the ego loves to judge, to evaluate, to see things as good or bad, better or worse.*

- **Fear** – *the ego is based on fear: of differences, of each other, and ultimately of love. True love is the death of the ego.*
- **Guilt** – *although it does a pretty good job of hiding this and then projecting this guilt out onto others, the ego is built on guilt. It is founded on self-attack and self-condemnation, not self-love.*
- **Specialness** – *the deep ego belief that we are not good enough causes us to try to make ourselves special in some way, but our desire to be special separates us from others, creating distance, not real love.*

When we look at the world, isn't this most of what we see? Guilt, condemnation, fear, battles and grievances. Isn't this what most of our news is about? Aren't these things what seem to make our world function? It can take years of tears to melt the hardness that we develop in this world, in order, we believe, to survive. Spiritual growth is a detox process. Our weakest and darkest places cannot be denied; they are sucked to the surface in order to be known and be released. Our shadow parts need to be brought to the light. Underneath is still our kinder, tender and gentler, inner selves. We may need to shed many tears. Tears for every painful loss. Tears for every humiliation and failure. Tears for every repeated mistake. Tears for every time we were unaware.

Often when we experience the weakness in ourself and in others, we are repelled and want to withdraw, either emotionally or by leaving the relationship. It takes courage to hang in. The answer may not be to change partners or friends, but to shift our understanding of the purpose of relationship and intimacy, from simply serving our own needs to serving a greater process of healing. Then we realize wounds are brought forth to be cured in order to *serve* love, not block the experience of love. Instead of negatively judging others, we become more compassionate and this is what heals us and the world.

So why bother? Because only through love can we experience the true fulfilment that lies within us. Only through love can we know our true creative potential. Only through love can we come alive and be the people we were born to be. And because love is the only thing that is real, on the Day of Judgment everything that isn't love will be stripped away. Only through love can we experience the joy and peace within us.

The power of love calls us to be ourselves fully, to become all that we are, to grow beyond our fears and smallness, and not to diminish ourselves. It is arrogant to think we are small and powerless.

2

OUR POWER TO PLAY BIG

*Deep within man dwell those slumbering powers; powers that
would astonish him, that he never dreamed of possessing; forces
that would revolutionize his life if aroused and put into action.*
ORISON SWETT MARDEN, 1850–1924, founder of *Success* magazine

Playing big is living our purpose and there is so much waiting to be
discovered within us. It is being willing to make a positive impact
on the people around us, to influence people's thinking and
attitudes. Never has there been a greater call for us all to step up
and be leaders in our own lives and in the world. As old systems
that have lacked integrity or been based on secrecy or win/lose fall
away, we need leaders who know how to build new systems based
on openness, trust and abundance. We are all being called to discover and create a new world and every step we take in our
purpose, with the intention of love and service, helps create this
world.

We are all full of spiritual gifts, creativity and love that the world needs, is perhaps even dying for. Playing big is about discovering and sharing what we have, it is about daring to shine, choosing to risk our significance, and live from love and creativity rather than guilt and fear. Playing big is also about showing *up* with natural authority and confidence, not showing *off*. It is turning up the volume on our soul, and giving ourselves to life, holding nothing back.

Many of us have been told to put other people first, but actually we need to ask for more blessings in our life first. This is not selfish, but effective. As they advise in aircraft, put on your own oxygen mask before you help anyone else. What good are we to others if we are suffocating? We need to activate the spiritual equivalent of an oxygen mask, whereby we breathe blessings into ourself first, raise our own consciousness, so that we have more to share with others. We are not called to sacrifice ourselves, but to move to a higher level where we can genuinely support and be supported.

Playing big is not necessarily about numbers, money, being famous or outwardly successful. It is about being the fullest and truest expression of ourselves in the world. Playing big is our connection to our own inner love, our own inner light, and when we make that connection it is almost inevitable that we will want to find ways of sharing that love out in the world.

Sarah Ban Breathnach puts it beautifully in her book *Simple Abundance*:

Only the heart knows what is really working in our lives. The heart is our authentic compass. If we consult her, the heart can tell us if we're headed in the right direction. But the heart also tells us when we've made a wrong turn or when it's time for a U-turn. For a lot of us, this is information we don't want to know. Knowing it might mean choice, and choice often means change.

When we connect ourselves more deeply to this feeling of inner truth, it will become the evolutionary driving force that will guide us through the whole of our life.

While our soul is always calling us to new levels of life, and greater authenticity, our ego can intervene in two ways. It may try to force us grandiosely towards unreal possibilities, then we fly too close to the sun, and then we crash and burn, or it tells us to stop thinking too highly of ourselves. Play small, it says, and tells us not to venture too far. Perhaps all our pain in life comes down to one thing – shrinking ourselves to a smaller size than we really are, holding back on our love and our gifts. Pain comes from forcing ourselves to be what we are not, and joy – the reverse side of this coin – comes from being naturally who we are. When we withhold what and who we are, *we* must suffer. What we have inside that we don't share can turn poisonous. We may seem to be giving a lot already, but we may be giving too much or too little of ourselves, while what is precious in us remains unexpressed.

PLAYING A BIGGER AND BIGGER GAME

Clive worked in corporate banking for many years as a very successful area manager, focusing on creating, managing and developing successful teams. Like so many employees and customers, he didn't like the way banking culture was heading. He saw it moving away from a real interest in people and relationships and towards valuing money and profit, and turning everyone into sales people. Whilst employed at the bank, for two hours a week he volunteered to work for a local hospice. He found that selfless service, connection with the people he worked with and helped, gave his life real meaning. He loved the connection and authenticity of the work.

He got more involved and the hospice management asked Clive if he would use his business skills to do some consultancy work for them. He agreed, did the consultancy work and submitted a report suggesting that they appoint a chief executive to oversee the work of the hospice. He was utterly amazed when they asked *him* if he would become the chief executive! His soul called him to do it, and he agreed. It allowed him to put what he loved at the centre of his life, still earn a reasonable income and move out of banking. He was definitely living his purpose.

In the past five years he has built a successful team at the hospice, with a staff of 100, including volunteers, and a budget of over £2 million, most of which was attained through fundraising. This is an incredible achievement for any hospice. When we spoke, Clive felt that he was at another crossroads. There was lots of politics, and his energy was lower than it had been. Five years after rising to his soul's challenge, he was beginning to feel restless again, but was not sure what was next. Something new was cooking in his soul, and it was calling him to move, but he wasn't sure how or where to. It was obvious that he had brought great commercial skills to bear on an organization that hadn't had someone with such experience before, and that not all hospices had the organizational skills that his did. He had managed to reach that enviable position of being able to combine his head and his heart in his work. But our purpose is not a static condition we can preserve. It is a continuously evolving activity, with questions asked over and over again. It's a process we live by every day; a process for listening and shaping the story of our life. While the essence is always the same, the forms it takes may change.

As we talked I shared a hunch with him. 'Would you like to help even more people by helping more hospices?' 'That does appeal to me,' he said. 'But how?' 'How about taking all you've learned and sharing it with a wider audience? How might you do that?' He thought for a while and then answered, 'I would love to consult for other hospices, sharing my experience and knowledge with them, and give talks and training. So many do wonderful work but don't know how to fundraise or organize themselves efficiently.' Suddenly in my mind I saw his future laid out. He was getting restless because he was playing too small. Why limit his influence to one hospice, when he could help many, and through that touch the lives, and deaths, of thousands more? It was almost arrogant for him *not* to play a bigger game.

Love wants to enlarge our life, and in doing so, help us enlarge the lives of others and re-create the world. This does not mean larger burdens or responsibilities, or simply more material or financial gains, but true spiritual enlargement, true joy. We have been told for generations that spiritual growth demands material sacrifice and self-denial. This is so untrue. To play big calls us to greater levels of support and partnership, not sacrifice.

PLAYING BIG IS EXPANDING OUR EXISTING TERRITORIES

You have the unlimited power of the universe within you, and so does everyone else. It's nothing to take personal credit for, or feel guilty about. Our real power emanates from a force that is in us but not of us.

MARIANNE WILLIAMSON, author of *A Return to Love*

We all have our own territories, where we are known and where we can have influence. Our territories are our families, our neighbourhoods, our work environment, our friends and wider communities. There are also the shops we patronize, the students we teach, our colleagues. But we can also have power and influence over people we don't even know and may never meet. There are nuns, monks and other spiritual people praying for you and me right now. We don't know them, but they are holding us in their hearts. You've probably donated to charities helping people or animals throughout the world, and your money has helped those

49

you will never know. I know that I have read and heard words that have changed my life in ways that the authors and speakers may never know. Mostly we will never discover the impact that our lives have had on other people. Our territory is already bigger than we could ever imagine. We will never know how many people hold us in their hearts.

Love wants us to expand our territory in two ways:

- *Expand the richness and depth of our existing life, to move to new levels of partnership, love and friendship with our family, friends and colleagues. Each of us has many places where we are limited by fear, anger, guilt, loneliness or unhealthy independence, and love is always wanting us to melt these so we can be more available to ourselves, each other and life.*
- *Expand the number of people that we befriend, help, teach, support and encourage. We can expand our circle of influence, but many of us react by saying, 'My life is busy and full enough already, I need less territory, not more!' This needn't involve more sacrifice, as with each step up we are also offered new levels of skill and ability.*

EXERCISE

✳ *Think about your territory for a moment. Who knows you? Who do you know? How many people know you and feel some kind of warmth and connection to you?*

SOMETIMES, WHEN WE TURN A CORNER, WE CAN FEEL LIKE WE ARE GOING ROUND THE BEND

Maturity and energy in our work is not granted freely to human beings, but must be adventured and discovered, cultivated and earned. It is the result of application, dedication, and indispensable humour, and above all a never ending courageous conversation with ourselves, those with whom we work and those we serve. It is a lifelong journey; it calls on both the ardors of youth and the perspective of a longer view. It is achieved through a lifelong pilgrimage.

DAVID WHYTE, author of *Crossing the Unknown Sea*

When we commit to something more fully, it may flush out our resistance, our egoistic self will kick in and subtly undermine us by whispering things like, 'But who are you? You are nobody special. There are people with better qualifications and experience than you to do this. You are not the best person for the job. You are inadequate. You are on an ego trip.' We may not find it easy to embrace this new territory wholeheartedly. This is an experience many of us go through on our journey in life, and unless we learn to recognize what is going on, we will hold back on our gifts and they will not be given.

Often when we choose to step forward in our life, we encounter resistance within ourselves. When Buddha sat under the bodhi tree and vowed to find enlightenment, every possible demon arose within him to scare and tempt him away from his goal. When Jesus was ready to start teaching, he went into the wilderness for 40 days and nights and faced a dark night of the soul. These are not the machinations of some external evil or force, but our own shadows, the workings of the deepest parts of *our own mind*. When we stay courageous and focused on our goal of higher awareness, all these 'negative' energies become transmuted and work *for* us rather than against us.

A while ago I had an experience like that. I had been invited back to South Africa to give talks and workshops in Cape Town and Johannesburg. Helen Burton, my friend and organizer there, kept me in touch with the interest, and a lot of media representatives wanted interviews. One day, not long before I went down to Cape Town, we were speaking on the telephone and she said, 'By the time you have finished the trip, you will be quite a celebrity here.'

Part of me was excited by that, and another part felt quite uneasy. Doubts started to surface. Was I just on an ego trip of self-aggrandizement? Was I just another author plugging and promoting himself? Not that there is anything wrong with that, but I wondered if I was straying from my true intention and my deeper purpose. I took some quiet time to check out my motivation. I do love the attention and the excitement but, even more important, I realized that I loved sharing. Far from this being a distraction, I saw that it *was* my purpose – to share with as many people as possible! When I aligned with my soul, I began to realize that I had actually *promised* to have fun, travel, inspire and be inspired. Far from being an ego trip, it was actually my soul's promise to do this. It was my destiny to play a bigger game.

That trip was one of the busiest schedules I had ever had. I was there for three weeks, but did most of the work in 13 days, and in those 13 days I did 8 public talks and workshops, 3 corporate breakfast seminars, 3 television interviews, a TV documentary, 6 radio interviews, 3 press interviews and 2 personal coaching sessions. Beforehand, I wondered how I would cope with it all. It seemed too much for me, something I could easily fail at or burn out from. But I ended up thoroughly enjoying myself and learned an important lesson: we can only crash and burn out when we rely on our own power and do not tap into a greater power. A few times I was tired, but I learned how to live in the moment and do what was right in front of me. If I thought about everything I had chosen to do, I would feel overwhelmed. When I focused on what was in front of me, I was present and not just able to cope, but to really enjoy myself too. I think we are often called to take on something that we feel is too big for us to do alone; then we come to realize that we need the help of others. In this case I had to rely heavily on Helen to support me and look after me. I needed to allow myself to become healthily dependent on her and other people, to recognize my own needs and see how I could meet them. On my own I couldn't have coped. Instead of thinking all of the right things to say to the right people at the right time, at times it felt as if I was simply a channel through which words were flowing. It was beautiful – and it was easy! It made me get out of my own way, relax, open up and trust.

As we start out on our journeys in life, we often believe we can go it alone. But we learn that we do need help, and acknowledging this is not a weakness but a true strength. Our path to greatness is not through our ego, but through surrendering to the strong hand of love working through us.

RADICAL DEPENDENCE

In western culture, where we are encouraged to be independent, not to let anyone have too much power over us, the idea of becoming dependent on a higher power seems like suicide. We sometimes face challenges that frighten us and yet we're reluctant to draw back. It is as if our soul is calling us to open up to a new, exciting and inspiring vision. The vision hooks us, we enrol on the curriculum and know that there are lessons to learn. And when we are called to face challenges, whether we know it or not, we're *putting our trust and faith in the higher power within us.* We are called to faith and trust, to surrender, ask for and receive from this higher power. We are called to face and overcome our feelings of inadequacy. As we do this our ego is likely to shriek as loudly as it can, throwing up its big guns to try and keep us playing at a smaller level. Our ego starts to show us all the ways we can fail, look stupid, get tempted in unhelpful directions, and we may think that the best thing we can do for ourselves is to step away and shrink back down.

What we probably don't realize is that we are *supposed* to feel like that! It shows that we are *precisely* on track! The feeling we are running from, and that is trying to sabotage us, is radical dependence. When we are not feeling dependent, we are trying to do it all alone. This kind of dependence shows us that we can best succeed by partnering with love or God or whatever higher power you believe in. Indeed, part of the process is learning to face our fear of dependence, so that we can become truly interdependent.

IF WE ARE RELYING ONLY ON OURSELVES, WE HAVE EVERY REASON TO BE ANXIOUS!

We are told that security comes from relying on ourselves, and then we begin to realize that our security comes from not relying on ourselves, but on our higher power. This secret can make us all extraordinary – radical dependence on love! It will make us feel very uncomfortable as we begin to turn a corner. We are called to turn all our theory into practice. We can read books on trust and faith, but the moment we are actually called to live by them, we step back and grab back all the control in our life for ourselves. *A Course in Miracles* teaches us:

> The recognition of your own frailty is a necessary step in the correction of your errors, but it is hardly a sufficient one in giving you the confidence which you need, and to which you are entitled. You must also gain an awareness that confidence in your real

strength is fully justified in every respect and in all circumstances . . . It is not by trusting yourself that you will gain confidence. But the strength of God in you is successful in all things.

Our real strength is to know and then experience that the power of God is literally within us, not as a vague concept but as a reality.

We live our best life when we learn to trust ourselves more and more, when we can bypass our ego knowledge and access our deepest wisdom. To hear our own wisdom, we need to be more comfortable with our own silence. It is only in this silence that we can hear the eternal whisperings of our own soul. When we do this we find an inner knowing, a sense of rightness that goes beyond words or logic and that needs no external approval. Any form of meditation will support this.

To start to live this way, start small. The purpose of life is not to engender more fear, but to dissolve fear. So start with small areas where you are willing to move through some fear to relinquish individual control for a greater power. Then move into new areas as you build up your 'faith muscle' and your confidence. As you begin to see how bigger hands are crafting your life, you become more and more willing to move towards radical dependence. And this is our lifetime's work. We all have many places where we are in control, and want to be in control, and we are scared and unwilling to surrender our control of these.

FIRST STEPS – GROW AS WE GO

It is easy to forget that everything we now know how to do and achieve we either once didn't know how to do, or it was something that frightened us. First steps are often bold, but in time the activity becomes natural and we wonder how we could ever have found it scary or difficult. Yet only those who know the invisible can do the impossible.

Sometimes, in order to shine and play a bigger game, we need to be put in a situation where we practically have no choice. Mary is an actress, and had been offered three days' work away from home: a day of rehearsal and two days filming. Her work until then had been mainly background and extra work, with a few featured and directed roles. Due to the inexperience of the director, she didn't get the script until she arrived on the set. When she looked through it, she was terrified. Not only was there more dialogue to learn than she had ever had before, but only two people were being filmed. She was very much in the starring role. She confided in me, 'If I'd known how much script there was, I would have said no, but as I was there, although I was terrified, I felt I had to give it my best shot. I didn't want to let anyone down. I have to say, I did do extremely well! I rose to the occasion, and it brought the best out of me. Everyone was very supportive, and we all wanted it to go well.'

SOMETIMES A PERSONAL CHALLENGE IS A CALL TO STEP UP

Have a think about some of the reasons you are not taking steps in your own life now. What do you tell yourself? If you step up you will:

- *create enemies and be attacked*
- *have to become a lot more political*
- *be shown to be imperfect in your own life*
- *have to shoulder lots of responsibility on your own*
- *serve your own needs and get out of integrity*
- *have to be responsible for more people*
- *lose so much of your freedom*
- *not survive financially*

Laura had breast cancer, and when I first met her just a year later she was vibrant, positive and happy. She told me, 'My cancer was really a funny-looking gift. It was strangely wrapped, but taught me so much. I used to be very fearful, and through my cancer I have had to face many of my fears. I am now much more at peace, and I realize that peace is the absence of fear.' She had survived and was now flourishing, and she explained to me, 'So many people I meet tell me I should share my story around my cancer, but thousands of women have breast cancer. Why should my story be any different?' I explained to Laura that her story didn't have to be different to be inspiring, but it did need to be authentic.

Her spiritual faith and belief had grown extensively. She could see that anything she could do to inspire other women, to give hope and reduce the amount of fear of cancer would be a great service, but she still doubted herself. She explained that as a child she had been made to feel unimportant, that she and her needs weren't important, and she was still finding that old conditioning difficult to let go of.

This is what so many of us do: we don't think that we are important enough, so our personal experience is not important enough, or our life significant enough, to share with others. But our life experience *is* valid. Whatever in our life can help others, we can share. It wasn't that Laura should or ought to help others. Guilt is never a helpful motivator, but she was moving towards valuing herself and her experience enough to shine a light into an area that for many people is dark and scary. She knew what she was called to do, and would do, but still resisted it.

When we don't recognize the calling and opportunity to step up in consciousness and success, we create a block, not just for ourselves but for others too. Because we are all connected, when we hold ourselves back we hold them back too, and vice versa, but there are some things that we cannot hold back: in natural progression babies become toddlers, toddlers grow to adults. Every day people are born and other people die. Life is in constant motion, yet we seem to be the only species who are able to choose to stop ourselves progressing or evolving in consciousness.

Great teachers do not just create more students; they create more teachers. The most powerful people are the ones who hold a mirror up to show others how powerful and amazing *they* are. To do this we need to be secure within ourselves, know that deep within us there is an abundance of gifts and go to that place of inner abundance regularly to refresh and renew ourselves.

FROM RIGHT AND WRONG TO OUR OWN INNER TRUTH

The greatest art is to be oneself. This naturally follows from living our purpose rather than living for approval. Mike was at a crossroads in his life. He had joined the armed forces when he was younger, and after leaving the army had gone into computer sales and marketing. He was successful but felt unfulfilled. When we talked about what he might want to do next, he didn't seem to have many ideas. I began to sense that he seemed to have an underlying fear of *making the wrong decision*. As uncomfortable as it was being stuck, it was at least familiar, and it was better than getting it wrong. It emerged that Mike's mother had been quite rigid, and thought in terms of right and wrong. This had been Mike's criterion for making decisions – *is this the right or wrong decision?* It usually induced a lot of anxiety in him: he was worried that he would make the wrong decision, and had an underlying fear of potential punishment. I suggested an alternative. 'Could you imagine the possibility of making *true decisions* that will take you beyond the paradigm of right and wrong?' Mike's usual style of thinking would not take him forward at this point in his life. He needed to develop a stronger sense of our own truth, not what is objectively right. No-one can tell us what is true for us, we can only discover that for ourselves. For Mike, it was about developing a greater connection with the child within him, with his own feelings.

We all need to develop a relationship with what we can't see with our eyes, but know in our heart. We need to learn how to develop our inner sense of what is true for us. This does mean taking more responsibility for ourselves. My friend Gregg Levoy, author of *Callings*, teaches us, 'The past shapes us, but by following the deep calling to heal ourselves and throw off old curses, we may be able to reshape our response to that past and perhaps even the way in which we remember it. Sometimes we're called to move backward so that we can move forward with a greater sense of ourselves and with greater confidence.' Mike was astonished at how, by recognizing a past pattern, he could shift dramatically and discover a whole new world of possibility, free of the self-tyranny of *getting his life wrong*.

PLAYING BIG IS OFTEN INSPIRED BY PASSION

Never underestimate the power of passion.
EVE SAWYER

Playing big is always motivated by a passion within us, something that we love dearly. Chantal Cooke is passionate about radio. 'How amazing it is,' she told me, 'to be able to enter people's lives through their radios, and be able to share ideas with them, uplift and educate them.' She always knew she wanted to own and run her own radio station one day, not just another pop radio station, but one that dealt with health, personal growth and environmental issues and was entertaining, educational and inspiring, balanced with great music from around the world. She wanted to change people's consciousness while entertaining them. So she spent her younger years working in any radio environments she could. She got her first job by putting her suit on and going around every media organization she could find in London armed with a bunch of CVs and she didn't give up until she was offered a job on the spot by one company.

She kept learning all she could and making connections, often holding down several jobs as both producer and presenter so that she could learn her craft. Deep down, she nurtured her dream, knowing that when the time was right, the opportunity for her station would become clear. Her passion and enthusiasm never waned. She met Kenny, who became her business partner, and they researched the idea of buying a station, but soon realized they couldn't afford it, although they knew its name – Passion for the Planet! Unlike a normal business, you can't just go and set up a new radio station, as they must all be licensed by the government. Chantal's opportunity came when the UK government announced a tranche of licences for the newly evolving DAB (Digital Audio Broadcasting) radio systems. She and Kenny managed to persuade a consortium to allow them to join and bid for these London licences and did everything she could to generate support for the bid, sending out 200 letters to solicit support for the station idea she and Kenny were proposing.

When it was announced that their consortium had won the licences and that one of the major reasons was the strength of the contribution made by the Passion for the Planet proposal, she was obviously thrilled. As she described it: 'That was one of those scary and exciting moments when we realized *this dream can come true*. We needed to decide we really were serious and committed, and we were, so we proceeded full speed.' Since then they have also won licences for many other parts of the UK, and began broadcasting on 10 September 2002.

Digital radio will become huge in the UK over the next few years, as analogue radio is phased out, and Passion for the Planet is poised to be a leading light in new radio formats. Chantal's own passion has created Passion for the Planet and its influence will be considerable. When I asked her where she thought most people failed in playing big and living their dreams, she told me, 'You've got to know where you want to go and just do it! It may be scary or feel overwhelming, you may have doubts and wonder about your own ability, but you will grow as you go along. Sometimes you will fall flat, but you can always get up again. The greatest reward for me is the freedom I experience to set my own goals, and do things that inspire me. And I love being able to touch the lives of thousands and hopefully in time even millions of people.' When I asked her what one tip she would give to others wanting to play big in their lives, she said, 'Talk to people who are passionate about what they do, offer to buy them lunch and ask for their help. I have bought dozens of lunches for people, and in doing so have learned so much, and created an impressive network. These people are passionate, and they can talk for Britain, and in doing so give you a great education for the price of a curry!' Our passion makes us unstoppable, and reawakens passion in others. It awakens potentialities which had hitherto lain dormant within us, raises our consciousness to new realms, and we begin to function along new dimensions.

EXERCISE

* Who are your teachers of passion? Who could be? If you don't know, seek some out. Read biographies or autobiographies of people who fascinate and inspire you.
* Stretch yourself outside your comfort and familiarity zones by having new experiences, for example go to a different kind of film, a dance class, try flower arranging or talk to refugees. Do something that is really unlike you and you have decided you would *never* do. It will stretch you and get you thinking differently.

PLAYING BIG IS NOT SELFISH

Although we appear to be billions of separate individuals each with our own mind, in truth there is only one mind, and we are all part of it, we are in it. All our thoughts have power. We may not yet understand this power but it is there. In *A Course in Miracles* we are taught that 'When we are healed, we are not healed alone'. This means that as we heal our fear and guilt, everyone benefits. Not only is love good for us, it is good for everyone. When we shine our own light fully, we can illuminate the lives of thousands, even millions. Love wants our life to be touched by as many people as possible, and wants us to touch as many people as possible. This doesn't require us to become evangelists or preachers.

EXISTING FULLY – OUR FEAR OF SHINING

For us to play big for love, we have to be willing to exist more fully. Many of us have grown up in homes where we felt there was not enough love, physical or emotional space for us. We have learned to *hide out* or be unseen as a survival strategy, fearing that if we are truly seen we will be found lacking. I have had big issues with my older sister, good old sibling rivalry stuff: not enough space for us both, competition, and not enough love to go around. My relationship with her has been a cause of great pain in my life. Since I have been writing about abundance and looking at what is going on in the world, I have begun to realize how I had projected onto her the view that she didn't allow me to exist fully, that I wasn't welcomed, and that she took up my psychic space in our family. Yet, when I was really honest, I saw that I had done exactly the same to her. I had tried to deny her the full space she needed, and I had tried to exclude her. Even deeper I became aware that I had not fully owned *my own* inner space, and had made her out to be my oppressor. Part of *me* was keeping me small, oppressing and suppressing myself, denying to myself my own right to exist fully.

I saw how although I have had abundance on a surface level, on a deeper level I have blocked plenty in my life as I have been in competition, and felt guilty that I wanted to gain the upper hand over my sister or other people. Also I have felt uncomfortable about taking up too much space in the world, and earlier in my life tried to pretend I hardly existed at all.

As we look around in the world, this kind of subjugation seems very prevalent. So many groups seem to want to eliminate each other and deny each other's right to exist. There is a deep belief that there aren't enough natural resources or love or money to go around. We need to understand that there is enough space for us all, that one group's existence needn't be a threat to the existence of others. Somehow we convince ourselves that who we are is not enough, that the only option is win/lose. Spiritual solutions move our understanding to one of win/win.

We may have compensated for feeling small in our family by trying to compete, by trying to become special. We may have inflated ourselves and become grandiose. We are still playing out a role to compensate for feeling small or insignificant in our past. It is important to understand that we can find a truer place of power within us, where we are not competing for space or attention, but simply taking up our natural space in this world.

There are incredible gifts waiting to be given to us, waiting for us to open to receive them, for us to move beyond the need to deserve and into a paradigm of willingness to receive. There is so much we are not asking for, or pretending we didn't deserve. But in learning to ask we open the doors to creative abundance. We are surrounded by benevolent spiritual helpers, who are just waiting to serve us. Instead of complaining, we should stop and ask for help first.

EXERCISE

✱ *Whose light do you think will be diminished or overshadowed if you shine yours more fully?*

✱ *Close your eyes and imagine your family. See any imbalance between you all energetically. Ask your higher mind to take you all back to a place of centre, where you are bonded, where there is flow between you, and you are all equally important. Ask for balance between you all. Do this as many times as you need to until you can feel a deeper peace.*

OUR POWER OF PERSONAL LEADERSHIP

There are three ways to lead people: example, example and example.

Anon.

We are all leaders because we are all rich and overflowing with gifts. A leader is someone who is willing and chooses to give their gifts again and again, to help others liberate their talents. Personal leadership is about living from our own authenticity, from our truth and our own values. It is looking at the world and knowing it is not what it could be, it doesn't always reflect the highest of human potential. Instead of moaning, criticizing, complaining or attacking, we must decide that we will do something creative in order to make the world a bit better. When we complain, judge or fight, we create 'stuckness'. When we decide to give our gifts, communicate honestly and make a creative contribution, we create flow and we give hope. We become accountable and connect with others. Indeed leadership is about increasing contact and connection with people. Command, control and distance simply don't work effectively any more, and maybe never did. To bring the best out of ourselves and others we need engagement, and to recognize the power of relationships. This will become our lifeblood.

Leadership is not about sacrifice or carrying the burdens of the world on our shoulders, or feeling guilty. True leadership is about greater creativity, support and happiness. It is about giving excess worries and concerns back to God. This is not abdication: it is placing our troubles where they can be dealt with. When we are weighed down with guilt and heaviness, we can't respond or don't want to respond to the needs of others. We may not even see the needs of others, or may even be repulsed by them. It is about stepping beyond our personality and taboos and leading the way forward for ourselves and others. It is about finding and sharing the way home, and that is always towards love, always towards Heaven.

Whatever you are offering in the world, don't only expect people to be peaceful and appreciative; expect people in pain; expect people to disagree with you and challenge you. They are there to help us reach new levels and new understandings, to keep us at the cutting edge of our creativity. As much as you are able, don't judge them, but be grateful to them for helping you stretch and grow. They are taking you deeper into your own genius. Difficult clients can be the ones who motivate you to a new level of consciousness. The ego loves to motivate through fear and distance; the spirit loves to motivate through engagement and rewards.

THE ILLUSION OF CONTROL

One way of controlling is by setting up rules and laws. Every rule is a place where we want it done *our way*. I never cease to be amazed by people's creative ability to break and get around rules. Too many rules kill creativity, stifle innovation and dispirit people. If we found a way of channelling this energy into more productive areas it would be amazing. Rules start from the premise that, if they can, most people will do something wrong. Our need for rules reflects our need to create rules to control groups rather than individuals. If one person does something wrong, then a rule is usually made that covers everybody, and we call it fairness. In my experience, most people will do the right thing when left to use their own judgement.

The most frustrated and unhappy people in the world are those who try to control everything. We want things done the 'proper' way, the way *we* want them done. Yet there are thousands of things we cannot control that can influence our life in a positive way. When we can understand this, know it *and not be afraid*, we are powerful. Being unable to control is not a failure, it is the door to real power. I am not sure we can even *control* a single person; but we can *influence* an infinite number. We can't control profit, but we can influence what creates profit. Let's not kid ourselves about our ability to dominate events and circumstances. Management is about control. Leadership is about influence.

Empowerment does not mean taking power from the top and spreading it throughout the company, it means giving everyone more power. Through skills, commitment, passion, love and energy, we all have power, now. This is not power we give, but power that others already have. Real power is creating an environment where people are encouraged to find their own power and use it for the benefit of all, not just for the few. This power is not sourced in authority, but in skills, commitment, experience, passion and inspiration. The real opportunity is to bring our power and other people's power *together* – not in a fight or power struggle but in a creative partnership to produce success for everyone.

OUR POWER TO DRAW OUT THE BEST IN PEOPLE

Most people want to do their best. I don't think they wake up in the morning and scheme to mess up their boss, colleagues, friends or family. Rarely do people give their best because a rule tells them they should. Most people give of their best because they are inspired to. If a workplace, family or community places no value on creating a space where people can express the best of who they are, then people's energy is more likely to be expressed unhelpfully. People are sacred, and their basic humanity cannot be improved upon. We need to draw out of them trust, love, creativity. We can improve work, but not people. Management can be a calling, a sacred trust in which the well-being of other people is put into your care during much of their waking time.

Real power begins on the inside, with self-awareness and self-acceptance. It calls us to make a transition from the external to the internal. Acceptance of ourselves as we are and things as they are is the pathway to power, personal authority, leadership and fulfilment.

BEYOND CONTROL AND COMPLIANCE

FORCING OURSELVES

'How do I discipline myself to make myself do the things I need to?' Tarik asked. Quite a reasonable question, on the face of it. He was director of sales for a big family company, and he had lots of responsibilities on his shoulders. We all need to know how to motivate ourselves, and follow through, but for him something didn't feel quite right. 'Do you want to do those things?' I asked. 'Not really, but I have to make myself.' 'Do you enjoy your work?' I asked. 'Not really,' he responded again, 'but a lot of people rely on me for their jobs.' So Tarik was forcing himself to do many things that needed to be done, but he didn't particularly want to do. This situation is familiar to many of us: we all have some areas of duty, but if the majority of our life is duty, we are likely to run out of motivation. Tarik's heart lay elsewhere; he was forcing himself into a role. Whole industries have grown up trying to teach us to motivate ourselves to do what we don't want to, and to make other people do what they don't want to. It's called management.

The greatest art of management and especially self-management is discovering what we are naturally motivated by, what we have energy and skills for, and then figuring out how to adapt our work and sometimes the organization to take advantage of these natural talents. Too often things work out in reverse. We try to force ourselves to do what we are neither good at nor motivated by. This is the old work ethic again – if we are not suffering, it's not really work. Our journey of personal power may involve going from pushing ourselves and being harsh on ourselves to loving, nurturing and inspiring ourselves. Our journey is towards a greater level of self-love. As we have seen, too often we force ourselves against our true nature, trying to deny our gifts and talents to conform to some external belief system or force.

Tarik began to be honest with himself, and realized that he really wanted to be doing different work. Together we began to put a plan in place so that he could start creating what he was motivated by, and transitioning away from what he was forcing himself to do. This was likely to take several years, but he really had little choice.

WHY ARE WE SCARED OF OUR OWN POWER?

With power naturally comes responsibility, and that can be a scary thing to deal with. It means being accountable for our own decisions, successes and failures. This can be an exposed place to be, and we may not want to deal with either the criticism or the acknowledgement we may receive. So we often create dramas and stories to hide our power from ourselves.

A great way to discover how we may be keeping ourselves small is to look at some of the judgements we have made about powerful people. Here are some questions to stimulate your thinking. Be very honest in your answers, or you may rob yourself of some very useful insights:

EXERCISE

What do you believe about powerful people? Which of the following can you relate to? They are . . .

Harsh, corrupt, hard-hearted, aloof, competitive, nasty, self-serving, interested only in material not spiritual realms, betrayers, demanding, manipulative, egomaniacs, not to be trusted, jealous, vulnerable to attack, fearful, out of balance or integrity . . .

Add your own terms to the list.

We can begin to understand that whatever we see and judge in powerful people we fear that we will become if we embrace more of our own power. Our ego creates fear after fear to keep us small. By taking back our judgements on powerful people, we can liberate ourselves to own our power with integrity.

MEDITATION

I know it is safe to be powerful

I know how my own power helps other people

Powerful people don't threaten me

I join with powerful people

I know how the authentic power of others is a blessing to me

I enjoy being powerful

Being powerful is a gift and blessing to myself and others

I enjoy taking responsibility for myself and others

I am powerful without force or manipulation

Power is an abundant resource

Each powerful person helps to create more true power

WHAT IS OUR GOAL FOR BEING POWERFUL?

It is very helpful to be clear about the purpose of developing personal power. We need to think about the influence we want to have and the impact we want to make; about what we want to create or initiate. Here are some questions to help you discover the purpose of your desire to be more powerful.

Within ourselves:

* Why do we want to be powerful?
* What changes do we want to make?
* What influence do we want to have?
* What do we want to transform?

In our immediate environment:

* Who do we want to help?
* How do we want to help?
* What do we want to provide?
* What support can we supply?
* Who can we give hope to?

In our wider world:

* What legacy do we want to leave?
* Who do we want to encourage?
* Who can we give hope to?
* What are we for?

WHAT IS THE SOURCE OF OUR OWN POWER?

We need to balance the ways we source our power, within us and from outside us. The more we try to source our power from outside ourselves, the less secure we may feel. Hannah was newly promoted into the role of news editor for a very successful magazine. She had started as a freelancer and now had a six-month contract, but was feeling insecure; she wished she had a full-time contract, believing that would make her feel better. As we talked it became clear that Hannah was very competent, but lacked confidence. She had experienced a difficult period in her career a couple of years before, and was still feeling a little fragile and did not trust in herself. She also felt she was operating in a vacuum. She needed guidance, positive feedback and ideas from her manager, but they weren't forthcoming. She felt a little as if she was hanging in mid-air and just waiting.

'What could you do to feel more secure?' I asked. 'I could ask them to give me feedback, I suppose, and I could ask them to give me ideas about how they see my news role developing,' Hannah responded. We met a few weeks later and she told me, 'Well, I asked for a meeting and got it, and they seem very happy with what I am doing. It also seemed to me that they are all so busy that they don't give my area much thought.'

Hannah was at a threshold. She was used to being told what to do, and was good at following through, but now she was being called to be an initiator, not just a responder. 'How about you create your area the way you would like it to be?' I suggested. A light seemed to go on in her head. 'I suppose I could. I have never been in this position before. I suppose I can come up with ideas, run them past people, cover the kinds of things I am passionate about, and really create what I want. I have a lot more freedom and power than I realized. Wow!' I suggested: 'Maybe that is your power and security, and what is likely to make you successful: your ability to be creative, come up with ideas and follow them through. Even if you don't get a full contract with your company, you can see that you are talented, creative, growing in confidence, and there are hundreds of opportunities available to you in the world. Employers will be lucky to have you, not just you lucky to get a job!'

Hannah was beginning to see where her power was – not in a full-time contract, not in the job title or industry sector, but *within her*. She was beginning to recognize her own creative abilities, her ability to get on with people, initiate ideas and work in partnership with other editors and teams.

THE POWER OF KNOWING WHAT WE WANT

Despite several decades of research, the most effective way to predict vocational choice is simply to ask the person what they want.

JOHN HOLLAND, career counsellor

Hannah found her power by shifting her thinking from *how can I please them and how can I fit in?* to *what do I want?* One of our greatest powers is to know what we want. It is that simple, but not always easy. Knowing, living by and doing what we want, with integrity, is the greatest principle for a happy, powerful and fulfilled life. Often we answer the question *what do I want?* with what we *don't* want, or redefine the question to accommodate what we think we can or should want, or what we feel we deserve. There is little to compare with knowing what we want, and making friends with our wants and desires is extremely powerful.

Leaders know what they want; they have goals for themselves which inspire and motivate them. But more importantly they want to know what other people want too, and help others achieve their goals. The best way to get what we want is to help others get what they want too. When we know what we want we can develop strategies and take action to get what we want. We can learn to deal with our own resistance, and the resistance of others. We can learn and grow, building self-confidence as we go.

Acknowledging what we want may take courage. It is important to let ourselves recognize our goals, even if we don't think we can achieve them, and even if we don't know how we could *ever* achieve them. For within wanting is a mysterious power of fulfilment. Here is a list of some things you may want. Add your own items to the list and keep adding as you think of more. Don't limit yourself but allow yourself to be free and open with your thoughts and desires.

- *I want lots of money*
- *I want to be creative*
- *I want to be acknowledged*
- *I want to feel I belong*
- *I want to feel fulfilled*
- *I want to be in charge of my life*
- *I want to be a mother/father*
- *I want to be a husband/wife/partner*
- *I want to feel like a true partner*
- *I want to experience real partnerships*
- *I want to be happy*
- *I want to be free*
- *I want fun and to feel alive*
- *I want to feel all my emotions*

Much of what we want are *things* but we also crave and enjoy experiences. We can't show the world experiences: the experience itself is between us and our own soul, and those with whom we shared the experiences. William Blake taught us, 'The soul is here for its own experiences.' Too often, we have been taught dogmas and ideas, and have not been encouraged to seek and value the experience of our soul and the divine. The mystic poet Kabir (1398–1448) suggests that the soul is here for its own joy, and that the desire for experience is the natural currency of our soul. Our soul longs for experience of the divine, which he calls 'the Guest', not just knowledge about it. He expresses it beautifully in his poem 'To be a slave to intensity':

Friend, hope for the Guest while you are alive
Jump into experience while you are alive
Think . . . and think . . . while you are alive.
What you call 'salvation' belongs to the time after death.

If you don't break your ropes while you are alive,
Do you think
Ghosts will do it after?

The idea that the soul will join with ecstatic just because the
body is rotten –
This is all fantasy.
What is found now is found then.
If you find nothing now,
You will simply end up with an apartment in the City of Death.
If you make love with the divine now, in the next life you will have the
face of satisfied desire.

So plunge into the truth, find out who the Teacher is,
Believe in the Great Sound!

Kabir says this: when the Guest is being searched for, it is the intensity
of the longing for the Guest that does all the work.
Look at me, and you will see a slave to that intensity.

WHAT IS YOUR RELATIONSHIP WITH YOUR DESIRES?

When you were young, were you encouraged to know what you wanted, and were you encouraged to find ways of having what you want? Or were you encouraged not to want too much? There are many popular expressions like *Those who want don't get*, and *Children should be seen and not heard*. We may have learned that our needs and wants aren't regarded as important.

> ### EXERCISE
>
> * *Who were your role models for being passionate about life – people who knew what they wanted and had what they wanted?*
> * *What messages, spoken or unspoken, did you get about your needs and wants?*
> * *Do you have any guilt about your needs and wants?*

Sometimes we have to search deep within us to discover what we really do want – our authentic desires. As Chuck Spezzano writes, 'Passion is taking such a bite out of life that when the juices run down your face, everyone licks their lips!' We are to love and experience life in all its forms.

OUR POWER TO GIVE OURSELVES TO LIFE

Attractiveness is a major leadership quality. Attractive leaders are people who give themselves fully, who know it is safer to be in contact with people, not distant and protected from them. They are learning to become more comfortable with their irresistibility and less afraid of it, and are learning how to retain their integrity. They learn how not to abuse their power and how to use their power to bless, inspire and encourage others. Instead of trying to consume people, they have more fun co-creating with them. They face and move through their fears of really connecting with people, because they know that is where the true power is.

Oftentimes we pick work or relationships where we know, deep down, we can hide out and not need to face our own attractiveness. This is a misuse of work and relationships, and can lead to deadness.

HOW DO WE DEAL WITH PEOPLE WANTING A PART OF US?

Deep down we may fear that when we shine, when we have the courage to be authentic, move beyond our defences and give ourselves to our life, we will become very attractive. We fear that when we are irresistible we will be overwhelmed. Our gut reaction is to defend and withdraw, but that is not the truth. We can learn to give ourselves completely without being a sacrifice. We can learn to use our own energy so that we can be an unlimited conduit for love, rather than just expressing a small amount. Crucial to this is learning how to set appropriate boundaries, knowing when to say no as well as when to say yes. If we are likely to give the shop away, we may need to learn to say no, so that our giving becomes truer, not sacrificial.

HOW DO WE DEAL WITH BEING ATTACKED OR OVERWHELMED?

'Life-affirming leadership is leadership that brings out the best in others or improves their contribution. Truly great leaders appeal to the best in people. They do not tell followers what they should be doing, but appeal to them to be the best they can,' says Margaret Wheatley, author of *Leadership and the New Science*. A major challenge of shining and becoming a leader in our own life is learning to deal both with our fear of, and at times the reality of, attack. How wonderful it would be if everyone loved and appreciated us – and we will experience that – but we are likely at some time to experience criticism, possibly ridicule, and people who may want to undermine us. The conventional view of leadership labels these people as our enemies. Visionary leadership is about being powerful without the need for enemies. True leadership doesn't need anyone to fight against, as it is motivated to create, not destroy, to join with, not distance from. Here are some ideas to deal with this:

- *Enemies are usually people we are not engaged with or connected to; there is usually an emotional distance, which both creates and sustains enemies. Enemies grow out of non-communication and non-engagement. A great point to remember is to stay engaged, connected and communicating with key people, so that this gulf doesn't come into existence. When there is a gap, negative fantasies easily arise to fill that empty space. Honest and authentic communication is the best antidote to, and dissolver of, distance.*

- *Look for the grain of truth in what our enemies say. What they say may hurt, but it may just reflect what we actually believe ourselves. They may be pointing out an incongruity, a weakness or an area we do need to improve. See the potential for learning and improvement, not just a chance to get defensive. If there is a grain of truth, be willing to adjust your own thinking or behaviour so that you have greater honesty and integrity. In this respect, our enemies serve us.*

- *Our enemies usually embody some hidden quality that we dislike in ourselves. We don't like it, so we bury it. Now we can only see it in someone else, and we sure as hell don't like seeing it out there either, which is why we try to harm or get rid of our enemies. Once we have this insight, we can start to pull back the projections we have made, for these sustain the energy behind enemies. We will learn a lot more about this in Chapters 4 and 5 on acceptance and owning our shadow.*

- *Our enemies are actually asking us for help. This may sound like a crazy thing to say, but A Course in Miracles teaches us that there are only two things going on in this world — love or fear, which is a call for love. That is all there is. If we are experiencing unloving behaviour, it can only be based in fear, as the only choices are love and fear. So everything is a call for love, not condemnation. We must not deny our desire to condemn, but must ask love to show us another response. I remember hearing the story of a minister who, leaving her church, was attacked by a man who demanded money from her. So centred in love was she that she gave him what money she had and said to him, 'I wish I had more to give you. God bless you.' Several years later, someone came up to her in her church, and said to her, 'I am the man that robbed you. What you said to me made me feel different about myself. I was in a mess, and your kindness to me when I was being unkind to you saved me. I am now turning my life around. Thank you.' That is the power of true leadership: love and kindness in the face of everything.*

MEDITATION AND PRAYER FOR AUTHENTIC POWER

To have without possessing is to be powerful

To act but not be attached to expectations is to be powerful

To love without conditions is to be powerful

To lead without dominating or controlling is to be powerful

To create and encourage creativity in others from within is to be powerful

To be inspired – and inspiring – is to be powerful

To accept without condoning is to be powerful

To touch the hearts of others with the authenticity of your own is to be powerful

To handle all your feelings with integrity is to be powerful

To forgive yourself for your mistakes is to be powerful

To show and extend your heart to others is to be powerful

To have the courage to look at and make peace with your own shadow is to be powerful

To love with all your heart is to be powerful

To not know and not be afraid to find your way is to be powerful

To act authentically with integrity is to be powerful

To be in awe of the deeper mysteries of life is to be powerful

To know that the more you share the wealthier you are is to be powerful

To know we all make mistakes and to be willing to correct them without punishment is to be powerful

To guide without interfering is to be powerful

COMMITMENT TO GIVING OUR GIFTS AND MAKING OUR CONTRIBUTION

Fear is part of the human condition. We may fantasize that people who have stepped into leadership roles no longer experience fear. The best leaders still go through fear, sometimes a lot of it. What distinguishes them is they have made a commitment that they will gift their message and share their gifts however they are feeling. When we are living our purpose, *the bigger our purpose, the bigger our fear*. The more people we can potentially help, the more our ego will try to force us into fear and playing small. Our ego urges us to delay our mission for thousands of spurious reasons: *you are not ready yet, you need more qualifications, you need to lose weight, gain weight, be old and wiser, be younger* . . . I am sure you can create your own list very easily. The crucial point is that our ego will tell us that now is never quite the right time, and we aren't quite the right person to live our purpose. Has your ego ever told you that *you are exactly the right person, perfect for this assignment, and this is exactly the right time?*

We need to recognize that feeling unqualified or unprepared does not disqualify us. Sheldon Kopp, author of *If You Meet the Buddha on the Road, Kill Him*, says, 'I have never begun any important venture for which I felt adequately prepared.' We are called to be willing to start, not perfectly prepared, and be willing to commit to each step of the way. You may have heard the story of Louise Hay, best-selling author. She wrote a manuscript about her insights into the links between physical ailments and our thoughts. No-one wanted to publish her! No publisher showed interest. Instead of giving up, she felt strongly enough to type several copies of the manuscript herself and start to sell them, and then she offered workshops on the subject. At first, only two or three people turned up. But she knew it was her purpose, and committed to it, and now that one book alone, *Heal Your Life*, has sold over 16 million copies and thousands turn up to her lectures. If you have read one of her books, you may well be grateful that she made her purpose more important than any fear or doubt. Her story is similar to thousands of others. She didn't wait until things turned out before she committed, she committed and then things turned out. Commitment holds a magic and mysterious power within it, which is why we are often scared of it. Remember, our ego tries to create fear around every gift we have. Commitment opens doors to freedom and helps us release ourselves from our fears, not create more of them.

EXERCISE

* *What can you start now?*
* *What are you prepared and qualified for, right now?*
* *What will you continue right now?*

Leadership and purpose are not in the *future*, they are *now*. Our ego will always make us prepare and procrastinate, while love is always telling us *here, now, this person needs your help*. We are ready now, and we develop our readiness by living our purpose. You deserve the fulfilment of giving your gifts and doing beautiful work, right now.

In my life, there have been many times when I have felt like giving up. It has all seemed too hard, I have been too scared, I haven't made enough money, I haven't had enough interest, people don't seem to have wanted what I offer, I have felt rejected or dejected. I have been very independent and commitment has felt like slavery. Freedom felt like keeping my running shoes by the door, always looking for escape routes and reasons to leave.

What I have learned, and am still learning, is that my ego's goals are always related to making me feel small, powerless and inadequate. My ego is always trying to get me to give up on my purpose. I have found it useful to ask myself, 'Well, if I gave it up, what else would I do?' and the truth is that there isn't much else I really want to be doing. So I realize the question is always one of commitment, my choice to keep going. The choice is always between remaining independent and becoming more inter-dependent. Each time I recommit, I find that something shifts in me: opportunities often manifest, but most importantly any fear or doubt in that moment begins to lift. Sometimes I just have to laugh at the silly thought that I would give it all up. I reconnect with that inner knowledge that I am living my own purpose.

Through commitment we are not inoculated against doubt, fear or feelings of inadequacy, but we are given the power to move through them. The greatest power is to realize that all these are just ego ploys to stop us giving our gifts. The answer is simple, if not always easy – keep giving! Give when we feel good, give when we feel afraid, give when we feel we have nothing to give, give when we feel we are useless, give when we feel inspired, give when we feel terrified, give when our heart is breaking. Our path is about learning how to give truly, without sacrificing ourselves. Through giving we join with other people, we dissolve a layer of our ego, and this is one of the most powerful healing principles. Our pain is caused by what we withhold, never by what we give. Through giving we get, through giving we help ourselves and others. We are here to undo our fearful thinking and giving our heart is the best way to discover and heal our fear.

It doesn't have to mean that we are trapped by what we are committed to, or that we are enslaved by it. Just because we are committed to something doesn't mean we can't change *how* we do it. In a committed relationship, or in our work, we often re-evaluate how we do things, what is working, what isn't working, what we are losing energy for, what new things are interesting and fascinating us. This is natural, and in fact very healthy, and is part of a dynamic and evolving relationship or purpose. We can find our freedom within our commitments, and don't lose our freedom by committing to what we love.

THE HIGHEST FORM OF COMMITMENT

The highest form of commitment is in essence saying 'Yes' to the truth of love and 'No' to the illusion of fear. When we say yes to our deepest heart's desire we send a very powerful message to the universe. It says to the universe that we are very serious, and when we get serious about serving the force of love, the universe gets serious about us and sends all manner of seen and unseen help. All sorts of opportunities wash up on our shore.

One of the extraordinary things about commitment is that it is not just a one-off decision: we are offered opportunities to commit and deepen commitment every day, and in each moment. We are always free to commit more deeply to the things we love and care about. Our ego will try and convince us to hold something back to save ourselves from pain. But as we realize that it is the holding back that causes our pain, we feel a natural desire to give ourselves more deeply. Will we love someone or something so much that we will give our all to them, and never give up on them? Will we keep giving through every level of fear, each disappointment, each layer of pain and every fear of rejection? That is commitment: to demonstrate that love is real and everything else is illusion. It is our life's work. It is the only thing that will do it for us.

Each time we commit, we are offered breakthroughs to new levels of love and abundance, trust and partnership. Within commitment there is the power to shift some of the biggest problems in our life. Without commitment, our progress is slower, and can even seem non-existent. Commitment causes us to be snakelike, shedding skins and being reborn. When things go well, commitment is easy. When our relationship seems to turn sour, when our business is struggling, the first thing that comes to our mind is not usually deeper commitment and deeper involvement – yet facing the fear and pain of doing this, over and over again if necessary, is what can free us. Every time we recommit, we move through a layer of distance and pain, into greater partnership. Commitment is giving ourselves fully so that we can receive fully. In committing we make our partner, our purpose, or our friends more important than doubt, self-attack or conflict.

Within each of us is an enormous creative spirit. It doesn't make us special; we all possess this power. We can learn to become inspired by our dreams and grow beyond our negative conditioning.

3

OUR POWER OF CREATIVITY
AND CREATIVE GENIUS

True creativity is being in union with our own divine nature.
Anon.

Genius is our direct connection to the divine mind, and is available
to each and every one of us. Our creative mind is connected to the
source and has answers to all our problems, while our ego will only
lead us into more cul-de-sacs. True creativity is something we *have*
to do, something we must bring into being. It is love bursting out
of us. Most of us have only glimpsed what our soul yearns to
express through being creative. We have barely charted or played
in the deep waters of our own being. Willingness to extend the love
within us through creative expression is our way of transforming
the world, for through creativity we can begin to move from the
life that was scripted for us by past conditioning, to a life of
autonomy and freedom. I am in awe of the beauty and mystery of
the creative process. When I look around the world at everything

that mankind has created and manufactured, I am astonished to think that all of it was once simply an idea in someone's mind. Indeed the whole world is the result of human imagination, and translation of the invisible to the visible is magical.

To create our dreams we need to be willing to journey on a daily basis into our authentic self. For much of the time when we are growing up we are taught to follow in the footsteps of parents and teachers, heroes and leaders. We are told what classes they think we should take, what sports we should follow, what our attributes should be, and what careers we should pursue. We are influenced to seek outside ourselves for inspiration and role models.

We have inherited so many beliefs that aren't ours, that stop us realizing our dreams. As we commit to doing what we love, old beliefs arise to get washed away. This is a natural part of our creative journey, as are the unearthing and undoing of unhelpful beliefs. When we can find ways of genuinely accepting and then moving on beyond these old beliefs, we can move into greater and more life-affirming belief systems, based on the principle of a kind, loving and supportive universe, not a frightening one.

There are a lot of creativity-squashing 'devils' inside most of us that we need to be willing to face. This is the other side of being creative – facing everything about us that is uncreative. Debbie Ford writes beautifully in *The Dark Side of the Light Chasers*: 'Shadow work is about opening your heart and making peace with your internal devils. It is about embracing your fears and weaknesses and finding compassion for your humanity. Give yourself the gift of your heart. As soon as you open your heart to yourself you will open your heart to all others.' Loving ourselves enough to give ourselves the gifts of our own creative self is a journey we are all on.

OUR POWER OF PERMISSION

I met Ali on a writing course I was running with my friend Jackee Holder. She hadn't written since she was 14 – about 20 years previously! Being a young mother, she had many calls on her time and had been put off by people who doubted her talent. We gave her and the other participants some exercises, and she spent about three hours writing during the day. When I spoke to her two weeks later, she had already finished the short story she started that day, and had entered it for a short story competition. I was thrilled for her and surprised.

It began to dawn on me that we all need permission from someone we respect in order to go ahead with new creative activities in our life. Sometimes all it takes is for someone consciously or unconsciously to say, 'Yes, you can do this!' to make us reach for our dreams. Whether it's friends, parents, therapists, coaches or inspiring role models, so many people can give us permission to succeed creatively in our life. The psychologist Carl Jung said that the biggest damage to a child's emotional health is the unlived life of the parents. Conversely, our own life fully lived can, often unknowingly, give permission to thousands to follow in our footsteps.

EXERCISE

* *Who has given you most permission to succeed creatively in your life?*
* *Who do you admire that you could seek permission from?*

One of the greatest purposes of life is not, as our ego would have us believe, to consume, but to create. The human imagination is the source of everything physical and is the most valuable and powerful tool we have at our disposal. As William Blake observed, 'Everything begins in the imagination.' Through imagination and action we bring our world and our dreams into being. It is the passport we create to take us into the real world. Imagination is where the divine mind penetrates the mortal mind and our only limits are those we create ourselves. The inspirational writer Napoleon Hill taught us, 'First comes thought, then organizations of that into ideas and plans; then transformation of those plans into reality. The beginning, as you will observe, is in your imagination.' The imagination is where all invention is born, and it needs to be unleashed with sensuality and abandon.

WE DON'T KNOW

At some point in our life we begin to wonder if there isn't something missing, whether the life we are living is in fact ours or one that we have been conditioned to live. We wonder what happened to that inner voice, that sense of adventure. In Willy Russell's film *Shirley Valentine*, the main character, in the midst of a midlife crisis, asks, 'Why are we given all these dreams if they aren't supposed to come true?' This is a feeling many of us share. We have inner longings, excitement, senses of possibility, and then wonder if we are just deluding ourselves and daydreaming – or might we be nurturing the seeds of our own greatness? The honest answer is *we don't know.*

Too often we try to control our future by telling ourselves that an idea is *not* going to work out. Or we can decide that we can find out, we can discover, we can venture into unknown territories in life and see what they hold. We can realize that the future can be full of possibility and opportunity, not just problems. Some of our ideas may be fantastic; some may not. I was once asked if I thought that anyone who wanted to be an astronaut could be, if they were determined enough. I answered that of course for most people becoming an astronaut is a fantasy, and may be a way of avoiding reality. But *some* people do become astronauts. Not long ago, South African Mark Shuttleworth fulfilled a childhood dream and became his country's first astronaut. Recently I saw an interview with Rani Manicka, a Malaysian woman living in Surrey in the UK. For years she had been working as a waitress in a pizza restaurant. Having never written before, not even at school, she had decided to start writing fiction, based on her grandmother's experience under Japanese occupation in the Second World War. She just went ahead and wrote a book out of nowhere! She took it to an agent who said it was very good, but too violent. So she wrote another book, which she called *The Rice Mother*. Again, she showed it to an agent, who took it to publishers who sold the UK rights alone for £300,000! Amazing for a woman who had never written before then suddenly got inspired to write. But the important thing was that she didn't write to get a big deal, she wrote to tell the story of her family's life: the material success was a by-product. We have no idea of the possibilities that are waiting just under the surface. The veil between fantasy and possibility may be very thin.

Sometimes it takes a leap of faith to get things going. You can bet that if Rani had taken professional advice it would have probably been *forget it!* If she had said to people, 'I am going to write a book, although I have never written before, and am going to get an enormous advance as an unknown author,' most people would have laughed at her and told her she was fantasizing, and seemingly rightly. The truth is we don't know where our dreams will lead us, we have to find out by stepping out into the unknown. We don't know the unexplored and undiscovered gifts and potential hidden within each of us.

INSPIRATION IS OUR ETERNAL CREATIVE COLLABORATOR

To be creative is to be in conscious contact with another realm of ourselves. It does not derive from the everyday 'I' that we use to pay the bills and drive to work, but from greater power. The artist Pablo Picasso described this in a letter to a friend: 'At the beginning of each picture there is someone who works with me. Toward the end I have the impression of having worked without a collaborator.' We are in an invisible but very real partnership with a force of inspiration that at first can feel separate from us. As we follow and trust our inspiration, it becomes more integrated and we simply experience it as a part of ourselves.

Inspiration is cultivating a space within us and an environment around us that encourage ideas to come to us. We need a space that holds and supports the germination of ideas – a space of emptiness: if we are full, how can more be added? Too often we are afraid of emptiness, of not having lots of distractions, of not being busy and having our time structured. But empty hands are receptive hands, they can receive and hold. In the Buddhist tradition, the Zen mind, or beginner's mind, is to know we don't know and not to be afraid. We are not limited by preconceived ideas, and are open to all possibilities.

THE POWER IN UNCERTAINTY

What we may fear most is not knowing. We demand certainty from a world that cannot deliver it. We want to know how it is all going to turn out and forget that whole purpose of adventure is embarking on a journey, the outcome of which is unknown. We need to learn to become more comfortable living in a state of not knowing. Dream builders develop a new relationship with uncertainty. We are afraid to fail, afraid to really succeed, afraid to be wrong or make mistakes. Perhaps the whole quality of our life is determined by our willingness to learn to live *with* uncertainty, and the realization that we and our own power, creativity and resourcefulness, as well as our willingness and ability to learn, are our greatest certainty. We cannot eliminate uncertainty from our lives, we can be certain of that! To know that if the stock market crashes, your partner leaves or your business goes through a tough time, you have within you the resources to cope and even flourish is truly powerful. We all have a need for a degree of structure and predictability, but too much structure and our spirit is suffocated.

OUR POWER TO DREAM

I truly believe that we should never give up on our hopes and dreams. The path may be rocky and twisted, but the world is waiting for that special contribution each of was born to make. What it takes is courage to follow those whispers of wisdom that guide us from the inside. When I listen to that, I expect nothing more than a miracle.

MARILYN JOHNSON KONDWANI, founder of a cosmetics company
for black women

Dreams are simply thoughts. We can dream with our mortal mind, which gives us dreams of fear, guilt and pain, or we can dream with our divine mind, which has the power of love and creativity behind it. We don't always know if our dreams will come true, or how long they will take to come true.

Some dreams are with us all our life; many we have in childhood and only reclaim later in life. Some dreams have died within us and need to be brought back to life. Our dreams are manifested for the highest good of ourselves and others. They can be a gift to the world. Our dreams rub off on other people, reminding them of their own, inspiring them to remember and live from the highest place within them. Many of us simply don't know people who *are* living their dreams, but when we do it's infectious. Too often we try and content ourselves with wondering what might have happened rather than discovering what we can make happen.

When I was a young boy, I looked at Jaguar cars with a longing, thinking how much I would love to have one. But I came from an *ordinary* suburban family, and *people like us* don't have cars like that. Only *special* people do, and I wasn't one of those special people. So I accepted that I would never have one. I guess you know that feeling. I always looked longingly at them, and fantasized *maybe one day . . . ?*

Not so long ago, my own car was beginning to get too old to maintain, so I needed to buy another one. I looked around at the sensible cars, but also kept looking at the prices of used Jaguars, and then talking myself out of that idea. I could only afford a secondhand one, and it would be too expensive to maintain . . . Suddenly, Chris, a friend's father, who was in the process of retiring from his used-car-dealing business, called out of the blue. 'I have just taken a Jaguar in part exchange. I sold it to the guy in the first place, and he has lovingly maintained it. It is in beautiful condition, and is only £2,500! Are you interested?' I had a mixture of conflicting feelings, both excitement and anxiety.

Part of my anxiety was that I was a *spiritual* person – was I *allowed* to have a beautiful car!? I realized that I wanted to integrate my material and spiritual needs, that they need not be at odds. I joked: under this spiritual exterior, there beats a materialist heart! I love both, and to deny spiritual or material pleasure is untrue.

My partner Helen and I went to look at it, and I immediately fell in love with it. It was the car I was born to drive! Almost without hesitation, I decided I would buy it. By the time I drove home, I felt it had been mine for ever. But apart from having a beautiful car, there was a deeper significance involved in the transaction. It was a dream that I had let go, that I had told myself I could never have. This car represented a shift from fantasy to the dream becoming a reality. Something began to stir and awaken in me, as I asked myself, 'What else have I told myself I can never have, that maybe I could have? What other dreams have I had, that I could bring back to life?' The Jaguar became a symbol of something much greater and more profound.

RECLAIMING OUR DESIRES

Getting that car was a desire of mine, and fulfilled desires are one of the greatest motivators for more creative action. Get into the habit of acting on your desires, even in small ways. Desire can get bad press in the spiritual world, but a life without desire is boring and mechanical. In the Hindu religious tradition, Shakti is the goddess who embodies desire, and guides us from one fulfilment to another. Our passion cannot fade, it can only be suppressed. Boredom is simply the mask we use to cover internal conflicts. We cannot eliminate desire, but when we try to suppress desire it turns into fear. We fear and criticize other people's desires. When we own our desires we start to bring ourselves back to life, we are willing to take risks to achieve our desires and we begin to taste the nectar of fulfilled desire. When we are bored, is it any wonder we feel frustrated? We are not admitting we have desires. We all do. We swap desire for apparent security and safety, and then wonder why we aren't happy. We get through boredom by re-owning our passions and desires, by opening to some of the very things and people we have feared and resisted.

HOLDING OUR DREAMS IN OUR HEARTS

When you were growing up, did you have someone who was holding your dreams in their heart? Most of us didn't, we have probably had more dream bashers than dream builders in our life. An exercise I love doing in workshops is to get people to break into small groups and name one of their dreams to the rest of the group. For many people, this alone is powerful. They take it in turns to tell each other, 'I hold your dream in my heart.' To know that someone *else* knows and cares about your dream, cherishes it, and holds it in their heart is incredibly powerful. For many of us, our dreams are so precious that we are afraid to share them for fear of them being ignored, ridiculed, or in some way rubbished. It can take great courage to share and courage to seek loving support.

EXERCISE

* *Find someone to join forces with. Know each other's dreams and hold them in your hearts. It must be someone you are willing to join with and trust that much.*

OUR DREAMS START WITH A CALLING

The concept of dharma, or purpose, holds that there are no spare parts in the universe. Each of us enters the world with a unique perspective and set of talents, which enables us to unfold an aspect of natural intelligence that has never been expressed before. When we are living in dharma, we are in service to ourselves and to those affected by our choices. We know we are in dharma when we cannot think of anything else we would rather be doing with our life. One of the greatest services we can perform for another person is supporting them in the discovery of their dharma.

DR DAVID SIMON, colleague of Deepak Chopra

We have within us the power to find and follow our calling. We may feel called to help people, heal people, nurture, love or inspire people; we may feel called to share our love of the natural world or help in the search for a cure for AIDS. No matter what our calling, it will fill our heart and leave us inspired.

MOVING TOWARDS A VISIONARY LIFE

Integrity must precede vision . . . If your vision does not have a strong integrity base, expect disaster down the line. Begin by focusing on integrity, and your visions have a great deal of power in the world . . . It produces alignment in yourself.

GAY HENDRICKS and KATE LUDERMAN, authors of *The Corporate Mystic*

We will confront our past conditioning, our inherited memories, as we follow our callings. Our goal is to move towards a place where we are not *acting from or reacting against* the past, which means we are still prisoners of our past programming. Our true power to create arises not in the past, but from moving into the present moment and discovering the power of *now*. Only *now* can we be free, only now can we truly create, not when we are reliving or acting from the past. This is vision leaping the abyss to love, and leaving a bridge for others to follow. Dr Chuck Spezzano says, 'If you are not living in a visionary life, you're living a life dictated by the past, if you're not happy, it's just a life dictated by old programmes, old patterns, with old unfinished business around.' Vision allows us to create reality, not merely react to it. Without it we have no direction in which to marshal all our resources. With vision we can perceive obstacles as challenges, not as stumbling blocks.

Many of our failures in life are failures of vision. By contrast, a clear vision is the first step on our road to success. Many people are too thin-skinned to keep their visions flourishing when they encounter resistance, and it's important to recognize that the better the idea, the more resistance it is likely to stir up within us and around us. Visionaries who shrink from conflict often try to keep their resistance under the rug, only to find that it surfaces later covertly. We must learn to deal with our own resistance and the resistance of those we encounter. The philosopher and mathematician Bertrand Russell said, 'The resistance to any new idea increases by the square of its importance.'

The greatest part of our calling is not necessarily related to achievement; it is more to do with who we become in the process. The true test of our calling is *how much love am I giving?* A visionary life brings something into the world that doesn't already exist; it is an act of love to make the world more inspired. The writer Nikos Kazantzakis says that 'By believing passionately in something that still does not exist, we create it. The non-existent is whatever we have not sufficiently desired.'

OUR DREAMS ARE FRAGILE AT FIRST

We tend to think of dreams as childish. We use this as a derogatory term, calling someone a dreamer as a put-down, and, sure, we can dream unrealistically. We can be daydreamers, and not turn thoughts into action, but all thought is creative. As I go through life, I wonder more often to myself, 'Who am I to judge whether someone else's dreams are realistic or not?' Knowing how easily fragile dreams can be shattered with thoughtless words, I am careful. As the Irish writer W. B. Yeats put it, 'Tread softly, for you tread on my dreams.'

At the beginning, dreams are tender and fragile things, easily stepped on and damaged by a variety of forces. When there is so much doubt and cynicism, so many material forces calling us to be 'practical' rather than creative, our dreams barely stand a chance. Sometimes we aren't sure how to respond to these callings from within, which are easy to label as impractical and useless. Too often it is hard for us to know and trust that a world of dreams, instinct and imagination will fit into the rational and orderly world that we usually inhabit. We may not even be sure we should have an *inner world*, we don't know what the relationship and interplay is between our inner and outer worlds. Often we are unsure if we should share our inner world with other people. Writer Annie Dillard articulated this well when she said, 'There is something you find interesting, for a reason hard to explain. It is hard to explain because you have never read it on any page. You were made and set here to give voice to this, your own astonishment.' The most demanding part of living a creative and imaginative life is the discipline of staying attuned to one's own innate sensitivity. This is finding what we are curious or passionate about, fascinated by, and that we are willing to stick with above all else.

WITH OUR DREAMS COMES IMPATIENCE

As our soul gives birth to our dreams, our ego gives birth to a twin force – impatience. Sometimes our soul opens up and gives us a glimpse of something so beautiful that we are captivated. What we don't know is that we may have some inner work to do to get there. But we haven't been betrayed, we've been enticed and engaged. Delays are not denials – we honestly don't know how long it may take for our dream to come to fruition.

WHY DON'T OUR DREAMS SEEM TO COME TRUE?

Dream lofty dreams, and as you dream you shall become.
Your vision is the promise of what you shall one day be.
Your idea is the prophecy of what you shall at last unveil.
JAMES ALLEN, author of *As a Man Thinketh*

Our cherished dreams and wishes don't come true for various reasons. We

- *never move them from fantasy to action*
- *take wrong action*
- *try to achieve our dream on our own, fail to ask for help from a higher power or from people who can help*
- *give up too soon*
- *take advice from the wrong people*
- *take too many precautions and hold back on commitment*

WE NEVER MOVE THEM FROM FANTASY TO ACTION

We daydream and fantasize but never really commit to making our dream happen. We stay in the comfort zone of keeping the idea in our mind, and never take the risk of really giving it wings. We may even get as far as doing some research to look at viability, but don't implement it. We treat our dream as an academic or intellectual exercise and don't keep our dream in our heart where it will become most powerful. We may think our dream is of no importance in the big picture, but as the novelist and poet Maya Angelou once said, 'If one is lucky, a solitary fantasy can totally transform one million realities.'

WE TAKE WRONG ACTION

Too often we don't have a clear strategy for achieving our dreams. Although much of our success is likely to come through synchronistic meetings and unlikely coincidences, we need to plan too, and know how to start. What new habits do we need to develop? What must we do on a daily, weekly and monthly basis to build up energy and get us into the flow? This isn't always smooth. As Gregg Levoy wrote in *Callings*, 'In making the leap from vision to form, you will suffer setbacks, occasionally severe. At our first steps towards authenticity – or love or compassion or any calling – every devil in hell comes to meet us. Only when you try vision in the world can you test whether it's true.' We need support and determination.

WE DON'T ASK FOR HELP

We confuse issues by mistaking the needs of our ego for our heart's dream. We then might ask for love to get behind *our* brilliant ideas, and can end up feeling disappointed and let down. What we should be doing instead is going deep within ourselves to discover what *love's* plan is. Spirit is always whispering to our soul, when we are willing to listen. This is surrender, when we are called to, and become willing to, implement love's plan, not our ego's. Then we are not just implementing our own dream. We become truly powerful, as our dreams become expressions of love. Far from having to sacrifice, we can then fully receive and share the benefits of love.

WE GIVE UP TOO SOON

Delays are not denials. Too often we impose our own time scale on our dreams, and judge their success or failure from our own limited perspectives. We don't know what would have happened if we had continued another three months. Sometimes we may be tempted to give up just as we are about to succeed.

WE TAKE ADVICE FROM THE WRONG PEOPLE

The mystic and poet Rumi cautioned us, 'When embarking on a journey, never consult someone who has never left home.' Everyone has an opinion; many fewer people have valid experience to share with us. When I was considering leaving the corporate world to start my own business, dozens of people wanted to share their opinions and advise me. Looking back, I realize that none of them had ever done what I was planning to do. Well-intentioned as they may have been, I needed to speak to people who had travelled the path I was considering. Too often, we ask for opinions from people who are not qualified to give us their advice. In the nicest possible way, ask if they know what they are talking about. I have seen so many people's dreams sabotaged because they have taken the advice and opinions of someone who is fearful and not qualified by their experience to comment.

WE TAKE TOO MANY PRECAUTIONS AND HOLD BACK ON COMMITMENT

Understandably, we often hold back from committing to something fully until it works out, and in doing so we miss the vital key, which is that our dreams are likely to succeed only when we have committed fully to them. Often we step out so far into the sea and then stop. This isn't how we learn to swim. We swim by building up little by little and then reaching the point where we let go of safety and plunge fully into the water. As we discovered in Chapter 2, there comes a time when we are called to take on something that we can't do alone, and that we know we can only succeed at if we commit fully and trust in a higher power than our ego. We don't trust the universe or ourselves enough. That is where we often get caught: we hold back and in holding back we rob ourselves of the success we deserve. Dr Chuck Spezzano writes, 'A certain flow will emerge because when you give yourself 100%, things come to you easily. Doors open. Opportunities occur. Luck happens. No problem can withstand the power of your choice to give yourself 100% . . . Total commitment creates a state of vision in your life.'

WITH OUR DREAMS COMES A SHADOW

Our dreams are not sinister, but there are many parts of us that are often not in alignment with our dreams. For every part of us that wants to build a future, be happy and successful, there are other parts of us that may prefer to hold onto the past, stay in control and not run the risk of criticism. There are forces *within us* that are not friendly to our dreams. We may need to acknowledge our own cynicism, our own doubt and fear, not in order to stop us, but in order to be honest. We must find ways, not of fighting these forces, but of integrating them so that we can move forward in a more whole fashion.

Too often we focus on the achievement of our dreams, not on how they call us to grow in order to achieve them. We focus on the outer without recognizing that just as much work needs to go in the inside. We may have to deal with disappointments, feelings of unworthiness, self-attack and our need to control. But this is not a distraction, it is an integral part of the journey. It is how we open our heart, develop compassion for ourselves and become kinder to ourselves. At the end of our lives we need to let go of everything material, but what we don't lose is the love we have shared. The one constant in this world is the miracle of God's love and its reflection in our human hearts. The love is eternal; everything else is transient.

WE NEED MORE PRACTICAL DREAMERS

We need more dreamers who do not just see what *is*, but can see what *could be* too, to cultivate the soil of their imaginations and show us possibilities for the future. We need dreamers who can turn their dreams into practical ways of living, or who can work with people who can help them do that. Robert Schwartz, founder of the School for Entrepreneurs in America, talks about many entrepreneurs as being practical dreamers. 'Entrepreneurs are the principal instigators of social change. Without new products and services, nothing changes. Without certain works of art – the creation of entrepreneurial writers and painters – new ideas would not circulate and nothing would move.'

TURNING UP MORE FULLY

In order to learn how to 'turn up fully' for someone else, we need to know how to turn up fully for ourselves. If we didn't feel seen, loved or appreciated when we were growing up, we may feel wounded: we may be carrying resentment, anger, hurt and pain, all of which become ballast to our dreams. We may be using up so much energy fighting within ourselves that we hold ourselves down at a lower level of consciousness rather than soaring to the heights that love calls us to.

We can't give of ourselves when we don't think we are anything worth giving; we can't extend the love within us if we don't believe it's there. To think it is *not* is arrogant. Low self-esteem, although widespread, is delusional. We are one in the spirit of love; we are all hosts for God. It is how we were created, there is nothing we can do to change it. Our goal is simply to accept that: sounds easy, and is our lifetime's work.

This means that we all have much to give. I think we barely know what there is within each and every one of us that we can extend and share. We've barely scratched the surface of our infinite potential. All of us are channels through which loving energy would flow freely if we awakened more fully. And there is no more powerful way to be grateful for our gifts, or to increase them, than by sharing them. We will be given as much power in the world as we are willing to use on behalf of our higher power. We are channels for love, and it is the love that is most important. When we pray to be of service, to become that channel, we initiate the flow. It is not our job to judge the size or value of our gifts, we must simply move out of our own way to become more willing, more effective channels. When we are ready to do that, we are guided by its light to greater places and higher paths and what emerges are plans and schemes that far surpass the limited perspective of our mortal minds.

RELEASING THE LIMITS

Our personal and collective evolution towards our goals is about stretching our credibility; realizing that what we thought was perhaps unbelievable is actually possible. The children's TV series *Catweazle* charted the adventures of a man who suddenly found himself living 400 years after his birth in a world of cars, telephones, TV and radio. To him, this was magic that often terrified him as he clung to his old worldview, and even today there are still millions of people on our planet who know few technological things and who would agree with science fiction writer Arthur C. Clarke that, 'Any sufficiently advanced technology is indistinguishable from magic.' A large part of our journey towards putting love at the centre of our life consists of stretching the limits of our conditioning and logical mind, to realize, know and experience that there are greater forces at work than our conscious mind understands. *A Course in Miracles* reminds us that 'We are under no laws but God's.'

When I first met Brian, he stretched my credibility about what was possible. His career for 18 years had been as a ticket collector for London Underground. He joined a six-month course I was running, and set himself some goals, which included changing careers and moving home. A part of me wondered whether he was being naïve, and whether I should caution him to lower his sights.

As the course progressed he became involved in some work with Doreen Virtue, a healer and angel therapist. He went to attend a workshop of hers in America. Brian resonated deeply with this work, and as he consciously engaged with and asked for angelic help, amazing things began to occur in his life. He had shared an interest in living on a houseboat on Tagg's Island, a beautiful lagoon in the River Thames near Hampton Court. He also said he would love to become an angel therapist himself, helping people connect with their angels, running groups and helping one-to-one.

By the end of the six-month course, Brian had given an umbrella name to his work, 'An Amazing Adventure', had moved from his home in Forest Gate in east London to a houseboat at Tagg's Island, as he had dreamed, had taken early retirement from London Underground and started his own business giving angel readings, talks and workshops to help people to tune into their own angelic help.

Brian became my teacher and my inspiration! I attended an evening he ran on working with angels, and he seemed to put his heart out, to say *This is who I am* and be open and defenceless. He is a real beacon. Brian is an expert in gratitude and in receiving. He has built a team of kindred spirits, who are both creating and living their dreams. He has dream builders and dream bashers around him. He receives their support and offers his own generously.

It wasn't until afterwards that Brian shared the source of his dream with me. 'Dreams are buried in our childhood and when they are unearthed they are nuggets of gold,' he told me. 'Our inner child never leaves us and is always reminding you of your un-realized dreams. I was eight years old and had celebrated my birthday by being released from hospital after undergoing an operation. My mother was told that I needed to have 30 days' convalescence and suggested Southend-on-Sea and Canvey Island, mainly because of the then invigorating air. My father was a painter-decorator and was often being laid off work, so money was scarce, but because my mother sold off a few of her clothes and a benevolent aunt generously donated needed funds, I was able to go with my mother every day to Southend or to Canvey Island. These were halcyon days for me and many dreams were sown during that September of '47.'

Brian went on to tell me how his dream of living on a houseboat was seeded. 'One such dream began when I was a child, on a visit to Canvey Island, at a place called Benfleet Creek. While walking by the creek I became fascinated by the boats that were moored there, and bemused. "Why do the boats have curtains at their windows?" I asked. "Because people live in them. They are houseboats," explained my mother. My eyes began to light up, my imagination went wild and I can remember a sense of awe and magic. Yes! I want to live on a houseboat! So the dream was sown in my mind in just a few magical moments, moments to a child that mean anything is possible. Whenever our family went on day trips to a seaside resort, I would ask if there were houseboats there, but there never were, and eventually I gave up asking. Yet stored in the recesses of my brain was an image of that houseboat. It was to be 50 years before that memory was awoken.'

ASSOCIATING WITH FELLOW DREAM BUILDERS

Most of us have experienced dream bashers, not dream builders, in our lives. Whether in our own families, at school, work or in relationships, we often hear more voices encouraging us to be safe and *not* take risks, rather than venturing our heart. To preserve and build our dreams and our active imagination, we really benefit from support and encouragement, from association with like-minded people, some of whom are further along the path than we are, so that we can be inspired and affirmed by them, and learn from them.

We are afraid of not being understood, of having our dreams trampled on or of re-enacting old feelings of shame. Often it feels safer to keep our dreams to ourselves, and yet we harbour a deeper longing to know and discover what life there is in our dream. Is it a dream or a fantasy? What is the difference?

One of the roles I feel honoured to fulfil for many people is to be a midwife to their dreams. In my personal coaching practice I meet people who have the courage not to have given up on their dreams, or who re-engage with old dreams. I recognize that I may be the first person who has ever really listened to their dream, supported and encouraged the possibility. I don't mean that I am special, but that I am affirming them in a way that they may not have experienced before.

CREATIVITY ALLOWS US TO KNOW AND SEE THE MYSTERY OF OUR OWN SOUL

One of our deepest longings is to have our presence made real in this world in order that the mysteries we harbour within us may become known to us. Through creativity we can see our own soul made manifest. Through human creativity, divine longing can come fully alive. One of the reasons I love to write and to teach is to discover what I know! By writing and speaking I find what is inside me. When we are creative, our inner world comes out and we can get to know ourselves and develop a greater intimacy with our own souls. Writing for me is an act of inner intimacy. The inherent abundance and generosity of our inner realms always want to be revealed.

Being creative is not about living a reasonable and sensible life. When too much of our energy and attention goes to the surface needs of our life, we rob ourselves of knowing our own mystery. As William Blake told us, 'Mysteries are not to be solved. The eye goes blind when it only wants to see *why*. The soul is here for its own joy.' The excitement of inspiration, the emergence of a new idea, the sense of not knowing what we are creating or what it means until it's done are our soul's pleasure. We hunger not for explained meaning, but for our own direct experience of our soul. We long for this connection to ourselves, through which our soul finds a new shoreline between the visible and the invisible, where entire new worlds can come into being.

THE EMERGENCE OF IDEAS

As I started to write this book, I had some idea of what it would be about, but no structure and not much detail. I went on holiday to start writing, and as I committed to write (I had to, there was a deadline to meet!), ideas emerged into my consciousness, structure and chapter titles became apparent, poems that I read 10 years ago have popped back into my mind for me to use to illustrate points, and stories have come to me. I am in awe of this process! The alchemy of something coming from seemingly nothing amazes me. I am in awe of the intelligence that is within all of us, the greater mind that makes itself known through us.

Regardless of the quality (or not) of what I have written, I feel blessed by the generosity of spirit that is giving me so much right now. There is no other way for the creative intelligence behind everything to work than through our own mind, and it is always wanting to do so. Only we stand in our own way. In each moment so many ideas and opportunities could be coming our way.

OUR POWER OF FOCUS

If there is one thing that excellence in sports and excellence in work have in common, it can be summed up in a single phrase: focus of attention. Focus is the quintessential component of superior performance in every activity, no matter what the level of skill or age of the performer.

TIMOTHY GALLWEY, author of *The Inner Game of Work*

We need to learn to focus on creating what we desire and want to create, and what we want more of. The Nobel Prize-winning Buddhist teacher Thich Nhat Hanh suggests that within us all are seeds of every quality, and that we can actively choose to nurture the seeds of goodness, love and compassion and not foster the growth of hatred and anger. By focusing our attention we make contact with everything in our world and by this means alone things become knowable and understandable to us. Thus, attention is critical to all learning, understanding, and proficiency of action. It is only when we are giving our full attention to what we are doing that we bring all our resources to bear effectively. Why? Because when we are giving full attention, self-interference is neutralized. In the sharpness of focus, there is no room for fears and doubts.

Too often our focus in life is on the things we *don't* want. We focus on problems, not solutions.

A SUCCESS FOCUS

Try this fun little exercise:

EXERCISE

* *What are the four areas that are working best in your life right now?*
* *What could you do to create more of those good things?*
* *What four of your qualities contribute most to your success?*
* *What could you do to amplify and enhance those qualities?*
* *Who are the four greatest supports in your life?*
* *How could you create more support?*
* *What are the factors that you think will contribute most to your future success?*
* *What are the greatest sources of power in your life right now?*

Did you find it easy to answer those questions? They represent a shift of focus in the way many of us think. It sounds so simple, but the idea is to *focus on what works in our life, and do more of it!* We can also look at what isn't working, and see how we can improve this, but too often we concentrate on eliminating what we don't want in the mistaken belief that this will automatically create more of what we do want. The only way to develop more of what works and what we want is to focus on it, expand and develop it.

We all have self concepts that we have judged and buried. On our journey to power we can face and integrate our shadow parts and free ourselves to be more of who we truly are.

4

OUR POWER TO OWN AND INTEGRATE OUR SHADOW

By healing the dark nature, vast amounts of personal power and ability can be reclaimed, for much of the ordinary powers of human beings is now hideously crippled by the personal dark side. These crippled areas, in effect, represent vast resources of contaminated and stagnant psychic energy. As one progresses on the path, each confrontation with 'evil' is an opportunity to grow stronger. This is desirable, for the repressed personal devils also grow stronger until one breaks through to the God in the centre.

WILLIAM CARL EICHMAN, Jungian analyst and author of *Meeting Darkness on the Path*

When I met Charlotte she was in her mid-thirties, with a career in the media, but was bored and frustrated. She'd been on a couple of writing courses, but hadn't followed through on any writing, although she had lots of ideas. She described her desire to write as *pathetic.* As we talked, I discovered that Charlotte had grown up in a working-class family in Birmingham, where the focus was on making a living and surviving. She had wanted to be creative, but she was encouraged to believe that being creative was a middle-class luxury, for people who had loads of money and time. She judged it as an indulgence, and buried all her desire for it, but now that creativity wanted expression. She was in an internal battle. She longed to be creative, but had judged it harshly. In her mind, the only option was to become one of the people she had despised earlier in her life, which wasn't attractive, yet her desire to be creative would not be silenced. It wanted to come out of the shadows of the psyche and see the light of day. 'Do you know any people that have kept the integrity of their working-class roots, and still been creative?' I asked. Her face lit up. 'Yes, one,' she replied, and when I suggested that she do some research, and find more, she began to get quite excited. Part of her longed to redeem her creativity from her shadow, but she couldn't see how to do it without *selling out* on her roots and integrity.

Most of us embark on a growth path either because we are in pain or because something inside us is calling to us, telling us that there is more richness than we are currently experiencing. We sense that there are buried lives within us, striving for expression. Shadow work is concerned with unmasking that which we have rejected, hidden away and denied. Unexamined shadow disempowers us, destroys relationships, squashes our spirit and holds us back from fulfilling our dreams and potential. In short, shadow work is all about transforming our dragons and revealing our authentic power.

There is incredible potential within us, but there are forces at work that seem to hold us back. We need to unmask these forces, to remove their destructive power and build our life. We have to integrate this new positive energy to help us build our life. In the shamanic tradition this is called soul retrieval work. In *The Road*

Less Travelled, M. Scott Peck said that in his experience most people came into therapy because they wanted to know they were *nice* people. Fewer people are willing to examine where they *aren't nice*, but those who do reap the rewards of real authenticity and a richer life.

I find it very useful to *depersonalize* the shadow. This does not mean that we are absolved of responsibility for it, but it gives us a little distance to see how we can turn our lives around. Everyone has a shadow side; it comes with the territory of being human.

Our shadow contains the parts of us that we have been ashamed of, tried to hide and deny. Strangely, our shadow also contains many wonderful qualities that we didn't believe it was possible for us to have – such as spirituality, wisdom, trust, love, spontaneity and creativity. In short, our shadow is the person we would rather not be or can't be. It contains those aspects that we have believed are not safe or acceptable to our family, friends or colleagues. We may even have thought that our very existence depended on us hiding certain parts of us and relegating them to our shadow side. Our shadow is buried deeply in our consciousness, hidden from ourselves and others. The message we get from this hidden place is, 'There is something wrong with you. You are not OK. This is what is not lovable or acceptable about you. This is why you are guilty and not worthy.' It has been said that up to 96 per cent of our energy and our traits are hidden in our unconscious. What a storehouse waiting to be reclaimed! Nobody ever told us that the riches of our soul, our most valuable qualities, lie in the very place we least want to go to – our own dark side. The key to the peace, happiness and fulfilment we are longing for is already hidden within us.

SHADOW FIGURES

Shadow figures turn up in our life bearing gifts for us. A shadow figure is usually anyone that we have a strong emotional reaction to – either because we dislike them intensely, or because they remind us of some wonderful quality. They show us what we don't realize we have buried away in our shadow, and when we understand this, we see the gifts they bring us. They hold up a mirror for us. They may highlight talents we can't see in ourselves; they may shine brighter than we ever think we can; we may even be envious of them; they may be people who love us more than we have ever been able to love ourselves. They may also appear as bullies, tyrants or pains in the neck; they may be people who keep turning up in our lives in different guises. They are often called our unflushables!

We may long to live in the light, but to do so we must integrate that which we have hidden away. We must be willing to continually expose and explore the hidden aspects of ourselves. Much as we would like to, we cannot be human without having a shadow. If you can't see, ask your family, colleagues and friends. If they are willing to be honest and you can listen without defence, you can learn a lot about your shadow. By definition, we cannot see it, but the nature of our shadow is often very clear to those around us.

We may think that in order for something to be divine it has to be perfect. The truth is that to be divine is to be whole, and to be whole means to be everything – light and dark, saint and sinner. Can you imagine that your mind has over six billion parts to it? Only when we understand this can we begin to know what Carl Jung meant when he said, 'The gold is in the dark.' To be reunited with our sacred self, we need to discover our own gold, in our own dark.

Most of us think that we need to be perfect to be loved. We grow up in families where we get *don't be* messages – don't be angry, don't be naughty, don't be selfish, don't be unkind, don't be noisy, don't be a nuisance. These bad qualities become our shadow. Then we project our perceived shortcomings onto others. We say to others what we should be saying to ourselves, and we judge others to hide the fact that we are actually judging ourselves.

EXERCISE

* *What were the major don't be messages that you received when you were growing up?*
* *How did they affect you?*
* *How are they still influencing you now?*

We start off with our mind as a mansion with thousands of rooms, so many different traits and qualities, energies and abilities. By adulthood, we have closed the door to the majority of them, and we call that being civilized. Every door we close adds to our feelings of inauthenticity and unworthiness. The rooms are still there, but we have no access to them. We *can* open them again: that is our power beyond measure. As the American writer Henry David Thoreau told us, 'Direct your eye right inward, and you'll find a thousand regions in your mind yet undiscovered. Travel them and be an expert in home-cosmography.' We are beginning to know the thrill of discovering the treasures of outer space, while overlooking the greatest treasures of all that lie in our inner space. There is nowhere else to go other than within our own being. There is no God outside us, only the God within us. All of us is in God, and all of God is within us. Carl Jung, one of the pioneers of shadow work, told us that to rediscover a deeper source of our own spiritual life, 'We are obliged to struggle with evil, confront the shadow, to integrate the devil. There is no other choice.'

Our shadows are hidden so well from us that it is impossible for us to see them. But when we understand projection, we can begin to see the beauty of the shadow. How else could we see what we've buried, if we can't see it out there in the world? How could we know our own vastness if there wasn't the world to project onto?

Our richness would remain hidden for ever. Psychologists say that much of what we bury has been hidden by the age of three or four. Imagine 30, 40, 50 years later trying to find what we have buried. We would have no idea where to look if we could not see it out there, through the eyes of other people.

Many of us have grown up believing negative messages about ourselves, and have felt disempowered because we have become scared of *ourselves*. We are afraid that if we look too deeply inside us we will see what is horrible about us. We fear ourselves more than anything. We fear what we have repressed. But whatever we repress, we lose access to its polar opposite too. When we deny our anger, we lessen our tenderness; when we deny our ugliness, we lessen our beauty; when we deny our violence, we lessen our softness. Because there is the imprint of all humanity within us, we need to acknowledge that we are capable of being the greatest person we have ever admired, and the most dastardly. Our first reaction on meeting our shadow is usually to want to turn away, and many of us have spent vast amounts of time, money and effort trying to distance ourselves from our shadow. But the world is our mirror, so what we have not made peace with will always stalk us. The parts we have rejected are the parts of us that most need our attention. What we learn to forgive in ourselves, we can forgive and accept in others. The biggest problem for most of us is that, in deep places in our mind, we don't love ourselves, we even hate ourselves. We can learn to give all that we are permission to exist. It is as if what we don't own begins to own us. What we don't use begins to use us.

We bury parts of ourselves, and hide them behind another inauthentic mask. We have a secret and guilty fascination with our shadow. Some of us are attracted to the light, others to the dark. We become impostors to ourselves, and then wonder why we don't like ourselves.

Instead of repressing what is in our shadow, we need to have the courage to bring it to the light. We need to reveal what we have kept concealed, to own our shadow, to acknowledge that a quality or a trait belongs to us. The great paradox is that by embracing the very traits we have been afraid to acknowledge we become truly powerful. The energy we put into suppression and denial can cripple us. When this energy is available to us, we can build our life and be more truly successful. It is what is hidden in us that is our treasure. A life dedicated to our goodness is a life making visible all the rich seams of existence we have kept hidden from others.

To understand the value of the journey to reclaim our shadow, this is what we need to understand:

- **Our shadow holds only treasures and gifts** – *what we judged within us and sent into exile only becomes dangerous when it is unintegrated and unloved. When we can begin to own and love our shadow parts, we see that each and every one has a gift and a treasure for us, something that will enhance our life and the lives of those around us. Our shadow wants to build our life and make us happy: it wants us to experience our glorious totality.*
- **Owning our shadow is our path to freedom** – *what we repress and deny we have become a prisoner to. Our prison bars are made of shadow. What we integrate and own becomes part of us. By knowing we contain the dark and the light, the good and the bad, we become free and are able to help others be free.*
- **Nothing about us is unacceptable to love** – *we think our shadow parts are unlovable and unacceptable. To unconditional love, to God, nothing is unacceptable. What appears not to be love is simply a call for love. Owning our shadow is the journey towards knowing and experiencing the unconditional love that is within each of us, now and eternally. It is the understanding that there is a light within us that shines through all darkness. The purpose of the darkness is to show us the power of our own light.*

In essence our shadow exists to teach us, guide us, show us and give us the blessing of our entire selves. All that we have denied and repressed is desperate to be loved, brought home and integrated into us. That is why sometimes things seem to get worse, and even reach crisis point before they get our attention and we take action. Our shadow will speak louder until we hear it and acknowledge it. It has a natural buoyancy, and wants to rise to the surface of our consciousness. Our shadow can show up as war, conflict, power struggles, chronic 'stuckness' and pain; even as our own illness and death.

One of the greatest motivations for doing shadow work is to free ourselves from our own fear and judgement, primarily of ourselves. It is to break down the walls we have constructed and see who we really are. Shadow work takes us on a journey to change the way we see ourselves, others and the world. It leads us to open our heart to ourself and all those around us. As the poet Henry Wadsworth Longfellow reminds us, 'If we could read the secret history of our enemies, we should find in each man's life sorrow and suffering enough to disarm all hostility.' To begin, we have to know our own secret history, and disarm our hostility towards ourselves. The mystic poet Jalaluddin Rumi told us, 'By God, when you see your own beauty, you'll be an idol of yourself . . . The source is within you and this whole cosmos is springing up from it.' This is not narcissism, but an acknowledgement that we were created in love and blessing, by a creator who did a pretty good job! All our shadows may be a result of the fear of our own power and beauty, our attempt to hide own our magnificence, our inability to own our divinity.

Shadows have no mass, they are insubstantial. Our fear that they are real is what gives them substance. As *A Course in Miracles* teaches us:

All that is veiled in shadows must be raised to understanding, to be judged again, this time with Heaven's help. And all mistakes in judgement that the mind has made before are open to correction as the truth dismisses them as causeless. Now they are without effects. They cannot be concealed, because their nothingness is recognized.

IDENTIFYING OUR DARK SHADOW

Little Child, you think you are chained to your shadow. It is but a dream. Awaken and you will see that you are free.
JERRY JAMPOLSKY and DIANE CIRINCIONE, authors of *Wake Up Calls*

The first part of shadow work is discovering what is in our personal shadow, what embarrasses us and what we hide from others, and often even from ourselves. With this knowledge, we can begin the process of integration. When we start doing this work, we need to have great kindness and compassion for ourselves. Increased awareness can be an excuse to beat ourselves up even more. 'I am even worse than I thought I was!' can be one response to shadow work. Its purpose is not to increase guilt, but to release us from guilt.

Here I explain several methods for outlining what is held in our personal shadow and wants releasing.

DISCOVER WHAT QUALITIES AND TRAITS YOU WOULD HATE BEING IDENTIFIED WITH

If someone was describing you in a newspaper article, what would you get really upset if they described you as? What would you be most ashamed of anyone discovering about you? What trait do you put most energy into defending against? Here are some examples to get you going:

Greedy, selfish, mean, competitive, sly, underhand, unkind, uncaring, nasty, hateful, abusive, manipulative, controlling, deceitful, weak, hostile.

IDENTIFY PEOPLE IN THE WORLD THAT YOU HATE AND DESPISE

Who are the people you least associate with? Who most punches your buttons? Who do you have the strongest emotional reactions to? Take 10 minutes to write a list of all the people you either know personally or know about. Leave nobody out, even those closest to you. If you are not honest, you rob yourself.

Then, begin to think about these people and write down next to each person the qualities or traits that you see in that person.

BEGIN TO OWN AND RECOGNIZE 'I AM THAT'

Begin to tell yourself that you *are* those qualities. For example, say to yourself, 'I am selfish, I am selfish, I am selfish.' Notice your feelings. Initially you may well feel very awkward and resistant. But keep going. The purpose is not to feel bad but to integrate, to lessen and even dissolve the charge that already exists within your psyche. Resist judgement, and instead accept.

I don't know about you, but I have spent much of my life chasing the light, only to be confronted with more darkness. I have come to realize that this is the natural evolution we go through on our spiritual path. Carl Jung showed the wisdom of looking at our shadow when he wrote, 'One does not become enlightened by imagining figures of light, but by making the darkness conscious.' Only by delving into our darkness can we reclaim our power, our brilliance, and the ability to make our dreams come true.

It does take incredible courage and compassion to do the work of owning what we have previously disowned, ignored, hated, denied or criticized in others. It is the greatest humility, but it opens the door to our authentic power. It takes an open heart towards ourselves to accept that we have every aspect of humanity within us. But the more we open our hearts to ourselves, the better our life can get. When we are reluctant to do our shadow work, we are not excused the lessons; instead we will attract people into our life who will act out more forcefully what we are unwilling to own. We cannot escape the lessons, although we can delay the timing. When we embrace it internally, we no longer have to create it externally. When we embrace the parts of us screaming for attention, they will guide us to the next step of the transformation of our life.

ACCEPTING OUR LONELINESS

One of the hardest parts of being human is loneliness. I remember Anita Roddick, the founder of the Body Shop, once saying that she thought loneliness was one of the greatest diseases on the planet. I think she is right. Yet it is a subject that we are often reluctant to talk about. There is a stigma attached to it, like a disease. Loneliness is somehow a failure, it demonstrates an inadequacy within us if our life is not constantly full of interesting times and people. But we don't recognize that loneliness has little to do with whether we have a partner or how many friends we have. Some people say the worst kind of loneliness is when they are in a supposedly intimate relationship, or have a great circle of friends, yet still feel isolated and separate from them. Indeed, having the opportunity for connection sometimes magnifies our feelings of loneliness.

Many of us go to great lengths to hide from our loneliness, keeping busy, moving fast, gathering lots of acquaintances, in order not to have to face that feeling of void within us.

There is a big difference between being alone and being lonely. Being alone can be joyous and liberating, allowing intimacy with ourselves. Being lonely can be the worst experience. Caught inside a prison of our own making, not knowing how to break out, we feel futile and despairing. It feels like a place of living death. When I am lonely I also feel a level of self-attack, that there is something wrong with me and that being alone proves I am a failure. 'If I really was a success, then I wouldn't feel lonely, so I must be a failure.' Loneliness is horrible, but then to judge that we are merely in pain compounds the pain. We get further out of the flow and life seems hard, even pointless.

Yet I have come to understand that loneliness is about the most independent place we can get to, a place born out of lack of connection with our own soul and lack of connection with those around us. It is one of the ego's greatest seeming victories. 'God doesn't exist, you have been abandoned, relationships don't work, and love isn't real. Just die,' it whispers to us. It takes great courage to visit these wasteland places within ourselves, where we feel so disconnected. But even when we feel alone, we have never been abandoned. In the Buddhist tradition, there is a being, a Bodhisattva, whose purpose is to sit in hell until all souls are freed from it. Lonely hell is not a punishment, it is just a place in our mind, another great ego illusion. It is certainly an experience many of us know, but there are ways through. Here are some ideas:

Acceptance – As I was writing this, I was sharing some ideas with my friend Steve who runs Alternatives. We laughed when we realized that at times when we feel lonely, we both tend to withdraw and not tell anyone how we are feeling. We may talk about it afterwards, but not at the time, because we both feel ashamed. Not judging loneliness is itself healing. When we meet it with less resistance or distraction, its hold weakens; when we fight it, it is strengthened. Simply to be able to say 'I am feeling lonely' without shame or defensiveness and with no demand that anyone fix you is powerful, and can begin to dismantle the wall. When I am honest and share my feelings I find myself immediately feeling more connected to people, to myself, and less lonely. We can very easily judge ourselves and doubt that anyone wants to hear about our unhappiness, but there are always people willing to accept us more as we accept ourselves.

Be honest about what you feel is underneath – Underneath loneliness is often another emotion like anger, rage, pain, guilt or grief. Because we are not sharing that emotion, we cut ourselves off. Be honest with yourself about what you are feeling underneath the loneliness. Have the courage to feel that emotion more fully. Sharing true emotion with others creates connection.

Recognize your deeper agenda – The ego wants to keep us separate. Painful as the feeling of loneliness is, it can also cover something we are even more afraid of. Be willing to acknowledge that underneath we often have an investment in staying separate. We are trying to prove something to somebody. Subconsciously, well out of our awareness, we are often trying to get revenge on someone. They didn't do something properly, and our loneliness is our revenge. Ask yourself intuitively who your loneliness is a message to. Who got it wrong?

Recognize your deeper fear of joining – If we are honest, there is often a part of us that would rather sit alone than face the fear of really loving, being loved, and being included. Do you think love or fear created loneliness? Loneliness is essentially one of the most successful ways the ego has of not joining. It is our fear of connecting at its most outrageous. We are not being excluded from any good thing, even Heaven, except within our own mind. Remember that love is the principle of giving all to all, so think about how you are excluding yourself from the good things you want.

Our spiritual path is not about avoiding loneliness, or despairing in our loneliness, and is not about thinking that our loneliness somehow makes us special or noble. It is about facing the experience and ultimate illusion of loneliness and recognizing that it is just an ego ploy to hide love from us.

IDENTIFYING OUR LIGHT SHADOW

Our light shadow contains all the parts of us that we think are too wonderful, extraordinary, successful, bright, loving or kind to be any part of us.

Here are several more methods for discovering what is held in our personal shadow and wants releasing.

IDENTIFY WHAT QUALITIES AND TRAITS YOU HAVE TROUBLE BEING IDENTIFIED WITH BECAUSE THEY ARE TOO GOOD

If someone was describing you in a newspaper article, what would you get embarrassed by if they described you as? What would you feel arrogant about if anyone discovered this about you? What trait feels too amazing to be part of you? Here some examples to get you going:

Beautiful, lovely, successful, abundant, healing, light, creative, joyful, happy, divine, Heavenly, confident, a winner, a champion, a saviour, supportive, powerful, a genius

IDENTIFY PEOPLE IN THE WORLD THAT YOU THINK YOU COULD NEVER BE LIKE

Who are the people you usually put on pedestals or worship? Who do you most admire? Who do you feel most unworthy to associate with? Take 10 minutes to write a list of all the people you either know personally or know about. Be as honest as possible, leave nobody out, even those closest to you.

Then, begin to think about these people and write down next to each person the qualities or traits that you see in each person.

BEGIN TO OWN AND RECOGNIZE 'I AM THAT'

As before, begin to tell yourself that you *are* those qualities. For example, say to yourself, 'I am love, I am love, I am love.' Notice your feelings. Again, initially you may well feel very awkward and resistant. But keep going. The purpose is not to feel arrogant but to integrate. Resist judgement of yourself again, and practise acceptance instead.

If our life is not working as we would like it to, it makes simple sense that either we are being held back by the lead boots of past conditioning, or we have disowned some aspect of our power and beauty. Or both. Most of us are cut off from many beautiful aspects of ourselves, parts that would make our lives much easier, successful and fulfilling if we could reconnect with them.

OWNING OUR SHADOW BUILDS CONFIDENCE

The greater our shadow, the more need we have for defences, and the more fearful we are. We fear our own attack thoughts coming back at us. The more we take back our projections, the safer and more confident we feel, because the less we have to defend. Our defences actually weaken us, rather than strengthen us.

Often we idolize other people: we project our own genius, power, success and creativity onto them, leaving ourselves feeling *less than* them. While we may not all be David Beckham, S Club 7 or Liz Hurley, there is some genius in all of us. How could there not be? It is wonderful to be able to appreciate other people's gifts but if we belittle ourselves in the process, then we are letting our fear diminish us. Yet again, we are robbing ourselves.

True gurus, other shining lights, are not there to shine over us, but to shine with us, to remind us of the light within us. They remind us of what we have forgotten. They help us awaken.

In his brilliant play *A Sleep of Prisoners* Christopher Fry expresses the true call we are now facing:

> *The human heart can go to the lengths of God.*
> *Dark and cold we may be, but this*
> *Is no winter now. The frozen misery*
> *Of centuries breaks, cracks, begins to move;*

The thunder is the thunder of the floes,
The thaw, the flood, the upstart Spring.
Thank God our time is now when wrong
Comes up to face us everywhere,
The longest stride of soul men ever took.
Affairs are now soul size.
The enterprise
Is exploration into God.
Where are you making for? It takes
So many thousand years to wake,
But will you wake for pity's sake!

We are called to awaken to our spiritual nature. Our life, and the world, are transformed as we make peace with our shadow. Once we have, we no longer need to work so hard to try to be what deep down we believe we are. We are able to transform our fear to genuine peace. We can glory in our true self, and we can become free. We find our innocence again, because love is the inclusion of everything, and the condemnation of nothing. As Neale Donald Walsch tells us in *Conversations with God*, 'Perfect love is to feeling what perfect white is to colour. Many think that white is the absence of colour. It is not. It is the inclusion of all colour. White is every other colour that exists combined. So, too, is love not the absence of emotion (hatred, anger, lust, jealousy, covetousness), but the summation of all feeling? It is the sum total. The aggregate amount. The everything.'

OWNING BACK OUR PROJECTIONS IS EMPOWERING

I used to be employed in the corporate world, and I have always wanted to teach about love in business, about how to transform the consciousness with which we work, and how love is the most powerful force in the world, not just in business. Yet, as with so many of my gifts, I have hidden this under huge layers of fear and judgement. 'Business people don't want to hear about love, they are only interested in money and outer success,' I told myself. Yet when I was honest, I realized that I was attacking myself. What I was afraid they would do to me, I was already doing to myself. I had projected my *hard-heartedness and criticalness* out onto business people.

I had recently read *Fast Company* magazine, which deals with high-growth and often high-tech businesses. A headline caught my eye. 'Love is the Killer App', it said. Inside was an extract from a book by Tim Sanders, a senior executive with Yahoo.com, describing how he believes that love is the most powerful force in business. I had one of those inspired and frustrating moments when I thought, 'That's great, and I want to be saying that!' I got angry with myself for how I always play a little small, am always defending rather than being defenceless. I realized that self-attack wouldn't fulfil me, but stepping into greater leadership would.

A couple of months later I had another opportunity to put these ideas into practice. I had been invited to South Africa and one speaking engagement was a breakfast presentation to 400 business people in Sandton City, Johannesburg. I knew the message I wanted to share, but would I have the courage? Would I allow myself to be authentic and real in front of 400 successful business people? The answer was 'Yes', and I was surprised by how relaxed I was. When I became more defenceless, I felt quite at peace. Getting up to talk I hardly felt nervous. Having owned back my own projections, I was not scared about my own attack thoughts coming at me. I was able to speak from my heart to their hearts, and I did a good job. I read them poetry, talked about love and abundance and how we need to change the consciousness with which we conduct business, and how business has a greater purpose than money and financial survival. I had a great time and had excellent feedback from the people there. Being willing to have a positive impact on the world around us is very powerful.

EXERCISE

* *What criticism or judgement do you fear people would make of you if you were more of a leader in your life?*
* *What do you get excited about and fear about having a greater impact on the people around you?*
* *Recognize that you are already doing that to yourself.*
* *Close your eyes and relax. Imagine that you are meeting that most critical part of yourself.*
* *Don't defend but imagine yourself being fully open to that part of you. Don't resist, but surrender.*
* *Allow that critical part of you that you have been trying to defend against to melt into you and work with you for your success. Let the intention go but absorb its energy, so that you become more whole.*

Sometimes when we recognize that our power is not to change the world but to change our own mind and our own thinking, we can experience a temporary feeling of helplessness, while a part of our ego dies away and allows our true self to shine through. Every time we integrate a projection, a part of our ego does dissolve, as our ego is founded on projections. Our ego projects out onto others, and the love within us simply extends itself.

The purpose of every emotion we have and every trait we possess is to help show us the way to enlightenment. Our shadow work shows us where we feel incomplete, and teaches us about love, compassion and forgiveness, for ourselves and others. We do shadow work in order to be whole, which means to become more at peace, which means to end our suffering. When we truly embrace our shadow, it heals us. What is integrated becomes healed, and what is healed becomes love. Peace is not choosing not to harm your enemy, it is seeing that your enemy is in fact your brother or sister. *A Course in Miracles* teaches us that, 'The holiest of all the spots on earth is where an ancient hatred has become a present love.' Each of us has so many of those spots within us. Healing transforms us. When we change our perception and begin to see that the entire universe is within us, we can accept our own magnitude.

My friend Adam is a GP and very involved in the Life Training seminar programme in the UK, the USA and South Africa. He told me once, 'I think one of the things I find most challenging is accepting the many different sides of myself and other people. At times I feel so powerful, clear and strong, and at other times I feel like a weak and needy little boy, just wanting Mummy! To accept that I am both so strong and powerful, and can also be so vulnerable, still shocks me at times.' To accept our vulnerability is a great strength. We can become in awe of ourselves and each other, and see ourselves for the miracle that each of us is. Then we can stop hiding from ourselves, and then we can stop hiding from the world, and play our part more fully in healing and helping the world. We can embrace both our human vulnerability and our spiritual strength.

SUCCESS – THE SHADOW BLESSING OF FAILURE

We are not taught how to fail and how to lose with dignity and awareness. Our so-called and imagined failures become the doorway to profound success in our lives – success that is not measured by commonplace standards, but by the currency of depth of being, compassion and wisdom. In fact, failure and loss have the possibility to be among humanity's greatest tools for a process of radical internal transformation that is deeply satisfying as well as enduring. The very experiences, events and emotions we fear most and attempt to avoid are frequently our greatest opportunities – openings we often pass up because our apprehension keeps us from learning to experience failure in such a way that it is transformed into invaluable gain.

MARIANA CAPLAN, author of *The Way of Failure – Winning through Losing*

When I met Todd, he had held a number of successful positions, and been made redundant from his current City job. He seemed cheerful and he was using this time to look at how he could integrate more of his spiritual values into his work and life, as they had become more and more important to him. But something didn't feel quite right, and he explained to me that he had been struggling with self-esteem issues. I asked him, 'Is there a part of you that *doesn't* feel a success?' 'Oh, a huge part of me feels a failure. Sometimes I feel that in my daily working life 110 per cent of my energy is going into trying to hide that part of me that I dread anyone seeing. I fear being exposed. So much energy is going into defending rather than creating my work and career and being successful.' This feeling doesn't necessarily have any basis in reality, but is based on our belief about ourselves. We can be extremely competent and still believe we are a failure.

Todd's example is not uncommon. Most of us can relate to the feeling of hiding, feeling a fraud and the fear of being found out. We try to conceal or eliminate the failure parts of ourselves, but they won't go away. They need our love and acceptance. Todd recognized that he had grown up in a family and culture where *losers* and *failure* were not tolerated, so had to spend a lot of time and energy hiding those parts of him. He learned to be harsh on himself, push himself, and be intolerant of certain of his own traits. Over a period of time Todd was able to start loving those parts of him that he had pushed around and judged harshly. He built up relationships with them. Several months later he explained, 'There were parts of me at war with each other, but as I have begun to heal them, I feel a new strength in me. I have discovered that the path to my wholeness is through my brokenness.' A Christian, Todd shared with me an excerpt from 2 Corinthians in the Bible: 'My grace is sufficient for thee: for my strength is made perfect in weakness . . . for when I am weak, then am I strong.' He had been scared to go to his weaknesses, but when he did, he found healing and comfort and, paradoxically, new strength.

One of the greatest shadows in modern western culture is that cast by the light of success, and that is the shadow of failure. I think about how few people I meet feel truly successful, despite how much time and energy we put into being successful and how much we seem to adore success. We are so focused on it that we see what appears to be failure as a very negative thing. Perhaps we need a new definition. In my book *Unconditional Success*, I proposed the idea that success was not just the good feelings that we all want, but our willingness to embrace all that we don't feel good about, all that we try to hide. Loving ourselves even in our apparent failures may be the greatest step in our spiritual growth. I wonder, did Mother Teresa, Gandhi, Buddha or Jesus think they were a success? I doubt that the question was ever big in their minds. They were simply concerned with being their true selves, living their purpose, being authentic and following their inner path.

Some of the most valuable times in my life have come when things haven't appeared to go as I wanted them to, what I have called failures. My ego has loved success and hated failure, but my soul seems to know that there is food in both. Where I stumble and fall, there often lies a treasure for me, if I am willing to change my perception. My disappointments become openings to greater understandings and self-love. All our failures that are offered up to a higher purpose, whether we call it God, transformation, love or whatever, can become food for our soul, raw material for our authentic growth and a greater step towards integrity.

Failure is an unavoidable aspect of every human life and we all know it, yet so often we run from it and are repulsed by it. Yet we also have an intuition that somewhere within us lies the possibility of really coming to terms with failure such that it becomes a kind of fertilizer for the soul – a soul that thrives on the *reality* of human experience as opposed to an unattainable fantasy. If we are honest with ourselves, we recognize that we have failed often and in many domains of life, both concrete and subtle, and in these places we often feel pain and even shame, and want to hide away. Then there are subtler domains of failure, where our egoistic identity fails us again and again because we are not who we think we are, or who we think we should be. All of our ideas about ourselves are destined to crumble one after another as we deepen our self-knowledge. Our ego *is* the absence of true knowledge of who we really are. Sogyal Rinpoche, author of *The Tibetan Book of Living and Dying*, informs us that the result is: 'a doomed clutching on at all costs, to a cobbled together and makeshift image of ourselves, an inevitably chameleon charlatan self that keeps changing, and has to, to keep alive the fiction of its existence'. We are so much greater than any sense of success or failure. Most of us don't want to do the spiritual work because we don't want the slow process of being ground down. It's very unpleasant, very painful, to be liberated from all that we thought we were. That's what suffering on the path is all about: the ego giving up its belief in autonomy and its belief that it is the ruler.

Success and failure is a meaningless distinction in the domain of our soul. What our ego sees as failure, our soul may regard as a huge success. For the only real failure is that of our own perception, our own ego-based imaginings of what it means to succeed in life. For most of us, this often takes many years to realize, and meanwhile we must fail many times in order to be humbled into gratitude for the reality of what life provides us with, all the good, the bad and the ugly that comprise the texture of human experience.

EXERCISE

* *How do you feel about failure? Be very honest.*
* *Who do you see as losers?*

LOVING OUR INNER LOSER!

A painful aspect of my own journey has been the recognition that within me there are parts that I have dismissed as failures, losers, helpless victims who are never going to amount to anything. I tried for many years to place as much distance as I could between myself and these parts of me. My drive for success can become my tyrant. But I began to realize that these parts needed my love and acceptance, not rejection and punishment. To recognize how harsh I have been on myself has been excruciatingly painful yet in time liberating. I no longer avoid and judge people who appear to me to be losers, because I know there is a part of me like that too. They need help, sometimes, to be educated. I saw that I succeed not by trying to eliminate the loser in me, but by loving and supporting him, listening to his needs and his gifts of understanding.

If we believe that success will offer us avoidance of or an escape from suffering, it is understandable that we should want success, and this is an honourable motivation. *Conscious suffering* is the process by which the human being makes an intentional choice to move into any number of domains of human suffering to achieve personal or spiritual transformation. Through this we learn to transform our imagined failures into fruits for the soul. In ordinary suffering, we consider suffering as undesirable: we avoid it at all costs, and when we have to encounter it we contract and turn away from it. In conscious suffering, however, we appreciate the capacity of suffering instead of running away from it. We shine the light of our awareness and inner strength upon it and, in so doing, it changes.

> *There is a process of alchemy, or transformation, that takes place in the human body when we accept loss. The* athanor *was the furnace used by the alchemists of old in which they turned lead into gold. They took something people did not see as valuable and turned it into riches. In this same way, our loss can be alchemized into an understanding of human nature, into compassion, into clarity.*
>
> MARIANA CAPLAN, author of *The Way of Failure – Winning through Losing*

We say 'Yes' to life either when we have failed, lost and fallen on our faces enough times to know that we can't do it right and that life won't work in the way the movies promised it would, or when we have glimpsed God long enough, or frequently enough, to trust God to do a better job than we are able to. In opening to failure on its own terms, a new kind of success becomes available. We realize that we are standing on more solid ground, stronger than any definition of success or failure. We discover that there is a quality of self-worth that lies beneath all gains and losses. We begin to grasp our unconditional value. There is a place to dwell within ourselves in which our happiness and contentment no longer depend upon the flow of continually changing circumstances. When our ground is taken away and we find we are still standing, we begin to discover something we might call groundlessness. We see that the moment of success is totally artificial, as our true self can rejoice at all times and in all circumstances, for we are our own source of all satisfaction and of all our own success.

When, through loss after loss, we finally become available to life as it is, instead of how we are attempting to force it to be, the measure of our success changes. We no longer calculate our personal value by whether we think the universe is conforming to our personal desires, needs and preferences, but by the depth to which we are able to embrace the fullness of whatever we are given. When we start to undermine the very notion of failure itself, then we change. The change may be imperceptible at first, but it does happen.

EXERCISE

* *What losses have you transformed into success?*
* *Who has inspired you by transforming a failure into a success?*

The path to power lies in acceptance, not judgement. To truly love is to understand this, to accept everything and judge nothing. It is important to recognize that we have the power to do this.

5

OUR POWER OF ACCEPTANCE

Pain only exists in resistance.
Joy exists only in acceptance.
Painful situations which you heartily accept become joyful.
Joyful situations which you do not accept become painful.
There is no such thing as a bad experience.
Bad experiences are simply the creations of your resistance to
what is.

JALALUDDIN RUMI, 12th-century Persian mystic and poet

Whatever we accept brings us closer to love and what we judge stands between us and love. Acceptance is a dual-level process: acceptance of our own boundless and spiritual nature, and the love and acceptance of all the egocentric limitations of our humanness. Trying to accept the light while running from our darkness only strengthens our feeling of being bad and having things to hide. Accepting our human frailties without reaching for a higher truth

143

condemns us to living at a disconnected, lower level. Facing our ego patterns head on and fully without defensiveness can seem one of the hardest things to do. But when we start to accept our patterns we put ourselves on the spiritual fast track. We can begin to transform and liberate ourselves from our weaknesses, and evolve to higher states of being. We no longer fight, we accept and move beyond our previously limited horizons.

When we go to war on our ego, our fear celebrates, because in the fight it grows stronger. It is perfectly understandable that we don't want to condone voices of self-attack, calls to sabotage and failure, insecurity and resistance within ourselves, but cracking the whip on them makes them work harder still. They fight for their life, and feed on our fear. This is what the author of *Boundless Love*, Miranda Holden, calls the kamikaze method of enlightenment. When we bury what we're scared of, it is like burying dynamite and at some point, usually when we least want them to, our old patterns are likely to explode again. It's best to bring them to the light of our awareness and defuse them in safe conditions. True acceptance is not giving in but giving up what doesn't serve us. When we realize that our beliefs and attitudes are our choices, and can take responsibility without beating ourselves up, we open the door to new and more empowering choices.

We run from negative self-concepts because we fear them to be true. Without an understanding of unconditional love and acceptance, and of our essential wholeness and goodness, looking at our darkness is indeed scary. Funnily enough though, many of us feel more comfortable believing in our badness than in our essential goodness. We are very reluctant to give up our self-attack and harsh beliefs. The only way to see the insubstantial nature of our dark stories is to metaphorically hold the hand of love, God or whatever aspect of divinity we resonate with. We can ask for help to shine through our own darkness, to see that it was only ever clouds that obscured the light in us. We can ask to dissolve the clouds and all our shadows then have no mass: it is only our fear that they are real that gives them substance. Jerry Jampolsky and Diane Cirincione remind us in their book *Wake Up Calls* that 'Darkness occurs when we witness each other's fear, while Light begins to emerge when we witness each other's Love.'

DIVINE LOVE ACCEPTS ALL AND SOMETIMES SHAKES OUR FOUNDATIONS

Love cannot help what we keep concealed, hidden or denied. We must be honest about our thoughts that seem dark, fearful and unloving – not to put ourselves down, but in order to start liberating ourselves. Divine grace contains not a single shred of judgement, however hard we find that to believe. Spiritual teacher Ram Dass wrote a book called *Still Here* after he had a severe stroke. He had been through dreadful pain, yet could see the hand of grace at work; grace undoes every attachment that is not love. It is fierce but liberating. A friend of mine recently experienced a very painful period in his life after a relationship turned sour. He described it as his *wrecking ball* time, a reference to the way they demolish derelict buildings. He thought he needed a course adjustment, a lick of paint to the building of his personality. He realized that his whole sense of himself was built on shaky foundations, and said he was being rebuilt from the bottom up. Although it seemed to come as a shock, he acknowledged that he had been resisting this shake-up for years, but now it had caught up with him.

It is completely safe to bring our dark or unloving thoughts to love, so that love can untangle them. Grace can and does undo everything, that is its purpose, and not on some future Judgment Day, but in each and every moment. But love will never violate our free will; we are free to continue in our patterns as long as we wish. Love can only respond to *our* invitation. When we are willing, love takes our hand and leads us out of the darkness and back into the light.

Perhaps the most divine act is to love ourselves just as we are, not how we think we should be. The paradox of life is that in our feeling of incompleteness, we are whole. We all have the power within us to judge or accept: the choice is ours. Fear teaches us that defence and attack are power, love teaches that acceptance is true power. Criticism creates deadness and stagnation, while acceptance creates flow. Love teaches us that through acceptance we can undo and transform our obstacles. *A Course in Miracles* reminds us, 'We must replace attack with acceptance . . . Let the peace that your acceptance brings be given you.' Acceptance is on everyone's side.

As we make peace with more of who we are, we become more content with ourselves and what we have in our life. In time we are led to a wonderful leap of faith, which is to have the courage to express our authentic selves in the world. We are willing to conceal less and reveal and celebrate more of ourselves. The trappings can be relinquished because the real thing is perfectly fine. Our need to justify and adapt begins to slip away: the need to be other than our authentic selves becomes pointless.

Within each of our souls are energies that spark and create the fire of life. It is light and dark, joy and sorrow, the divine and the devilish. The *Tao Te Ching* teaches us that 'the darkness is the gateway to all understanding'. Once we accept this we become natural, whole, attractive and powerful. The more we can love the many sides of ourselves, the more we cease the pain of trying to make ourselves into an ideal that doesn't exist. We become comfortable with our multi-faceted nature, and our ambiguities. We develop the wisdom to know that when we recognize and honour the darkness, this is part of our creative journey of empowerment.

In the Koran we are encouraged to give thanks and celebrate when we discover an 'unloving' and 'dark' part of ourself, and offer it up to God because now that it can be 'seen' clearly we can take better care of it. I believe that when we undertake shadow work of self-acceptance we are doing it not only for ourselves but for all of our human family and for the 'whole'. The dark and unloving parts of ourselves are also the most wounded and need to be revealed to us so that we can provide them with the loving care they need. The universe is always offering us opportunities in our everyday lives to reveal these wounded parts of ourselves.

The day after the bodies of Holly Wells and Jessica Chapman, the 10-year-olds who had been missing from their homes in Soham near Cambridge, were found, I was touched by an article written by Jill Craig in the *Sunday Times* in Britain. Herself a mother, she wrote: 'You think of all the horrible things an adult can do to a child, intentionally and unintentionally, of all the evil and violence that every parent suppresses in themselves when driven to extremes of anger or frustration by a child. No normal parent would ever really hurt a child and yet in some dreadful part of ourselves, every parent has seen this monster of potential cruelty rear out of the darkness.' I thought it was very courageous of her to write honestly and openly and, while not condoning violence, to understand that the *propensity* for violence lies within us all.

If you want to become whole,
let yourself be partial.
If you want to become straight,
Let yourself be crooked.
If you want to become full,
Let yourself be empty

Tao Te Ching

The light is not all positive, the dark is not all negative; the night is not the enemy of day, energy is not the opposite of matter – they are all aspects of the same whole. Opposing energies can exhaust us and cancel each other out. Within our own mind we need to start integrating these opposing energies, unifying them so that they can begin to face in the same direction. We need to create an attitude of wholeness, of inclusion, not exclusion. Every part of us we attempt to leave out and neglect will come back to us.

What is available to us when we allow our defences to melt and our gifts to shine bright is stunning. Enlightenment is not about becoming anything – we already are all that we seek. In fact, we are everything. We are the good and the bad, the divine and the diabolical, the insecure and the confident, the fearful and the courageous. Owning our shadow allows us to make peace with *all* that we are.

A NEW VIEW OF SHADOW WORK

Embracing our shadow is the ultimate act of self-love. Finding compassion for the parts of us that we have condemned, disliked or felt shame about opens the door to new levels of personal power, peace, confidence and authenticity. Rather than viewing our weakness, our smallness, our insecurities or our rage as enemies or as obstacles to moving forward in our lives, this process guides us to embrace our so-called defects as the powerful teachers that they are.

When we receive the gifts of our dark side, something truly miraculous occurs. Acceptance of these parts creates flow in our lives. To accept is not to condone or to encourage, it is simply to cease resisting. We can accept the reality of a situation without accepting its permanence. Then our sense of self-worth is less at the mercy of how other people feel about us. We find inner strength, our wounds are transformed into wisdom and strength. The parts of us we once believed to be our deepest flaws can be revealed to be our greatest assets. The parts of us we were afraid to show are seen for their beauty. For those of us who are already committed to spiritual evolution and the expansion of our consciousness, shadow integration is an invitation to go deeper – to see spirit and find beauty in each and every aspect of ourself. The darkest and most hidden parts of ourselves obscure the brightest light within us. This is the most courageous work we will ever do.

From an early age, we are more often taught to suppress and resist than to accept. We may have been taught to resist our vulnerability, or suppress many of our feelings, including those relating to fear or uncertainty; or we may have been shown how to resist failure and only value success. We may have been taught how to resist our own spiritual nature and value only the material. More commonly, we may have been taught to resist intuition and inner guidance, and value only logic and rational thinking. Through this kind of conditioning we have learned to value control and to resist trust and surrender. In short, we have been taught to be defensive; to resist *being* and to value hard work and struggle.

FROM JUDGEMENT TO ACCEPTANCE

Nigel was sales director of his family cosmetics company, and came to me to ask for help in implementing a more spiritual approach to doing business and motivating his staff. We talked regularly over a period of time, and I had begun to feel slightly uneasy, as the focus of attention was always on *How could he change his staff? How could he get them to be more effective and successful?* He was a very kind man, yet seemed to have some criticisms of his staff. As he got to trust me more, he levelled with me: 'Actually, my team is not performing as well as it could. I feel under a lot of pressure from my other family members, and am beginning to wonder whether *I may be part of the problem*.'

I acknowledged his honesty, and asked him to list all the ways that he thought *he* might be contributing to their reduced success. It was a humbling experience for him – he came up with a list of 20 different ways that he felt he was a cause of the problem. His list included recognizing he didn't know enough about aspects of the business; he started lots of projects he didn't finish; he didn't confront situations that needed dealing with; he was more distant than he wanted to be; and he lacked clear planning. 'I have tried to hide these things, and build a smokescreen around me. That has worked for a while, but it's not working any more.' On the verge of judging himself harshly, he was in the process of pointing the sword of judgement away from his staff and at himself. With help, and an understanding of acceptance and the true nature of responsibility, Nigel was able to move into self-acceptance.

I congratulated him on his willingness to identify his own weaknesses, areas where he felt less proficient than he could be. I sensed a breakthrough opportunity approaching. 'Do you see that you have been putting pressure on your staff to change, when really, deep down, you knew it was *you* who needed to change, become more skilful and proficient? You have been a defensive leader rather than a strong one. They too may need to develop, but your willingness to grow and develop will inspire them rather than pressurize them.' 'Yes, I had never seen that before. I thought I'd been judging them when really what I have been doing is judging myself. It has been more comfortable to make it about them, not about me, but I guess that is one of the privileges of being the boss!'

While it is a privilege, Nigel was seeing that it didn't fulfil him: this didn't help him succeed and, most of all, it didn't make him happy. Through his own guilt, he had become distant, although he knew he had a lot of affection for the people he worked with and wanted to be supportive. He had beaten himself up rather than given himself opportunities to grow, and his self-esteem had suffered. He had not become more empowered. His power came in shifting his thinking from *There is a lot I am lacking, I am not good enough* to *I can acknowledge my weaknesses, I can learn and grow.* Through self-acceptance, not self-attack, he was able to start changing. He moved towards problem solving because he recognized he had a problem. Resisting his own weaknesses caused him greater problems, and accepting his weaknesses led him to his own power.

Nigel had done what so many of us do. He had taken what he felt uncomfortable about, and focused these negative thoughts on other people. In doing this we really disempower ourselves. When we are relying on other people changing for us to feel different, we become a victim. As a result of this new awareness, Nigel was able to develop in a whole new direction. Because he felt weak in some areas, he had become defensive, and much of his energy was now going into maintaining his defences rather than solving problems and creating success. His judgement kept him as part of the problem, his acceptance freed him. With his new energy, he started to put a training and development plan together for himself, which freed him to help his staff develop too.

EXERCISE

✳ *Who or what are you most aware of judging right now?*
✳ *What qualities do you find unacceptable?*
✳ *Are you willing to accept that those qualities are also within you?*

ALL JUDGEMENT IS SELF-JUDGEMENT

As Nigel's example shows, one of the greatest ways we disempower ourselves is through judgement. All judgement is actually a form of control. Although we may seem to judge others, we are actually only ever judging ourselves. Our judgements keep us small, and although they *seem* to make us strong, they actually weaken us. One of the greatest ways we can re-empower ourselves is through moving from judgement to acceptance and this is one of the most challenging journeys we will make on our path. Every – yes, every – problem in our life comes down to some form of judgement.

WHY DO WE JUDGE?

We only judge others negatively when we forget love. We were created, and then returned the compliment by creating God in *our* image. We created a God that can be judgemental, angry and harsh. Again, these are *our* projections, and not the true nature of God. But love has a different concept. Love doesn't judge, it cannot judge and knows nothing of judgement. However judgemental we are of God, love sees only our innocence.

When we are very honest, we recognize that we all judge a lot. Byron Katie, in *Loving What Is*, reminds us 'Every true spiritual teacher that has ever lived on this planet has told us not to judge, yet thousands of years on we are judging as much, if not more than ever. Let's be honest and get our judgements out and take them back so we can liberate ourselves from them.' I like this honest approach, because it is working with what is. We all judge, and it can be extremely liberating to bring the judgements we keep in the dark out into the light and dissolve their power over us. We hide some of our judgements because we want to believe that we are nice people, and don't want to show how judgemental we really are, for fear that we won't be accepted. We *do* all make lots of judgements, and it takes emotional willingness and maturity to acknowledge them without beating ourselves up.

If we could have X-ray vision and see into our hidden and unconscious mind, we would probably be both shocked and saddened. We have made such big judgements of ourselves. In some ways we are keeping ourselves in prison, torturing ourselves for past mistakes, and in trying desperately to cover and compensate for this we are too hard on ourselves.

As we have already seen, owning back our projections is the most difficult and courageous of acts, and yet one of the greatest acts of service and liberation we can make today. We need to understand that fear is writing both sides of the story. Fear writes the story for the persecutor and the victim, fear writes the story of good and evil. Love sees no evil; it sees absence of love and knows that the cure is forgiveness, not condemnation.

WHEN WE DON'T ACCEPT, WE CREATE UNNECESSARY SUFFERING

So much of our suffering comes from the words 'should' and 'shouldn't'. So much of our pain comes from our judgement that events are not how they should be. They *should* have treated me differently, they *should* have loved me more, they *shouldn't* have done that, I *shouldn't* be feeling like this, I *should* be more successful. Our problems stem from not accepting *what is* or *what was*, and release from pain and suffering comes through accepting what is or what was.

When we judge instead of accepting the reality of our situation, we add suffering to pain. I have had times of feeling depressed fairly regularly throughout my life, when I would get so angry with myself for feeling depressed that I would say to myself, 'But I run the Alternatives programme, I have had dinner with Deepak Chopra, I have hung out with Susan Jeffers, I have been on loads of workshops, I'm an author. I *shouldn't* get depressed.' It took me many, many years to realize that I was actually causing even more pain for myself by not simply *accepting* my depression. When I learned simply to accept *I sometimes get depressed* without judgement, shame or anger, it became something I could live with, and much more manageable.

WE COMPENSATE FOR OUR JUDGEMENTS

Because we don't like our own judgements, we tend to hide them away, and even compensate for them, by acting the very *opposite* way to our judgement so that no-one will ever guess what is really going on inside us. For example, we may be prejudiced against a particular racial group, but end up being incredibly nice to them to cover this up; we may feel huge anger, and work with angry people to take the spotlight away from ourselves; we may dislike our boss, and end up helping her so that no-one would ever guess how we really feel. It wasn't until I had been involved in the spiritual area for many years that I realized how many judgements I'd made about some people, and why.

WE SOMETIMES TEACH WHAT WE MOST NEED TO LEARN

Having been involved in Alternatives at St James's in London for many years, I have met most of the leading teachers in the area of mind, body and spirit. On the one hand this has been a marvellous and blessed experience, and on occasion I have also found it a very challenging experience too, as I realized that there was a little part of me that had many demands and expectations about how speakers and writers should be, and made judgements about them when they fell short of my expectations. I have seen teachers of relationships who I judged to be aloof and unable to relate to their audience, teachers of fearlessness and confidence who I judged to be really scared; a teacher on health and detoxing come off stage and devour a ham roll and creamy cappuccino; teachers on un-attachment demanding many things before they would agree to conduct their talk; teachers on peace and meditation appear to be stressed out; teachers of selfless service requesting vast sums of money before they would speak.

JUDGEMENT CAN BE A BLOCK TO SUCCESS IN OUR OWN LIFE

In my early days I would secretly judge these people quite harshly.

Part of me wanted to feel very superior and imagine that I would never do anything like that. But as I became an author and a speaker myself, it began to dawn on me that I had enormous expectations that I would be totally perfect and completely congruent, just as I had with them. Although it felt like a demand on *them*, I began to see that it was actually a demand on me. I had such high expectations of myself. I felt the pain of *my own* judgements. I realized that if I had someone like me sitting in my own audience, I would be scared of me! I would be one of those critical people. I would have been my own stalker! I had this whole harsh and critical side of me that made me feel ashamed of myself. Then I judged this judgemental side of me as bad – which just made the whole thing worse.

The way through for me was simply to begin to accept that *nice Nick* had another side of him. It felt a relief to own that, and not to be ashamed of it; I had to accept it was just part of my personal shadow and as I brought this part of me to the light of day and stopped hiding it, its power over me became less. I began to reclaim its power, and the energy I had put into trying to suppress it. I could allow myself to be less than perfect: to be human. I also began to feel safer to *step up* and explore new paths in my own work. As I became less afraid of my own self-judgement, I had less fear of other people's possible judgement of me. This opened me to a whole new level of success, as I could be the authentic me and I needed to defend myself less. I was less scared of attack, and more compassionate of my own weaknesses. A portion of energy that I had been using against myself was now available for success and creativity.

EXERCISE

* *What secret judgements about yourself and others are you trying to hide?*
* *Would you be willing to bring that part of you out into the light and start to accept it?*

OUR NEED FOR COMPASSION
WITH OURSELVES

Personally, I find real *self-acceptance* a challenging and liberating dimension of my journey. Oftentimes I have been really harsh on myself, and have treated myself in ways that I would never treat anyone else! I beat myself up for past mistakes, what seem to be current failures, and all manner of other things. There are so many parts of me still calling out for love and acceptance. Hurt parts, wounded parts, unkind parts, abusive and nasty parts, tender and fragile parts, weak parts.

We tend to condemn our weaknesses a lot. Often I find that to love and support the fragile part of me, rather than push and force myself, is not easy. I often wish I didn't have all these vulnerable parts. In fact, the shame I have felt has led me to think that there must be something wrong with me! What I gain most healing from is the stories of others; then I realize that to be human means to be strong and powerful in some areas, and fragile and dependent in others. We begin to liberate ourselves only when we see that all our weaknesses come with the territory of being human.

A wonderful tool of acceptance is to *depersonalize* our ego, and to recognize that *we aren't different*, that having judgements is natural. Sometimes we want to be better than others, but although it can seem boring, to actually be *normal* and *average* is very liberating. Our problems, however difficult, are pretty similar to those of millions of other human beings on this planet.

The process of liberating ourselves goes like this:

- *Recognize that you judge other people.*
- *Own that you more than likely judge yourself to the same degree, for the same things.*
- *Begin to accept that.*
- *Begin the process of self-forgiveness, for your own judgements.*

156

- *Integrate the energy you have been fighting against into your mind, so that it is available for you to move forward.*

OUR NEED FOR ENEMIES

One of the great ways that the ego deals with its uncomfortable feelings is by creating enemies and projecting our worst feelings out onto them. We demonize them, express hostility towards them and celebrate their misfortune. It seems we cannot live without enemies, there is always someone we need to fight against. What we are unaware of is just how much *we need our enemies* to carry our projections so that we don't have to own them. When we create an enemy, we also create an enemy of our own peace of mind. Mostly we don't know it, but our enemies can actually do us a great service. Through them, we can see what we are projecting, what we are disowning in ourselves. It takes great maturity to be grateful to enemies. Our outer enemies point us at our inner enemies, which are really only parts of us needing love. The spiritual leader Mohandas (Mahatma) Gandhi reminded us that 'The only devils in the world are those running around in our own hearts.' Projection is not *wrong*, it is just a part of the ego and how it functions, and a normal part of being human. We all do it. *A Course in Miracles* teaches us that the ego – fear – projects itself, while love simply extends itself. Where there isn't acceptance, there is projection.

In truth we are the enemy within. I have often thought that some people are against me and unsupportive of me, and then when I am honest I find within myself painful places where I don't wish myself well, where I don't support my own happiness, and where I am against myself. I am an enemy to myself. I then projected this onto other people. By loving and supporting myself, I have blinded myself to the love and support that is available to me. It takes courage and maturity to accept how we are and to be willing to transform those places.

EXERCISE

* *Be honest and have a look at some of the places where you are not for yourself. Where are you against yourself? Where are you aware of being your own worst enemy?*

One of the greatest ways we can create enemies is around the area of evil. The perennial battle of human history is the battle of good and evil. The characters and context change, from Holy Wars to *Star Wars*, from the Inquisition to the war on terrorism, but the dynamics remain the same. 'I am good, you are bad. I want to get rid of you so that I can continue to feel OK about myself.' Nobody wants to be thought of as evil, so we are always looking for someone else to carry that burden. Elizabeth Kubler Ross, a writer on death and dying, has spent years helping people face death, and how to live well before death. She recognizes that there is a 'Hitler' in all of us, and that real growth happens when we admit this instead of denying it, judging it or trying to rid ourselves of it.

This doesn't mean that all of us are going to commit genocide, but it does mean that the energy of the diabolical is in all of us. But what we can recognize and accept in ourselves, we no longer need to judge in others. This doesn't make us bad, it makes us whole, and it makes us real.

It is one of the hardest acts of spiritual maturity *not* to judge evil, and not to condemn those who do judge evil, but to see it as an absence of love. This might be interpreted by the ego as condoning, but it is not. The ego says that you are either for me or against me, with no other options. It always sees a split – that is its nature. Acceptance sees only unity; it sees disconnection from the source of love, which requires correction not condemnation. This is perhaps the biggest lesson to be learned on this planet. Our lesson at this time in our history may be to recognize that success is not brought about by fighting and trying to eliminate evil, but by understanding it and healing it. One great act of human courage is to face the capacity for evil in all of us and to undo it, not project it onto someone else. Human power alone cannot manage this, but divine love *through us* can – that is its purpose. The spiritual path is the path of self-acceptance. The Buddha taught: *resist nothing*. Acceptance doesn't attack, it transforms. The *Tao Te Ching* teaches us, 'Give evil nothing to oppose and it will disappear by itself.'

NOT IN MY NAME

Rita Lasar's brother Abe Zalmanowitz was killed in the terrible attacks of September 11 in New York. Abe was on the 27th floor of the World Trade Center. He could easily have escaped. But he decided to stay with his friend Ed, who couldn't make it down the stairs as he was in a wheelchair. They died together as the first tower collapsed. Rita's world has changed completely in the last year. September 11 started it, but almost as important for her is September 14, because on that day President Bush made a speech which singled out her brother's heroism. Rita explained, 'I said to myself, "Of course they're going to use my brother's death and act to justify killing people in Afghanistan." And that horrified me almost as much as his dying.'

Rita was so distressed by the thought of innocent Afghans being killed that she decided to go there. In village after village she found homes destroyed, relatives distraught. She tried to give a letter to the US embassy, but was turned away. Since she's come back, Rita has been a passionate critic of the war on terror. She said, 'Americans want to believe that we're the best, kindest, freest, most generous people in the world. But all the aid and all the money that we provide is done in our self-interest. What are we accomplishing? We are just sowing the seeds of hatred for us and we're good people.' Rita's life has been turned upside down, and at the age of 70 she's become an activist.

An act of great maturity is to be willing to start to communicate with and understand our enemies, to see what their life is like, to make them into real living people, not just objects. This takes courage and it takes compassion, also to ourselves, to recognize that there are within us such places of pain and suffering that we want to inflict that pain and suffering on others.

It takes great courage to acknowledge our wounded parts, allow ourselves to feel the pain they cause us, and to process the accompanying thoughts and feelings so that we may 'own' them. It requires *so much love, so much understanding, so much tenderness* to ourselves. The more compassion we can have for ourselves, the more we can have for others. There is a light in us bright enough to shine away all darkness. We cannot see the suffering of others while we deny our own.

This is usually achieved not in one big leap, but by small steps. In Israel, Palestine, Ireland, Africa and other places of conflict around the world, there are thousands of people who are working to reconcile, to see beyond projections, and to lift the veil and begin to say, 'Beyond my projections onto you, I am beginning to recognize that you are not so different from me.' Our capacity to accept and forgive is incredible.

I met Anne Dickenson at one of my workshops, and she told me of her experience in Sierra Leone as an aid worker. Here is how she described some of it: 'One of the most inspirational things that has happened to me in my entire life was going to Sierra Leone. Yes, that Sierra Leone – war-torn, brutalized, unimaginable atrocities committed, Sierra Leone. Displaced people, refugees, camps, violence, amputees, hunger, war. Before I went, all those images came to mind. I was half expecting to meet lots of hollow-eyed people who had lost all hope. I asked myself if I would be able to cope with the shattered human spirit that I was expecting to find. Suffice it to say that I did not find a broken people. I found a determined, resilient people, who displayed a strong commitment to rebuilding their country. It was a heart-warming and humbling experience. Whilst the trauma, suffering, brutality and vast numbers of people displaced cannot and must not be denied, the other side of the coin is that I was overwhelmed by how many people spoke of their good fortune. "I am grateful to be alive", "I am thankful", "The consolation is that our lives were spared", I was told.'

She continued, 'But that was just the start. Not only did I encounter a remarkable positiveness, I also encountered a willingness to embrace those who had inflicted brutality upon them. I met a man who had had his home and small carpentry workshop (his means of livelihood) burnt down and looted. He had slowly rebuilt his home and his workshop and had now taken on two ex-combatants as trainees. He said, "We need to invest in youth and teach them skills so that we can all have a better future." [Unemployed youth had been an initial source of the rebel forces.] He was an exceptional man, but not an exception to the rule. I met villages where some of the people had lived rough for years, hiding in the bush by night, sneaking into their villages by day to try and cultivate a few food crops. Rebel forces usually attacked at night. With peace returning and ceasefires holding, both the displaced and ex-rebels were returning to their villages. In that homecoming, pain, shame and terror were being met with dialogue, with openness, honesty and with forgiveness. People told me that my coming to their village was an act of love and that their hearts were filled with joy. And what of my heart? It was overwhelmed. I don't think I can ever express how much faith in humanity those people have given me.'

While Anne was a giver there, she has also received enormously. All over the world in every second so much healing is happening. Where we find acceptance, we also find joy.

It is easy for us to look *out there* and see the visible conflicts and horrors of the world. But they can only happen out there because somehow we are doing those things ourselves, *in here*. Our power lies in knowing that we can always bring it back to ourselves. We can look for our own inner conflicts and battles. What parts of ourselves are we attacking and terrorizing? What parts of ourselves are we keeping in prison? What parts of ourselves are we abusing? Everything we do to love ourselves more, heal our open wounds, *does* help the world. Every wound *we* heal does make the world a little safer, it does ripple out into the entire human family.

OUR ACCEPTANCE OF OUR VULNERABILITY

The spiritual journey is one of continually falling on your face, getting up, brushing yourself off, looking sheepishly at God, and taking another step.

SRI AUROBINDO, spiritual teacher

One of my favourite prayers is 'Dear God of second chances, here I am again!' In a world where the prevailing belief is either control or be controlled, we defend our vulnerability. Here we erect our greatest defences, in order not to have to go back to those places. We avoid our vulnerability: we know the places where we can feel most pain, be most exploited and taken advantage of. Yet the defences we have built keep out life, keep out the goodness and connection that we seek. Through vulnerability we are broken open, we are freed and we are reborn. All new birth requires some rending, some breaking open. Mostly, we have trouble with our vulnerability. We prefer to keep our defences. They are predictable, controllable and familiar. Love never forces our defences down; it is never unkind, although it can feel tough. It will always show us where our defences are, so that we can choose to dismantle them ourselves.

GRACE UNDOES JUDGEMENT

To escape from the prison of guilt and judgement is a miraculous experience. When we release judgement, love is restored, and it is truly graceful. It is blinkers being removed from our eyes, it is seeing with new eyes. *A Course in Miracles* reminds us, 'Grace is acceptance of the Love of God within a world of seeming hate and fear. You are loved and accepted . . . The fact that God is Love does not require belief, but it does require acceptance. It is indeed possible for you to deny facts, although it is impossible for you to change them.' Often it seems that it would need a miracle – and miracles are just waiting to happen through us, when we are willing.

One of the most moving and profound experiences of life is the realization of how loved and accepted we are. When I experience grace I often feel tearful as I let the next level of God's acceptance of me flow in. It is the acceptance of oneself and of the infinite nature of God's love for his own creation – me and you. Grace is the love of our creator, unconditionally given, unearned, and requiring only our willingness to accept it for us to be released from the prisons we have created in our minds.

Grace is not just an idea. Once we've experienced it, our life begins to be transformed. Most of us know the song 'Amazing Grace' but we may not know the story behind it. It was written by John Newton, who was born in 1725, the son of a commander of a merchant ship. At the age of 11 he went to sea with his father, and they made six voyages before the elder Newton retired. In 1744 John was impressed into service on a man-of-war, the HMS *Harwich*. Finding conditions on board intolerable, he deserted but was soon recaptured. He was publicly flogged and demoted from midshipman to common seaman. Finally at his own request he was exchanged into service on a slave ship, which took him to Africa. He then became the servant of a slave trader and was brutally abused. Early in 1748 he was rescued by a sea captain who had known John's father. John Newton ultimately became captain of his own ship, one which plied the slave trade.

Although he had had some early religious instruction from his mother, who had died when he was a child, he had long since given up any religious convictions. However, on a homeward voyage, while attempting to steer the ship through a violent storm, he experienced what he was to refer to later as his 'great deliverance'. He recorded in his journal that when all seemed lost and the ship would surely sink, he exclaimed, 'Lord, have mercy upon us.' Later, in his cabin he reflected on what he had said and began to believe that God had addressed him through the storm and that grace had begun to work for him. For the rest of his life he observed the anniversary of 10 May 1748 as the day of his conversion, a day of humiliation in which he subjected his will to a higher power. He continued in the slave trade for a time after his conversion; however, he saw to it that the slaves under his care were treated humanely.

He decided to become a minister and applied to the Archbishop of York for ordination. The Archbishop refused his request, but Newton persisted and was subsequently ordained by the Bishop of Lincoln. He was given the curacy of Olney, in Buckinghamshire. Newton's church became so crowded during services that it had to be enlarged. Here is the text of his original hymn, composed between 1760 and 1770.

Amazing grace! (how sweet the sound)
That sav'd a wretch like me!
I once was lost, but now am found,
Was blind, but now I see.

'Twas grace that taught my heart to fear,
And grace my fears reliev'd;

How precious did that grace appear,
The hour I first believ'd!

Thro' many dangers, toils and snares,
I have already come;
'Tis grace has brought me safe thus far,
And grace will lead me home.

The Lord has promis'd good to me,
His word my hope secures;
He will my shield and portion be,
As long as life endures.

Yes, when this flesh and heart shall fail,
And mortal life shall cease;
I shall possess, within the veil,
A life of joy and peace.

The earth shall soon dissolve like snow,
The sun forbear to shine;
But God, who call'd me here below,
Will be forever mine.

ACCEPTING OUR DIVINITY AND UNCONDITIONAL LOVE

We are called to accept our divinity, with humility and without arrogance and embarrassment, and to recognize that, quite simply, we are spiritual beings, now and eternally. We are loved unconditionally. To accept our divinity is to accept our innocence, our freedom from having been judged by the creator. We need to stretch our imaginations to envisage a God whose love is infinitely tender, who takes us in her arms and looks at all our condemnations of ourselves, all our judgements, all our guilt, and all our fear, and says, 'But you are my loved child, you are mistaken if you think you could ever be anything other than that,' a God who is on everyone's side, who would find nothing about any of us unacceptable. Many things are meant to be removed from our lives, but through love and acceptance, not judgement. Most of us have felt lost, and we all feel pain, sometimes loneliness. But at every moment there are angels and guardians watching over us to keep us safe and protected. Invisible forces bless us and guide us home.

ACCEPTANCE OF BOTH THE MASCULINE AND THE TRUE FEMININE

Today we are being called to a greater acceptance of the power of the sacred feminine, the divine feminine principle. It seems that the last two millennia have seen a world dominated by male ego, unchecked by its feminine counterpart. A dominant masculine and a subjugated feminine are distortions of the true power of their energies. The feminine way has been demonized and almost crucified in many spiritual traditions, causing a great imbalance in life on this planet. The Christian Church has done a pretty good job of trying to eliminate the sacred feminine, largely because it knew just how powerful it was. But it was man, not God, that created the concept of original sin. Instead of being the sacred life giver, feminine energy became an enemy. As the author Marianne Williamson says, 'crucified not so much by men as by spiritual ignorance born out of the terror of the forces of love on the dark side of the moon'.

The power of the feminine must be vast for us to be *that* afraid of it. The power of true union of masculine and feminine is overwhelming, which is why we have created so many problems around it. True union of any kind unleashes enormous spiritual power, and opens the door to the divine in both men and women. The power to create new life is a miracle, and miracles are only supposed to be of God. But through new life we know our own sacred abilities, thereby leaving the Church out of the loop. That is why union has been so belittled by the authorities: in order to obtain and maintain power over people.

OUR POWER TO ACCEPT OUR POWERLESSNESS

Accepting our impotence at times can be humbling. Knowing how much we don't know, understanding that there are some parts of ourselves or others that we are unable to change, keeps our feet firmly on the ground. Powerlessness can also be the gateway to a new vista. Sometimes it signals that we have been on the wrong track – we have been trying to use our own ego power when that will never be enough. Ultimately, we are being called to place our life or areas of our life under a greater power and when we accept this invitation we can truly become powerful beyond measure.

OUR POWER TO ACCEPT THE NOW

When we accept the present moment, when we find nothing to resist, we are at peace. When we are aware that there is a plan that we may not know and a greater force than our own mind running the show, we are at peace. We know how rich this moment is when we stop resisting it. We needn't give a script to Heaven. We are known better than we know ourselves: our every need is acknowledged. Heaven has not lost our file, and knows better than we do what will make us happy. Divine intelligence knows all that we don't know about ourselves. We don't have to know the details. There is an intelligence that orchestrates for us, when we let go enough and let it work fully.

All that isn't invested with love can be undone and transformed. What we accept, we can transform, as love is the power of transformation and the way through which judgement, fear and guilt are undone.

6

OUR POWER OF TRANSFORMATION

There is nothing your holiness cannot do. Your holiness reverses all the laws of the world. It is beyond every restriction of time, space, distance and limits of any kind. Your holiness is totally unlimited in its power because it establishes you as a Son of God, at one with the Mind of his Creator . . . you have dominion over all things because of what you are.

A Course in Miracles

What we have acknowledged and accepted, we can begin to transform. Love *can* transform everything that is not love, and within each of us now is the miracle consciousness that has been available to every sage and saint across the ages. *A Course in Miracles* teaches us that 'The holiest of all the spots on earth is where an ancient hatred has become a present love.'

How do we know when we have transformed a situation? We feel a profound and abiding peace. Change is not the same as transformation. We can change partners, where we live, who we work with, but our underlying motivations and emotional patterns may remain completely *unchanged*. True transformation is concerned with consciousness rather than circumstances alone. Transformation is getting to the core dynamics in our mind that are the root cause of our pain, suffering and lack of empowerment, and this is our life's work. It is going to the sources of fear, guilt or lack in our own minds, and weeding them out. True alchemy is the transformation of the energy of fear into the power of love, and this mysterious alchemy is available at the heart of each of us.

I loved the honesty of a woman I once met on a workshop. She had been complaining about men, saying that all men were the same, and how difficult it was to find good ones. She had been challenged to think about *her* attitude to men, rather than men themselves. As a result she suddenly had a glorious insight moment and shared it with the group: 'I have just realized that if I don't transform my attitude to men, I am just going to keep getting the same problems in a different pair of trousers!' She could change the man in her life, but if she didn't change her attitude to them she was going to be in trouble! Insights like that are so liberating. She was able to start tracing back her own thinking to its origins in her father and brother, and begin to change her mind about men.

If we are always waiting for others to change, we will always, to some extent, feel stuck and victimized, but when we understand our ability to transform our own thinking, we have power. You and I do possess within ourselves, at all times and in all circumstances, the power to transform the quality of our lives. That seems a pretty bold statement to make and it is, but it's important to remember that it is true, and that this transformation stems from learning to trust and accept ourselves. There is a power in each of us, a piece of Heaven which remains whole and unbroken, irrespective of our life experiences and circumstances. This cannot be damaged or harmed by anything of this world.

There is a grace in each of us, miracles at the heart of all of us.

FROM CHANGE TO TRANSFORMATION

*To change, a person must face the dragon of his appetites with
another dragon – the life energy of the soul.*

JALALUDDIN RUMI, 12th-century Persian mystic and poet

Change is usually motivated by self-criticism and the change is an
attempt to get away from what we have judged; it is not usually
initiated from a place of peace. Paradoxically we usually resist
change when it is imposed, and are most willing to change when
we feel accepted as we are. Change is viewed as a movement from
bad to good, defined by and usually initiated by someone other
than the one who is making the change, and this often creates
resistance. When there is acceptance, there is less resistance,
because we are positively motivated and *desire* to change, to free ourselves from old patterns. When we choose to take responsibility for
our own change, we put ourselves in a more powerful position. While
change is about doing, transformation is as much about *undoing*. It
is not achieved through conscious effort alone, but through willingness to have it done through us and within us. We become willing to
let go of what isn't true, and what no longer serves us. There is a large
element of letting go and surrender in transformation.

We can change a lot of our thinking consciously. We can choose
to think more positively, focus our mind in new directions, and that
can be very powerful. But at other times we need deeper change, as
the cause of our thinking is hidden away in our deeper mind. Many
of our unhelpful thinking patterns have been etched into our
unconscious minds, and unless we address that level, it's a little like
putting a sticking plaster on a cancer, or moving around the
deckchairs on the *Titanic*. We may feel we are doing something,
but what we are doing is ineffective. Our ego wants to think it is

doing something, when it might actually be more effective to *do* less, and *be* more. We need to address that level of our mind too. This is one reason why hypnosis can be so powerful: it reprogrammes our deeper mind, undoing unhelpful thinking and establishing more true and empowering thoughts.

In Joseph Campbell's book *The Power of Myth*, he coined the term 'hero's journey'. He spent his life searching for the connections between the myths and stories of change that crossed historical and cultural boundaries. He discovered that certain themes are repeated in many cultures and appear to be deeper threads linking all of humanity, reflecting the overall path that we take from birth to death regardless of our individual circumstances. Campbell described the commonalities of our overall life path in terms of the steps of the 'hero's journey' – the sequence of events that seems to be shared in the epic myths of every culture. According to Campbell, these steps include:

- **Hearing a calling** – *this relates to our identity, life purpose or mission. We can choose either to accept or to ignore the calling, but this calling will move us beyond the world we know, into new lands.*
- **Accepting the calling** – *leading us to confront a boundary or threshold in our existing abilities or map of the world.*
- **Crossing a threshold** – *this propels us into some new life territory that forces us to grow and evolve, and requires us to find support and guidance. It is an initiation, whereby our life will no longer be the same.*
- **Finding a guardian or mentor** – *something that often comes naturally from having the courage to cross a threshold. As it has been said, 'When the student is ready, the teacher appears', so we naturally attract support and fellow seekers.*
- **Facing a challenge or demon** – *we meet our shadow, the unacknowledged parts of ourselves. Demons are not necessarily evil or bad; they are simply a type of energy or power that we need to learn to contend with or accept.*

- **Transforming the demon** – *through alchemy we turn lead into gold; this is typically accomplished either by developing a special skill or by discovering a special resource or tool.*
- **Completing the task** – *for which we have been called. Finding the way to fulfil the calling is ultimately achieved by* creating a new map of the world *that incorporates the growth and discoveries brought about by the journey.*
- **Returning home** – *as a transformed and evolved person. We then have the gifts for ourselves and others, we become leaders, teachers and mentors, helping our community evolve.*

This is not a one-off process, but something we may experience a number of times in our life, and in smaller ways fairly regularly. Unfortunately in western culture we lack wise elders to help us, so too often we don't recognize and honour this process, and thereby create a spiritual poverty.

OUR TRANSFORMATION FROM BEING HEAD LED TO HEART LED

The great secret to the spiritual life . . . is that everything we live, be it gladness or sadness, joy or pain, health or illness, can all be part of the journey toward full realization.

HENRY NOUWEN, 1932–1996,
Catholic priest in the Netherlands and United States

Joanna had been successful in human resources, but was really beginning to feel that it lacked something. Although her job was ostensibly all about people, it lacked that true human touch, and was really about logic, systems and rationality. Amongst other things, Joanna had trained in Reiki healing, and had found that had triggered quite a profound shift within her. She was on a transformational journey. She was much more interested in the people side of things, but wanted to genuinely connect with, serve and help people in a way that was meaningful to her.

As often happens when we are making these subtle but more fundamental shifts, Joanna was finding it easier to be clear about what she *didn't* want rather than what she did want. She knew the corporate land was no longer for her, but she didn't really know what was her. She felt anxiety and fear, as there seemed to be deeper forces at work within her, beyond the desire to climb a career ladder, be evaluated, get ticks in the right boxes and make money. So many of us are conditioned to deal with uncertainty by knowing where we are going, setting goals, and being busy. Otherwise, we fear, nothing will happen. There are times when we do need to be focused and active, and at other times we need to allow the river to carry us, rather than make our own plan.

When we met, Joanna was struggling a bit. 'I don't really know what I am supposed to be doing,' she told me, 'I feel a bit cut adrift. I have taken some steps, I have now resigned from the corporate world, but am not quite sure what for. When I meet people at parties and they ask me what I do, I feel a bit defensive. I want to tell them what I used to do, because I don't really know what I will be doing. I am realizing how much of my identity has been tied up in the job, the status and money. Those things don't motivate me so much now, but what is next?'

Joanna had been used to being driven and motivated by her head and by logic: '"Get a good job, apply yourself to it, play the corporate game and your life will be OK" is how I was brought up,' she told me. She had pushed herself, quite harshly at times, as she had believed that this is what she was supposed to do and needed to do in order to be successful. But the forces that had motivated her were not the ones that were motivating her now. She wasn't who she had been, but neither was she who she was going to be! We are all like caterpillars, constantly trying to emerge from cocoons of inherited conditioning and beliefs about ourselves. But how do we become a butterfly? We must want to fly so much that we are willing to give up being a caterpillar.

'Seems to me that you are at a threshold,' I suggested. 'How would you describe where you are standing?' Joanna pondered this question, and then said, 'I guess I am finding a deeper motivation, that is less about money, and more about soul. I am not even sure what that means, but that is the best way I can articulate this. I want to move from hard work to heart work.' As we've seen, Joanna was so used to having a plan, having her future mapped, being in control, trying to eliminate major insecurities from her life, and being pretty focused. Now she found herself with few plans, a lot of uncertainty, not really in control, and experiencing a mixture of excitement and fear, peace and doubt. She had lots of questions, but not enough answers, and the biggest question was, 'What should I be doing?'

I think one of the biggest mistakes we make in any transition is that we are really asking ourselves, 'Please tell me what I should be doing, even if I don't know why I should be doing it!' We put the *what* before the *why*. We are reluctant to delve into our deeper selves, to trust our own sense of what is true for us, to take responsibility for our choices and decisions. This is natural, as we are educated most of our life to think in material terms and to listen to the voices of the world, not our inner voice. Our logical mind only thinks in material terms – how am I going to make money, pay the bills, what about the job market, how do I remain employable, what will people think of me?

The material world has too little space for those bigger questions that can only be answered from *within*. These are the questions that logic and rationality cannot answer, but that *are* answered by developing a greater dialogue with our own heart and soul. I suggested to Joanna, 'The question is less about what to *do*, and more about how you want to *be*.' She smiled and acknowledged this, but then asked, 'How do I work out how I want to *be*?'

EVOLUTION AND UNFOLDING – THE NEW WAY OF BEING

What Joanna was in the process of discovering and experiencing for herself was a whole new way of being in the world. She was being called to swap the power of her conscious mind alone, whose currency was business plans, control, certainty and linear career progression, for the adventure of apprenticing herself to the power of her soul, to a force much greater than her conscious mind. While her conscious mind was asking for answers and understanding before entering new waters, her soul was calling her to dive in. The threshold was putting her faith and trust in the newly discovered power of her own soul. At this point, our ego will offer us scary thoughts, telling us to go back to the old ways and our old sense of security. But when we are willing to hang in there with our discomfort, new shoots of inspiration and guidance, new life begins to appear within us, out of seeming nothingness.

CREATING OUR OWN MAP

Man's spiritual journey is a long sad arduous journey, an adventure through strange lands full of surprises, difficulties and even dangers. It involves a drastic transmutation of the 'normal' elements of the personality, an awakening of potentialities hitherto dormant, a raising of consciousness to new realms, and a functioning along a new inner dimension.

R. A. ASSAGLIOLI, founder of Psychosynthesis therapy

What Joanna was concerned about was that *she no longer had a map for her life.* Her future was no longer mapped out for her but it was inside her, deep in her soul, waiting to be revealed to her. She was learning to listen to her deeper wisdom. Too often we see education as a cramming in of information, unaware that within us we have our own store of wisdom and knowledge. Within us, love is our own great teacher, waiting to lead and guide us, when we are willing to listen. Too often we project our wisdom outwards onto gurus and the like. Good gurus are wise, and only intend to remind us of our own innate wisdom that we have temporarily forgotten. Some gurus do want to shine over people, rather than with them, and have got their egos too invested in this.

Joanna was at a crossroads, where she faced choices. Would she get scared and go back into the known and familiar even though she knew she didn't want that any more? Or would she move forward into the unknown, aware that although it was new territory for her, millions had travelled before her, and were also travelling now, and that she was being guided by her inner compass and wisdom? Joanna chose to listen to the voice of love within her, not succumb to her fear. On our journey in life we have to align our personality with our soul, and learn to live with the tensions between them. Like the North Star, our soul is a guiding light: it is not outside but inside us, and represents our authentic feelings. We develop and are guided by an inherent sense of what is right and true for us, an emotional intelligence. Rather than trying to override our feelings, we learn from them, so that their energy is available to us.

THE TRANSFORMATIONAL POWER OF SPIRITUAL PARTNERSHIPS

You are each bound to your world only by the gravity of your unhealed relationships. It is those whom you have put out of your hearts that bind you to hell.

JOEL WRIGHT, *The Mirror on Still Water*

Joanna had a very loving husband who completely supported her in her journey and in her uncertainty. The greatest opportunity we have for growth and happiness is within a partnership. A spiritual partnership is when two or more people come together for the conscious purpose of their spiritual growth, which in essence simply means to be happy. In the face of true intimacy and acceptance, all problems can be healed. It's not what the relation-ship *looks* like that is important, but its purpose and intention. Through our choice, every relationship in our life can have a holy purpose. There is nothing that surpasses the power of a true partnership, it goes beyond appearances and invites us to consciously know and choose to remember that we and our partner, child, employee, boss, client, friend, neighbour and colleague are also precious souls. Everyone in our life is a divine being, looking for love and fulfilment as we all are, and when we remember that, we can open the door to miraculous relationships. The purpose of spiritual partnership is to pull the greatness out of each other, but in that process, a lot else may have to surface first. Relationships tend to stimulate all our control issues, all our negative emotional patterns. But we shouldn't be afraid to confront these issues; just because we don't feel comfortable, we shouldn't jump out of the moving carriage and hinder the journey. Better to settle in for the ride and see where your journey may take you.

One of the spiritual partnerships that I have found most power-ful and that has inspired me most is that of Lency and Chuck Spezzano. They have a happy marriage, two great children, they are both creative in their own right and are both living their purpose. They run healing workshops around the world both together and separately, and have written many books between them. The power of their relationship and their work has touched the lives of hundreds of thousands of people on the planet. They have a relationship that has been hard won. Together they created a therapeutic model called 'Psychology of Vision', a powerful blend of psychology and spirituality, and have learned to be successful in their lives and relationship by falling into all the traps, then find-ing graceful ways through, and sharing these ways with other people in books and workshops. They have totally committed to healing the problems that inevitably arise in their relationship as they go.

As Chuck explains in *Change Your Mind, Change the World,*

When a couple works their way through the power struggle and deadness stages of their relationship and reach partnership, they have done so by joining in love thousands of times. They have accomplished this because at some point they committed to their equality, which always brings about love. This re-establishes the lost bonding and by the time a couple reaches partnership, they have healed most of the competition, reached a balance of the masculine and feminine sides and a more natural balance in their relationship and life. If a couple keeps joining in love they will reach stages of leadership, vision and mastery together and while each partner may demonstrate one stage more than the other, they typically move through the stages together. In mastery a new level and greater balance is brought about as God comes into the relationship in a lived way. Most of the roles and false jobs are given up as more and more is put into God's hands. Life becomes more simple and balanced.

A HIGHER PURPOSE

Spiritual partnerships have a greater purpose than simply getting our emotional and material needs met. Within them, we can discover and let down the defences that we have spent a lifetime building, and give birth to our creativity and our power. In a spiritual partnership, all is revealed, our glory and our brokenness. We can face the shadows and integrate them. Our heart may need to be broken open first, before we can truly join with another human being. When we are willing to educate them to a higher purpose, they become *holy* relationships. Sometimes all Heaven can be let loose in a relationship, but all Hell may break loose first. When we don't have a higher purpose, and aren't bonded with our partner, our relationships can gradually deteriorate into pure self-interest, not joint interest when things go wrong. We compete, not co-operate, we lose sight of joint goals and shared vision. We think that for one to win, another has to lose.

THE JOURNEY FROM INDEPENDENCE TO INTERDEPENDENCE

Heaven is reached two by two, by being in relationship.
Anon.

For many of us, our journey around relationships goes something like this. We start off our life here being completely dependent and our life is a journey towards *inter*dependence. Many of us experience some difficulties *en route*. We may have a difficult childhood, and out of that pain or disappointment we decide to become *in*dependent. Unhealthy independence is characterized by the John Wayne syndrome of believing we don't need and shouldn't need help from anyone else, being an untrusting lone ranger. We believe we should be self-reliant. Independence *feels* safe: it protects us from being hurt again, or so we think. Independence keeps out a lot, but at worst we cut ourselves off from true contact. We cut ourselves from the life-affirming and regenerating human love that makes our life meaningful.

In a relationship, the independent person is the one who appears strong and doesn't need anything. They have covered their own feelings and needs, and may appear attractive because they seem to be together and confident. But independent people can become blind, almost living in their own world, unaware and disconnected from the people and world around them. In effect, this lack of awareness makes them very vulnerable as they miss the problems around them, keeping themselves in a vigorously defended cocoon of denial. This problem can arise in the business world too. The experience of a major UK company in recent years is a typical example of what happens to large organizations when they become blind and, instead of being connected to their world, don't see the signs of what is coming down the line. They just set up bigger defences. They went from being worth billions of pounds to becoming almost worthless in a very short time. Their leaders seemed totally disconnected from the world in which they operated, and were unresponsive until it was too late. I am not making points about individual personalities here, but the patterns and dynamics at work.

As we've seen, what happens in organizations also happens to individuals in their private lives. When we become disconnected from our partner we may not see the warning signals. We don't respond, so the distance grows. Then one day we are shocked to discover that they are having an affair or have simply decided to leave. Because we missed the signals, we talked ourselves into believing everything was OK. Whether you view yourself as the dependent or independent type, the important thing to remember is that we must never be complacent when it comes to relationships. Making the effort to truly understand and embrace the reality behind the façades presented to us can bring wonderful and longlasting rewards.

PARTNERSHIPS ARE BASED ON CONTINUAL JOINING

True partnerships have their foundation in joining together. True joining is not about bodies or bank accounts; it is about joining in heart and mind, in spirit and soul, making nothing more important than love. In doing this we create a sacred place where we invite a mystical third party into the relationship – the spirit of love. All true power comes from joining. As Christ said in the Bible, 'When two or three are gathered together in my name, there am I', meaning that all Heaven can be let loose when we consciously join together with the intent of love. When two souls join together we create a safe place for the light of love to enter, in which alchemy and transformation can begin to occur.

It is the choices we make about their purpose that can make relationships so powerful, rather than what these relationships seem to be about on a surface level. Spiritual partnerships can be in business, in the community; between lovers, family, parents, children, friends, coaches or therapists; in politics or government. Their appearance is less important than their purpose.

THE POWER OF INTEGRATING OUR SEXUALITY AND SPIRITUALITY

The Holy Spirit uses sex to heal us . . . It is only when sex is a vehicle of spiritual communion that it is truly loving, that it joins us to another person. Then it is a sacred act.

MARIANNE WILLIAMSON, author of *A Return to Love*

Our ego creates huge problems because our sexuality and spirituality are so closely connected and are both so powerful. They are both about connection and union. When we have them, we radiate irresistibly, and can shine with a bright inner light. But in our culture, on the whole when people shine, either we want to try and take a part of them for ourselves, or we attack and criticize them. A great challenge of modern living is to be able to feel a strong connection to our irresistibility, to our sexual passion, to our sensuality, without using it as a weapon, a way of manipulating or gaining power over another person. We may fear that if we are that open either we will be abused or hurt, or we may end up using that wonderful power without integrity. But to be sexually open with integrity, to step through our fear and guilt and truly join with another through sex is a healing gift.

Just think about how religion has been used to control and suppress sexuality by making it evil and wrong even though sexuality and spirituality are both expressions of the life force. Both are gifts from the creator. The ego's purpose is to generate enormous guilt and shame in our lives, to hide this power from us. It tries to stop us dead on a deep level; although our life may seem to progress on the outside, there is a lack of flow, even a deadness, on the inside. The Oedipus complex creates huge guilt and shame, and is designed to hide our gifts of aliveness and innocence, to hinder us from being truly attractive, and even irresistible. Dr Chuck Spezzano in *Change Your Mind, Change the World* writes: 'The oedipal conspiracy is used by the ego to block or stop altogether many of the good things of life. It is meant to block your purpose, your destiny and your greatness as a child of God.'

A COMMITMENT TO OURSELVES

Our emotions are the force-field of our soul, and when love comes along it invites us back to life. By facing our emotions we are forged in the heat. We may need to become comfortable with our discomfort as we grow, shed and learn. Indeed, to transform our life, sometimes we have to be uncomfortable for quite a while, even years. We need to be willing to commit to the change we want, commit to truth, all the time, not just when it is easy and convenient for us. We need to dig down to the roots of our problems. This commitment is the catalyst for our transformation. We must not shrink from our discomfort and pain, but embrace it. Rather than trying to control everything we must surrender to the healing journey. Paradoxically, we are weakest when we are defensive and not ready to let love open us; the places we *least* want to go to are often the gateway to love's healing strength. Most of us have no idea how many layers of pain there are in us, how much guilt we carry or how many parts of ourselves we dislike and even hate. It takes true commitment to heal and transform, for our denials can be powerful and deadly. But our commitment to overcoming them through loving and forgiving ourselves can overcome anything.

If we give our relationships a sacred purpose, a sacred place in our life, they can become healing environments rather than emotional torture chambers. We can learn to commit and to work through, instead of running for the door and the next relationship. We can begin to grasp that the universe is set up *for our healing*, and this will lead us to relationships where our unloved places are exposed so that we may love them. Instead of cruelty, we can begin to see opportunity. Instead of criticizing each other's wounds and emotional stuff, we can begin to support and help each other, knowing that we are actually on the same side. We begin to realize that unconsciously we have sought out relationships that will challenge us and then deliver us to our most soulful selves.

IN SPIRITUAL PARTNERSHIPS WE CAN BEHOLD EACH OTHER

In one tribe in Africa, all of the members start community meetings with everyone present greeting each other. One person says 'I am here to be seen' and the response is 'I see you'. This is a beautiful way of honouring the existence and presence of everyone there. At times we may be scared to be seen, afraid that behind the masks and defences we have so skilfully built up we aren't acceptable, we won't match up. But if we take the time and make the effort, we can see the courage, the beauty, the innocence within each other. Then we can say, 'I see you, and accept you for who you are.' Each time we see and reflect the glory of another, *we* are strengthened, and so are they. When we invite the mystical power of love to be present, we are asking for miracles and transformation. Robert Bly describes what happens when we invite the mystical third to be present in our relationship. He suggests that the relationship itself has a life of its own:

> *Every breath taken in by the man*
> *Who loves, and the woman who loves,*
> *Goes to fill the water tank*
> *Where the spirit horses drink.*

We must learn to live and love in two worlds, in this world of matter and the mystical world of love, of spirit. No love is ever lost or wasted.

STAGES OF RELATIONSHIP

There are four main stages that we are likely to continually experience and continue to recycle throughout our relationships. Going through these stages is how we grow, learn and evolve, and by deepening our understanding of the stages, we restore our ability to resolve our issues and illuminate the purpose of our life and our relationship. These are the ways we discover our gifts and the shadows that hide our gifts. They are all natural stages; we try to resist them but will rob ourselves if we do. Instead of seeing relationships solely as painful and problematic, we begin to see how they, like the whole universe, are exquisitely designed to heal us and restore our wholeness. We may need help to understand them, but relationships are the best vehicle for healing on this planet.

- **The honeymoon stage.** *Most of us know and love this one. It is the falling in love stage, when we see our partner free of our judgements, we* see them as great, beautiful and innocent. We project all our good qualities onto our partner. What we love about ourselves we see in them, and we feel all our good feelings. Their qualities attract us, they seem to have the missing parts of us. Together we are whole, and they can do little wrong in our eyes. This stage can last from days to years, in an intimate relationship, a business relationship or even on our spiritual journey. But gradually it slips away and we enter a phase where our partner begins to fall from grace in our eyes, we see their faults, and we begin to judge rather than accept them. Many of us have come to believe that the end of the honeymoon is the end of the relationship, when in fact it heralds a new beginning.

- **The power struggle stage**. In this stage we start separating out. Previously we had seen our good qualities in our partner; now we see bad qualities, and the differences once enjoyed now annoy us and irritate us. We start to feel some of our bad feelings, so we try to control our partner, as they are beginning to push our buttons. When we can understand that our partner is really only showing us the hidden parts of our mind, we get with the curriculum. We have found the key to unlock the healing potential of relationships. If not, we start to polarize, to see them as our enemy, hating their differences, attacking them and making them wrong. There is some excitement in our relationship, but it is a painful excitement. We fight for whose way and whose style is going to predominate. We look at win/lose scenarios rather than win/win. Often we say, 'We don't seem to have any-thing in common, we are so different.' Most relationships fall apart as a result of a competition and fighting over whose needs are going to get met. One of the greatest skills of relationship is learning how to take responsibility for our own needs.

- **The dead zone**. We look at our partner and wonder what we ever saw in them. Far from looking attractive, they now look distinctively unattractive, even repulsive, to us. We seem to have given all we have and the cupboard is bare. The relationship seems all but over, perhaps a shell of what it was. We may be together but feel like strangers. There is little true contact, and our roles are no longer working. We are called to greater honesty. This is *when the really deep and buried parts of us begin to surface, the parts we never wanted to have to look at again. It feels as if the answers must be elsewhere. This is when we may be tempted into another relationship or affair.*

- **Breakthrough to partnership**. *Every time we commit to ourselves and our partner and join with them, or take back a judgement, we create a breakthrough, a new level of love and connection, a new level of happiness and trust. We can have another honeymoon, which can last from hours to years. In partnership, we have built a container where we trust, where we appreciate differences rather than see them as a source of conflict. We see each other's intrinsic value.*

Relationships are transformational when we begin to understand that our partners mirror back to us what is hidden within us: indeed we are calling it forth from them, because we have buried it so deeply within ourselves. Certain people and situations keep showing up in our lives over and over again, until we recognize a trait within ourselves that attracts this kind of repetition.

IN RELATIONSHIPS, WE CAN GIVE EACH OTHER VALUE

In 2001 I was hosting a friend, Nancy Rosanoff from New York, for a talk in London, which coincided with her husband John's 50th birthday. He was with her and part of the purpose of the trip was to celebrate John's birthday. Nancy was giving an evening workshop, and John came along. I welcomed him and he surprised me by saying, 'I'd like to pay.' I said to him, 'Don't be silly, she's your wife, you don't have to pay to hear her talk!' but he insisted on paying. When I asked him why, he explained to me, 'We have been married for 20 years and I still learn a lot from my wife, she is still a great teacher for me. I want to value her and I want to value you for the work you have done in promoting her.' I was touched and inspired by how John showed his love and appreciation of his wife.

EXERCISE

❋   Is there a part of you trying to get something for nothing, rather than to give value to people?

❋   Is there anyone you are not valuing right now?

❋   How could you value them more, and appreciate their presence or contribution in your life?

When I stayed with my friend Jane recently, she was only weeks into a wonderful new relationship. She had been in e-mail contact with John for several months, they had spoken on the telephone and had just met for the first time. She felt that he could be her soul mate, yet some of her neurosis was already stirring up. Her envy, jealousy, insecurity and need to control were surfacing. That's why on one level we avoid intimate and conscious relationships – we know that just under the surface lots of issues are bubbling away. We feel the tremors from a distance. So we either seek someone who is not going to stimulate those feelings in us (good luck!) or we try and control our partner. We may try to work on ourselves so that we are sorted before we go into a relationship (good luck!). Our best bet is to throw ourselves into the relationship and grow as we go. The blessings and the lessons will come in their own perfect time. The spiritual teacher Ram Dass once said it was very easy for him to feel that he was enlightened when he was not in a relationship. But it only took a few months of being in a relationship for his neurosis and unresolved issues to start to surface.

OUR POWER OF COMMITMENT

Commitment is an incredible force. It can open us up and clear blocks, it can give us wings. Commitment is not a one-off decision, it is a regular and ongoing process. It is the constant choice to keep giving love and support to, and investing in, who and what we love; and it is the ongoing choice to keep opening up to receive more fully from who and what we love.

Commitment is not the same as sacrifice. Sacrifice is a form of slavery, but when we commit to what we love we are called to liberate ourselves. Commitment is not necessarily related to time. We can have been in a relationship for 25 years and kept our running shoes by the door. We can commit fully to being with someone for an hour, and that hour can be transformative.

A major belief of us independent people is that love traps us, that it closes the doors and removes our freedom. Our ego cherishes this belief to keep us away from commitment's transformative power. In truth, commitment *opens* the doors to freedom, sometimes straight away, other times a step at a time. Our life, work or relationships only fail when we withdraw our commitment from them, when we stop giving to them, when we stop receiving from them.

EVERY PROBLEM HAS A FEELING AT ITS HEART

Non-violence is the greatest force at the disposal of humanity.
MAHATMA GANDHI

All behaviour is motivated by some feeling or feelings, and all problems have a feeling, or a fear of a feeling, at their heart. Looking at September 11, we see that for years many countries had been expressing concern at US foreign policy and the globalization of business. Many people felt outraged and invaded by policies that

191

helped the US win at the expense of many other countries. There had been assaults on the US in Nairobi and Aden, but the American response has always been just to build bigger defences. Again, I am not talking personalities here, but patterns. This is what ego does. When we don't connect and hear concerns and seek to create win/win solutions, but simply build bigger defences, those bigger defences actually invite greater attack.

It wasn't until September 11 that many American people began to feel invaded and outraged themselves. Many probably still haven't made the connection that what *they* felt is how millions have felt about *them*. When they do, they feel an incredible poignancy and gain an insight into why things happen; their hearts open and compassion can begin to flow. While they lack awareness about the impact of their policies, hearts remain closed, and condemnation and judgement endure. This is not a political statement. It could apply as much to Israel and Palestine, to Ireland, and to hundreds of other places on the planet. It applies equally to our own relationships. We need to be willing to see beyond the behaviour to the feelings and beliefs that motivate the behaviour. Condemnation is a seemingly easy option, but it lacks compassion or understanding. We are still responsible for our actions, but need to understand what compelled us to act in such unloving ways. The solution is healing, not judgement.

Whatever is happening *out there* simply mirrors what is happening *in here*. Whenever we try to win at someone else's expense we are storing up problems, and we have to defend ourselves. Whenever we dominate, we create a backlash. Those we defeat dream of revenge, and we create an enemy. Only when we can begin to understand the dynamics of creating success for all, to understand that this is a planet of abundance, can we find *sustainable* solutions to problems. Only when we see that who we think is our enemy is merely a part of ourselves we have found unacceptable can we begin to make friends and solve problems.

There is a paradigm beyond right and wrong – it is the paradigm of understanding.

In the situation between, say, Israel and Palestine, both countries seem to want to deny each other's right to exist. Deep down both sides feel fear, as they do in Ireland, or in hundreds of situations throughout the world. When we are afraid, we defend and often attack. If we could acknowledge the feeling that motivates our behaviour, we could begin to truly feel and heal it. Once we know how bad we really feel, and are willing to face that feeling, we no longer want to try and pass it on to anyone else. Indeed, we will do our best to help others *not* to have to go through what we went through. We develop a compassion that guides us.

TRUSTING

A Course in Miracles teaches us that 'Trust would settle all things now.' Easy words, but most of us have plenty of evidence to confirm our deeply held belief that trust is pretty dangerous, and that control and defences are our best bet for safety and security. We put our faith and trust into something. If we put our faith in the power of fear by creating defences, then we put our trust in money and stocks, investments and other material things; it may be in power and control, weapons or high defences; it may be in status or position and the ability to influence; it may be in religion or some other form of moral leadership; it may even be in a football team, medicine, science, technology or a miracle cure. These are the things we make into our gods, the things we idolize. But when we put too much faith in them, we can become stuck in fear. When we don't know the boundless possibility within us, we can easily end up fighting over scraps, defending our patch, holding on too tight and causing ourselves stress.

LOVE

Help me remember that there is nothing
That could happen to me today
That you and I together
Cannot handle.
Thank you.

There is only one place to really place our trust, and that is in the power of love. When we place our trust in the boundless creativity, love, inspiration, ideas, forgiveness, inner resources and intelligence within us, our trust is well placed. We begin to lower a solid anchor that grounds and holds us in our endlessly changing world. It is a natural human urge to seek security, but we must see beyond our ego's need to distort that urge by looking for external props. When we are more anchored within, we can rise and rise again, even from the apparent ashes of our life. There *is* one guarantee, one constant throughout our life here on earth – us. We are there in every situation, we are the ones making the choices, we are the ones who are aware. Knowing our own boundless self is our guarantee. Friends, partners, lovers, jobs, stock markets, cars, homes, politicians and religious leaders come and go – but *we* remain. I am not saying we don't need help, what I am saying is that we can grow in awareness and experience of our own boundless creativity and realize that we are very resourceful. We learn that we can develop, we can be flexible, we can keep receiving inspired ideas to solve problems and move our life forward. When we know that within us are such incredible resources, the doors open to true fulfilment.

Trust doesn't just happen: it is our choice. In every moment we are choosing in what we will trust, and where we put our trust determines the source of our power. Choosing to trust, even when our circumstances seem hopeless, is transformative. When we direct our mind towards a positive outcome, we are truly trusting. We have all had times when we have had no idea how things would resolve themselves, but somehow, perhaps with our help, our problems were resolved, and perhaps we became even stronger. We don't have to understand in order to trust.

There are many ideas and theories about why we experience what we do in life. Why do murders and war happen, why rape and abuse, why natural disasters? Why do children die, and good people get harmed? I think we have a choice – decide that the world is harsh and meaningless, or trust that there is some greater plan in operation. Any meaning that includes revenge, attack, competition or getting even we can be sure is our ego. All meaning that involves forgiveness, letting go and healing we can be sure comes from love. In truth, we don't see the big picture, we can only choose to trust that everything that happens is happening *for* us and not *to* us. We can trust that there may be grace in every experience, no matter how difficult, that every lesson is somehow a lesson in love. Often, times when it felt as if a curse had been visited on our life became our greatest spurs to growth, and fertile soil for the growth of new perspectives, more resources and our greatest breakthrough.

But can we trust that this is *love's* plan unfolding for us? When we are feeling hurt, disappointed, betrayed, angry or wounded, it is hard for us to trust that life is supporting us. It is the time when we most want to reinforce or prove our belief that *life is a struggle, nothing works out, men can't be trusted* or *nothing good ever lasts* or any other of the fearful beliefs that we all harbour. It is crucial to recognize how we think and feel, but not to indulge in this for too long. Trusting in fear and reinforcing our victimhood robs us of power, even if we do find tremendous support and agreement for our beliefs.

Part of our unfolding is our willingness and ability to see the gift in more and more of what we experience, to be grateful even for the difficulties. The sage Sri Ramakrishna said, 'You can tell how evolved someone is from how grateful they are for all the gifts of God.' He doesn't say *some* but *all* the gifts. We have a plan for our happiness, we tell God what we think from our limited perspective will make us happy. Often we end up disappointed. We need to understand that God's will for us is nothing less than complete happiness, and that whatever is occurring is for that purpose; that although we can't see it, we are being supported. This is *real* trust.

I would love you to consider the possibility that whoever and whatever is in your life right now is your next lesson in trust and love, not a curse sent to irritate you. *A Course in Miracles* invites us to understand that 'All your problems have been solved'. Trust that there is a spiritual solution to every problem. When we begin to experience this, we start to receive grace from all situations in our life. There is a price to trust, though. It means we have to give up the cynicism that seems to have served us so well; we are called to let go of all our stories that we are unworthy of love and happiness; it will cost us all our ego's defences and strategies for safety; it will cost us our grievances and our unforgiven places. In return we will gain our heart back, and know how loved and supported we are. This is all we really want, and all we really need; by holding on to nothing we gain everything.

EXERCISE

* *Where are you being called to trust now?*
* *What is love calling you to do?*

OUR POWER OF INNER WISDOM

Within you lies all the knowledge about yourself, your challenges and problems, that you will ever need to know.

SETH, through Jane Roberts

Our path may be rocky and twisted, but the world is waiting for the special contribution each of us was born to make. It takes courage to follow those whispers of wisdom that guide us from the inside. The voice of love is within us at each moment: we need to be willing and able to listen and hear. It tells us we are safe, and will guide each step. There are many realms within us, benevolent support, and gentle and kind invisible hands tenderly guiding and holding us in our adventures. Many times we decide to follow a path that is not really our own, one that others have set for us or influenced us to take. Yet whichever path we choose, the price is always the same: we will pass through both difficult and happy moments. But when we are living from our heart, the difficulties that we encounter make sense. They are all opportunities to grow, to discover more about ourselves, to increase in compassion for ourselves and others.

When we trust our own inner wisdom, no-one has to be wrong for us to be right: we don't have to fight anyone. Our truth may not be their truth, but the world is big enough for both of our truths. When we are learning to trust ourselves, we may initially experience some conflict between our head and our heart, as our wisdom goes against external thinking and the world's wisdom. But that is part of the journey.

EXERCISE

* *Do you consider yourself wise?*
* *When have you been most aware of your inner wisdom?*
* *How do you know when you are going against your own wisdom?*
* *What are the consequences of not trusting yourself?*

Our souls lead us forward in our life, and will lead us all the way back to love as we learn to trust it more. To follow this path we need to:

- *learn to be willing to live in the moment – live in gratitude and awe of what is, now*
- *learn to sense what each new step is. As we move forward, each step is revealed. We are called to trust that our path is unfolding even when we can't see it*
- *recognize that our journey is one of awareness as much as of outer achievement. We grow in consciousness and inner riches; the outer riches follow.*

LOVE AND TRANSFORMATION ARE OFTEN IN THE SMALL THINGS

Love is in the small things, and perhaps love *is* the small things. But sometimes I wonder if there are no small things. We can so easily get caught up in wanting to make big changes in our life that we overlook the small changes that we make every day, the ways that our lives are constantly touched and transformed. Small and incremental change has a cumulative effect which is astonishing. The Buddha once said, 'Do not overlook tiny good actions, thinking they are no benefit; even tiny drops of water in the end will fill a huge vessel.' As the *Tao Te Ching* teaches us, 'We accomplish the great task by a series of small acts.'

THE RIPPLE EFFECT OF OUR DECISIONS

We cannot see the transformative consequences of our smallest action, so each of our actions deserves the same meticulous attention. Every action is an integral part of our life or work, and valuing it and giving it our fullest attention can make a huge difference in the way our life evolves. Harvey Zarren, a cardiologist and spiritual teacher, turned up to give a talk, only to discover that there was just one person who wanted to hear his talk! Instead of being despondent, he talked to the man and discovered that he was a senior manager in a health care organization. He decided to do the talk for the one man and this led to a major project that altered the direction of Harvey's career. Robert Holden, best-selling author and founder of the Happiness Project, tells of how only three people turned up at one of his first talks in the NHS, and two of them were in the wrong room! But he carried on and from his small beginnings huge success has grown. I can tell many such stories from my own life and career.

Ego can get so hooked up on the *big thing*, the *jackpot* or the *breakthrough* that will change your life, that we miss the beauty of the small and beautiful changes that can happen in every moment.

In his fascinating book *The Tipping Point*, Malcolm Gladwell researches and discusses how small ideas become big, even global ideas. One fascinating story he tells is of the revival in interest in Hush Puppy shoes. The company that manufactured them had been considering dropping the brand because sales had declined over many years. Yet suddenly there was an increase in sales, the shoes became trendy again, and within a few years the company was producing four million pairs a year again. Closer investigation revealed that four college students in the Lower East Side of New York had started to wear Hush Puppies, with the idea that they were so old-fashioned, they were trendy. These four students literally started the whole revival of interest, but they didn't even do it consciously. They just knew people who knew people and the whole craze took off. It is astonishing to understand the power of connection and of small and incremental steps, the power of compound growth.

OUR LIFE IS AN ACCUMULATION OF MANY SMALL THINGS

Our adult nature is determined by the thousands, perhaps millions, of small ways we are loved, encouraged, nurtured and appreciated, or criticized and discouraged, by those we grow up with. We are all the product of millions of acts of love and kindness, cruelty or indifference. We should never underestimate our power to make a change and to have an impact. Every kindness has a divine source. Did you know that the whole civil rights unrest in the USA in the 1960s was fuelled by Rosa Parks' refusal to give up her seat to a white person? This was not even an act of defiance, she said afterwards. 'I was just too tired to stand for the journey!' Yet that one act had enormous consequences.

Too few of us are taught the power of incremental change in our personal evolution. Thought is so fast that we can conceive and see in our mind's eye immediately, so we easily get frustrated when we have trouble bringing ideas into the physical realm as quickly as we imagine them. It is one of the challenges of being human and in a human body, to live with the time lag between thought and manifestation. The evolution of consciousness is speeding up now, and the time taken for ideas to become physical is shortening. With tools like the internet, what used to take months can now take minutes. Through new daily habits and practices we can make the gradual but powerful changes we want to.

GOING THROUGH THE FIRE

There is a light that shines in each of us that does away with all darkness.

JERRY JAMPOLSKY and DIANE CIRINCIONE, authors of *Wake Up Calls*

According to Dr Chuck Spezzano, deep within our minds are

places of such pain that when they surface we go through what he calls *sacred fire pain*; places of such excruciating pain that we feel we are literally dying. But the fire is not our greatest danger: it is a great gift, when seen correctly. Once we have been through the fire, we are less scared. We know the process: through the fire, burn away and emerge into a new level of consciousness, stronger, less defensive and more open.

Transformation is about piercing surface issues to reach the greater truth at the heart of our thinking. We may have spent a lifetime building defences against the pain and suffering we have at the heart of us. So many of us have unhealed emotional and psychic wounds within us. To allow our defences to be pierced to enable transformation is truly courageous. To go back to where we vowed we would never return is a heroic journey. Life supports us dismantling, not strengthening, our defences. The whole of the universe is invested in healing and the gentlest, but firmest, of unseen hands are always nudging us towards our dreams.

Once we decide 'I want more, I want the real thing, the gold of my own soul' we confront the ego and claim the joy and aliveness that is our birthright. We are choosing to awaken from our sleeping state to the truth of us. As Jalaluddin Rumi expresses it so well, 'Though we seem to be sleeping, there is an inner wakefulness that directs the dream, and that will eventually startle us back to the truth of who we are.' When we have the deep motivation and desire to declare that the limits of love in this world aren't enough, that we genuinely seek to lift the veil, then we have taken on the forces of fear, all of love's opposition in its many and often subtle guises. We have set ourselves on the path of liberation. But we have activated the forces of love too, and often the world opposes the ways of love.

As we walk the path back into the awareness of God, it is likely we *will* meet fire: the fire of cleansing. All that is fearful will be revealed to be released, all that has been hidden will be brought to the surface for healing, all our defences will be challenged. Why bother? So that we can experience the true gold. Out of the destruction is born creativity, out of the fire of defences, true strength is born. With love comes fire. You can have a relationship that lasts a lifetime, a business that functions adequately; you may have all the worldly signs of a successful life. Without the fire of initiation that takes our heart, breaks it open and then brings our life to a new level of understanding, we haven't really loved, and are only half alive. This isn't a call to a life of emotional drama and instability, but a call to a life of true growth.

Wherever there is opportunity for a deep love, real creativity, honest emotion and natural abundance, there will be a wall of fire, either an inner burning or an outer condition. Love and fire go together. Love is the great initiator. To the earthbound, fire means 'Stand back or you may get burned', while to the mystic it means 'Burn away what is false and be reborn, stronger and truer'. Fire is not a danger, but that which moulds us.

We need to learn to develop a greater sense of acceptance of pain. Too often we want to fix ourselves or others, not have to face the pain. But when we avoid pain, we rob ourselves of the potential and opportunity for growth. Yes, it does take every ounce of courage to face and accept what we had buried, and to go through the fire without any sense of the divine is difficult, if not impossible: it simply feels like a descent into Hell, and who would willingly do that unless they knew they were on the route to Heaven? But the fire is not punishment, it is cleansing, and we are not alone. Our hearts are always held safely, even in the midst of our pain, even when we feel alone.

NO PRIZES, ONLY RELEASE

There are victories whose glory lies only in the fact that they are known to those who win them.
NELSON MANDELA, author and former President of South Africa

The world gives prizes and certificates for many things, but turning the lead of our ego consciousness into the gold of spiritual consciousness is generally not one of them. Mostly the world doesn't even recognize this process, often calling it a mental breakdown and prescribing drugs to cure it. The prize is purely our own: knowing and experiencing the gold now within us, reclaiming a part of our own soul. When we are in partnership, we know the joy of experiencing a whole new honeymoon and level of friendship and connection where before it all looked bleak. When we go through the fire with our partner, our relationship becomes a sacred chalice, a place of rebirth and hope. If we haven't had a partner, we may now be ready and available for one. In our work, our success can reach a higher level of new opportunities, creative fulfilment, and greater confidence; old enemies seem more like friends now. We create a true team. When we have faced our own pain, we are less afraid of other people's, as we know we can go through it. We come out more whole, more compassionate, less judgemental and better able to help others. We come through with a warrior spirit, knowing that darkness is just an illusion and cannot sustain exposure to the light.

THE TRANSFORMATIVE POWER OF SERVICE

What do we live for, if it is not to make life less difficult for each other?

GEORGE ELIOT (Mary Ann Evans), 1819–80, novelist

Throughout history we have been shown how powerful acts of service are. By extending ourselves to help others *we* can be transformed. As we commit to contribution and service our conscious mind evolves and becomes more spiritual. True service is the conscious choice to make a contribution to the life of others, and is the most joyful of experiences. Unfortunately too many of us have been taught that service is sacrifice, and that to serve we must ignore or override our own needs to help others. This is not true. But it is transformative to think beyond ourselves, to touch, impact on and enhance the lives of others. When our conscious motivation shifts from *What can I get?* to *How can I help?* we begin to undergo a transformation, because we align with the spirit of love within us.

As we have seen, we may serve because we think people should be different or believe something different; we can serve because we feel useless or unworthy and want to feel we have value; we can serve because we want to 'buy' the love and approval of others. When we start serving we may have one or all of these motivations, and part of our path of service is to begin to purify these so that gradually we are able to transcend our ego needs and connect more to the love within us. Through service we can transform our awareness. We begin to find that truly selfless part of us that genuinely takes joy in helping others and understands that every act of service, however small, really does help to make the world a better place.

Jenny was in her late forties, married and with three teenage daughters. Seeing her daughters and their friends struggling with certain life issues, she felt compelled to help young adults navigate the difficult waters of parental pressures around school, career and partners. She was also aware that now she was needed less by her girls and she wanted to be creative, more purposeful and to achieve something. 'But am I just wanting to do something because I feel purposeless, because I feel like I made some mistakes in my life and because I want to help? Am I wanting to do this because *I* need to?' she asked. 'I think you have a mixture of motivations, and I think you need to accept that it is OK for you to do things for selfish, as well as selfless, reasons,' I suggested.

I sensed that within Jenny there was a true motivation – she truly wanted to improve the quality of the lives of others. That was her most powerful motivation. 'You don't have to have saintly motives before you can help,' I suggested. 'If we had to wait for that, very few things would ever get done!' In the Hindu religion, Bhakti yoga is one of the pathways to the divine, through selfless service. It teaches that as we serve all our ego motives *will* surface, but by committing to see, or wanting to see, the divine in everyone, and serving everyone with the consciousness that they are God in disguise, we begin to know our own God or Krishna consciousness. We will dissolve our ego consciousness through service.

CHANTING TO HAPPINESS

I have always been fascinated by the story of how the Hare Krishna movement came into being. The founder, Sri Prabuphad, had been a devotee of a spiritual master in India, and was told when he was very young that one day he would teach Krishna or God consciousness, the consciousness of love, to westerners. He had no idea how or when. His ministry didn't start until 1966, when he was already 69! Can you imagine this old man sailing to New York, having never left India before? He knew no-one in the West, and had only a few rupees, a food steamer, a few books and the address in Baltimore of a cousin he'd never met. Out of complete faith and trust in Krishna, and a desire to serve humanity, he came to America and simply started talking about Krishna consciousness to anyone who wanted to listen.

Slowly, as he allowed his happy soul to shine, he found people who were interested in the message and who enjoyed the chanting and meditation, and found that it gave some of them spiritual experiences that until then they had only been able to achieve through drugs. Gradually more people were attracted to the message. His ministry lasted only 16 years, until he died at the age of 85, but by then the Krishna consciousness movement was established, with centres in dozens of countries throughout the world. More importantly, its impact on the consciousness of the planet had been enormous, and all because of one man's desire to serve humanity. Reading his biography *Your Eternal Well Wisher*, I was struck by how Prabuphad never seemed to get angry at God, how he trusted God completely. He never judged God even when the circumstances of his life seemed to indicate that his ministry wasn't working. He completely trusted that the plan was unfolding perfectly.

TRANSFORMING *OUR* JUDGEMENTS OF GOD

The issue underlying our need to tell God what to do is our lack of trust. We're afraid to leave things in God's hands because we don't know what He'll do with them. We're afraid He'll lose our file. If we're going to set any goal, let us set the goal of being healed of the belief that God is fear instead of love. Let us remember that 'our happiness and our function are one'. If God is our goal, that's the same thing as saying happiness is our goal. There's no need to believe that God can't figure out the details or provide the ways to make it happen.

MARIANNE WILLIAMSON, author of *A Return to Love*

A friend of mine used to have a T-shirt on which there was a picture of God with his head in his hands, sitting in a psychotherapist's office. Above his head was a bubble that said, 'I blame myself!' Deep down, if we are really honest, we blame God for a lot. We think that God cannot be trusted, and that we have to run the show ourselves. Our criticisms of other people and ourselves can be hard enough to deal with, but perhaps one of the biggest taboo areas, and an unexplored area of our mind, is *the judgements we have placed on God*.

In *Die Fröhliche Wissenschaft* the philosopher Nietzsche said 'God is dead'. What he meant was not that most people believed that God had stopped existing, but that most people live *as if* God doesn't exist. How many people do you know who live in a state of constant peace and happiness, complete faith and trust? Not many, I would suspect. Even if we believe in God, we sometimes act as if God didn't *really* exist. We like to be in charge and live as if there *isn't* a higher power that can support, nourish, sustain and guide us. If we have grown up with a view of God as being punishing and angry, then we will be scared that God sees our faults and is after revenge.

Our fear is that if we surrender to love, we will lose too much. This is a great ego ploy, because we will actually *gain much*. Our ego has created this terrorizing story: the creator is harsh and cruel, don't trust him, pay him lip service, but hold onto your own control for dear life otherwise you are dead meat, cosmically frazzled! Lency Spezzano described her experience this way:

> I just finished a session with a fellow who faced his tantrum with God. Rage that creation even occurred; fear of love, especially fear of God's love, competition with others and ultimately with God. Many layers of terror, and defence mechanisms, sabotage, exhaustion, the notion that separation is probably a good idea. The spin of the mind's constant effort to control, and improve and categorize. And finally the recognition that the only way through is love, God's Love. In the past months most joining sessions have led to this basic human issue of separation from God. It takes real courage to lean into the rage and the terror involved in this issue but the result is life changing. It accomplishes the surrender of your bad attitude in exchange for Peace.

Often we are terrified to let go and trust God; we think it will be our death. And on one level that is true, but it is only our ego that will die, and it will only do so in order that more of who we really are can come through. Our ego has created wonderful and subtle ploys to hide what is true from our awareness. Often we are unwilling to surrender until we are on our knees, when we know our way isn't working any more. When we know we don't know, we are open to learn.

OUR TRANSFORMATIVE POWER OF CHOICE

The power of his decision offers it to him as he requests. Herein lie Hell and Heaven. The sleeping Son of God has but this power left to him. It is enough.

A Course in Miracles

Our power of choice is our greatest power, and the only thing that can never be taken away from us, whatever the circumstances of our life. In July 1998, five days after the finalization of a messy divorce, Theresa Ritzert was at home with her three children when her angry ex-husband broke into their home and announced that he would make her pay the price for divorcing him. He said he was going to kill all three children and then himself so that she would have to live in a lonely hell for the rest of her life. He went ahead and did just that – he shot all three children and turned the gun on himself.

Theresa's life was obviously devastated, and she was angry as hell with him, full of hatred, grieving enormously and just wanted to die herself. But then she began to realize that if she did that, her husband would have won. She began to see that she had a choice in how she responded. That choice was not just concerned with whether her husband would win or lose; she saw that she had choice over her own happiness. In the depth of her pain, she realized she could choose to continue living fully, for herself and for the world. She touched the power of who she was, and decided that out of her own pain she would choose, as much as she was able, 'to make a heaven on earth'.

As a result, she found a new partner who became her fiancé. She refused to live her life in revenge. She wanted to experience joy as much as she could for the rest of her life. She explained, 'I began to recognize that there was a higher authority than myself, and that maybe there was a plan for me that I couldn't see, but only trust. Maybe I am not qualified to judge.'

OUR POWER OF SURRENDER

Our ego doesn't believe in God; it thinks it rules the world, but it does like to *play* God! It likes to think it has usurped God's position, and has to defend itself against God. What this can block is that our spirit *is* the divine: it extends the love of God. Our ego thinks it has a different will from God and survives only by defying the will of God. Our ego tells us that if we surrendered to God's will we would lose our power and become a slave or a wimp, or have to do things we really wouldn't want to do, when actually we would align with our greatest power. Surrendering *will* satisfy our greatest need – we will be happy! Love has a plan that is probably very different from our own. Love's will for us is perfect happiness, and when we are unhappy it is because we have valued something more than love.

We defy love. Love tells us that we are beautiful, precious, accepted and whole, and we won't accept it. We say, 'No way! I know better about me! I am not good enough, I am bad, I am guilty, I am unworthy.' We so want to be right, even if it means that we are unhappy or suffering. There are places within us, usually hidden deep in our mind, where we value control more than anything. We won't surrender because we fear we'd lose our sense of separateness, thinking we'll become a slave to God, our partner or our boss, or that we'll lose our identity completely. The ego exists through separation, so will do anything to preserve that sense of separateness. We always control out of fear.

Our greatest courage is to *choose* to let our ego go, to *choose* love and joining over separateness. We can't be made to, but we can choose to. Here are some ideas on how to do that:

- *Joining. We do this by making a connection with someone else, and moving through whatever feelings, thoughts and beliefs we may have been using to hold ourselves back.*
- *Take back projections. Whatever judgements we have had about someone else, we must take them back and realize that we do that too. This will release both of us.*
- *Release our own guilt. When we feel guilty, we can't join.*
- *Give through our resistance. Every fear hides a gift, so if we give our gift despite our resistance, we will burn through a level of separation.*
- *Give up our need for specialness. Every place we want to be separate is a place where we value specialness over loving others.*

OUR POWER TO BE A CHILD AGAIN

Parents love giving all they can to their children; what they have they share. Their joy is to love and to give to the best of their ability. Our power comes from being a child again. Not childish, but childlike. We can be childlike at any age, with any responsibilities. It is a quality that is eternal within us. We can be a child to our parents, a child to our children. And we can be grown-up, mature and adult too. Childlike means having an innocence and a willingness to receive. When we are truly childlike again, we can be taken care of, we can be loved, we can receive fully. Love wants to give so much but we must become childlike again to see what is available. To be childlike is not naïve, it is innocent. It is letting people enjoy, love and appreciate us. Children need to love; the child in us naturally wants to love. We are hard wired for love.

We become disillusioned with our idea of our creator, religion, spirituality, gurus, success, fame or any other idol that we put our faith into. But none of these is God, they are all God substitutes. The truth of God remains, when we are willing to let go of our false ideas. We must let go of *proof* that God can't be trusted, and that our broken hearts and broken dreams are warranted.

The Snow Falls

The Christmas before last in my inner world
the snow was falling.
The snow falls and my heart is very quiet.
It walks the midnight woods at full moon
And the flakes fall down, hushing the world
In the abyss of silence.
My soul opens like a woman in love
I can finally hear God's words:
Be at peace.
All is right.
You are loved.
Not one soul shall fall
From my loving catch.
I know you totally.
I love you utterly.
In the moment that time and its dream ends
You will know
That you have been in my arms forever.
Do not fear.
When you awaken
From the lonely corridors of time,
I shall be there.
I am always there
Waiting for you to remember.
Look ahead, I am there.
Look inside you, I am there.
Look beside you, I am there.
Look behind you, I follow you,

Your faithful Friend,
Ready to catch you if you should fall.
Do not worry.
No weight is too heavy for me.
Unburden your heart.
Make room.
Let me in to love you.
I wait for you at home within
A light always burns.
I, dweller in the mists of time,
Stumble back into my life
Yet no longer alone
On the journey home.

by Chuck Spezzano

Deep within us is spirit, and prayer is one of the ways that we can align our mind and our heart with the divine. Through prayer we can dissolve our sense of separation and reveal the much greater power that lies within.

7

OUR POWER OF PRAYER

The place I go for help is deep within, to that level of conscious-ness that lies beyond the materialist mindset – to the God within. I have to ask God for help. I have to pray. When I pray in this way, I am not asking for divine intervention by an external God. Moreover, I am not praying for the world to be different than it is. I am praying for a different perception of the world. I am asking for divine intervention where it really counts – in the mindsets that govern my thinking.

PETER RUSSELL, author of *From Science to God*

Prayer is alchemical. It helps us transform our lower consciousness into a higher consciousness. As an airline pilot seeks a higher altitude when encountering turbulence, so prayer moves us to a higher ground of consciousness, not to *escape* the world, but in order to alter our worldview.

Prayer is greater than any religious tradition, and has been a tool of transformation since the beginning of time. True prayer is not for some distant God to come into our lives, but for us to realize that God has never gone away. The names may alter, but the principle is the same. Through prayer *we* are uplifted and brought to higher ground, and it is a vital part of the spiritual path. Prayer can bring incredible emotional, physical and spiritual benefits. Many studies show that every living thing responds positively to prayer. This is as true for plants sitting on a greenhouse shelf as it is for pets, or people lying in hospital beds: there is more than ample evidence of the power of prayer. Scientific knowledge accelerates the healing process, reduces the need for drugs and can help with mental health problems. Prayer transcends time and space. Here I want to delve into the mysterious power of prayer and see how we can harness it in our own life.

Let's begin with the world of work, as businesses can benefit from prayer too. Two friends of mine, John and Jackie, started a business buying properties in order to rent them out. Their intention was to harness spiritual principles to create a successful business by providing a wonderful place for people to live; to serve their tenants, thereby providing a good income for themselves. Before they rent out each property, they bless it. They also pray for their tenants every week, that their lives will be blessed, that they will be happy and that their work will be successful. They don't pray for 'things', they pray for a consciousness to which all things are attracted. John explained to me, 'In three years of operating, we haven't had a single bad debt, and we have good relationships with most of our tenants. In three years we've created a property portfolio worth over £3 million and substantial rental income.' How would our workplaces be different if we all prayed for each other's success rather than competing with each other?

Prayer is thinking with the mind of love, and that is why it is so powerful. It awakens the soul, opens the doors of possibility and helps us to penetrate the mystery of our own being. Prayer is a universal human practice – an essential element common to every person in every religious and ethnic group. Prayer is a bridge to the Absolute, one of the most powerful ways of connecting with something higher, wiser and more powerful than our individual ego self. It is how we touch, or connect with, that which is beyond ourselves. The aim of prayer is to release the present from its chains of past illusions, and for us to see with the eyes of truth.

Prayer links us to the deeper rhythms of life, the eternal order beneath the material surface. Through prayer we trade our small power for the great power that lies within. Prayer both does and undoes and is not the overcoming of God's reluctance, but the taking hold of God's willingness. John O'Donohue in *Eternal Echoes* talks in depth about prayer, and describes it as the bridge. Prayer bridges the gap between our sense of separateness, and our sense of unity and belonging. It helps us know the ground that we all stand on, the place where differences can dissolve. We begin to know that what is at the heart of me is also at the heart of you. All true prayers, in any religion, have equal power, and will be the same prayer. Prayer is intimacy with our own soul, and with the heart of the divine. In prayer our attention is diverted from the outer world and its claim and control over us. Through prayer we realize that our peace comes not from importing goodness from the outer world, but from discovering our inner riches.

PRAYER'S PURPOSE

Prayer is not meant to be a tool we use to attain a quick material fix in our life but then go back to living in the consciousness that led to our need to pray in the first place. The true purpose of prayer is to lift our heart and soul into a new consciousness, one aligned with our divine well-being and our soul's purpose, so that life becomes new and we see with new eyes. We are not just looking for a boon or a miracle (although those come along the way); we are striving to step into a new outlook that will bring greater clarity and effectiveness to all that we do, enabling us to be more truly powerful. As Alan Cohen puts it beautifully in his book, *Handle with Prayer*,

> We must pray not *to* God, but *from* God. Once and for all, we must recognize that the power of God is *within* us, and expresses itself *as* us. To handle with prayer begins with the premise that God is a God of love, we are blessed offspring of God, and it is God's good pleasure to give us all that our hearts desire.

The purpose of prayer is not, as commonly believed, to change God's mind, but to change *our* mind. God always and only ever knows our wholeness, innocence, lovability and worthiness. Prayer is very practical, because to look to love is to look to the realm of consciousness that can deliver us from the pains of life and can provide us with what we need to live purposefully. It is not about begging, trying to manipulate or do deals, but about the subtlest and most powerful of transformations within our own mind, our own sense of our self.

PRAYER AS A FIRST RESORT

When asked for the secret of her success in loving and serving so many people, Mother Teresa responded, 'Everything starts from prayer . . . my secret is very simple. I pray.' We tend to see prayer as a last resort, something we turn to when all else fails. We try prayer almost as a panic measure. When the world has hurt us, disappointed, shocked or disillusioned us, we seek refuge in prayer. Marianne Williamson tells us in *Illuminata*: 'No conventional therapy can release us from deep and abiding psychic pain. Through prayer we find what we cannot find elsewhere: a deep peace that is not of this world.' Prayer can soothe our deepest pain. What it offers us far exceeds all that we have asked for.

When we pray as first rather than last resort, we are aligning our thoughts with thoughts of real power, because we are praying that we bring forth our excellence, our beauty, our brilliance into the world like a beacon. Prayer is the superpower that releases the light in us. When we pray as a first resort we open the door to real success, which is recognizing and coming from the place of wholeness, creativity, abundance and fullness within us. We can pray in and for joy, love and happiness too as well as pain and suffering. You can give thanks for the blessings in your life, the friends, love, laughter, money, possessions, ideas and creativity you have at this very moment.

When we have a problem, we often try to fix it ourselves, thinking it through, usually trying out various forms of our own power and control, and only when these fail do we ask for divine help. We can begin to train ourselves to ask for help immediately we experience a problem. As soon as we perceive a problem or need, we can learn to step back from the machinations of our mind and become still for a moment. In the silence, connect with your higher power and turn the problem over, *right then and there*. We need not wait until we reach crisis point before we call in the power; the same power will head off the problem at an early and manageable stage. We will receive intuitions or guidance, or people will come into our life who will be the answer to our problem, or the problem may diminish, even melting away.

WE CAN NEVER ASK FOR TOO MUCH

We need to stretch our mind to conceive of a power that never stops giving, never withholds and never finds us too much trouble. We need to embrace boundlessness. Can you think of a creative force that is willing not only to help us a bit, but help us immeasurably, that not just accepts us, but adores us, that wants to bestow every wonderful thing on us? Think about this for a moment. A creator that adores us, that cherishes us, that holds us in such love and tenderness that we weep to realize and experience it. It may seem almost inconceivable to many of us, but this is unconditional love. Through prayer we can remember this presence, and come to know it as the ground we are always standing on.

FROM PRAYERS OF LACK TO KNOWING OUR FULLNESS

When we pray because we seem to be experiencing a lack, we are asking out of need. This is not wrong, but is an affirmation of weakness. *A Course in Miracles* teaches us that 'These forms of prayer, or asking-out-of-need, always involve feelings of weakness and inadequacy, and could never be made by a Son of God who knows Who he is. No one, then, who is sure of his Identity could pray in these forms. Yet it is also true that no one who is uncertain of his Identity can avoid praying in this way. And prayer is as continual as life. Everyone prays without ceasing. Ask and you have received, for you have established what it is you want.' We can learn to shift into prayers of fullness: the desire to know and live from our own strength. We can acknowledge our feelings of lack and weakness *and* ask to know our strength.

CREATING OUR OWN PRAYER

One of my joys over the last few years has been re-owning the power of prayer in my own life. This has inspired me to start creating prayers that resonate deeply with my own heart and soul. Here I share some of them with you. There is a greater selection at *www.heartatwork.net*.

A prayer to accept the love in us

Today I accept the Love in me

Without any arrogance or pride, I accept my divinity, my innocence

My freedom from guilt and fear

I accept the love and joy that I am, in which I was created

I am willing to let go of all imaginings that I could be anything else

Thank you

A prayer to work with love

As I go to my work today, may your loving spirit go with me

May my work be a vehicle for the love you put within me

May my light shine in darkened places

Show me how I may be able to forgive all whom I meet today

May I carry your light to all I meet

May I love myself so that I may extend that love to all I meet

Help me leave yesterday behind

Help me have new love, new creativity, new passion, new power

Help me remember that we are all here to lead each other from the darkness into the light

Thank you

A prayer for releasing self-judgement

I have created so many self-concepts

I have judged myself not good enough

I have criticized and attacked myself

All because I thought this might make me more acceptable to you

How silly I have been

You have simply loved, supported and accepted me without question

Your love has been the bedrock of my life and work

Only I have obscured that with self-created clouds

Today help me clear away my old self-concepts

Help me to forgive myself for such silliness

Help me see what you have always seen in me

Beauty, truth, love and innocence

Help me bring those qualities into my work, play and life

Help me be a shining beacon so that I may know you as my source

And help remind others of *their* source.

Thank you

A prayer for abundance

I let today be the day I remember the truth of abundance

That beyond this world there is a whole other world within me

A world where there is no lack, doubt or scarcity

I let today be the day I stop resisting and accept the power of my soul

I let myself grow in awareness of the love and beauty within

Today I am willing to accept the truth, accept myself however wonderful that may be!

I choose to share of myself, give and receive and am willing to face all doubts and fears

And to see that they are not true

I accept that the power of creation is in me now, always has been and always will be

I forgive myself for all my misconceptions about myself

And step into the glory that I am

Today I am willing to have it all and give it all

To hold nothing back

To shine my light and remember the holiness and wholeness that we all are

Thank you

A prayer for original blessing

I understand that I need to overcome the idea of original sin

Help me understand that it never was true

I give up the belief that I am separate from, small and powerless

I accept that within me is the shining glory of love's creation

Nothing less will ever satisfy me, but Spirit's intention for me

Thank you

Love knows nothing of unworthiness: that is a story created by our ego. Love knows only our value. We can't pray for our worthiness, it is already ours, but we can pray to see and accept it. When we feel unworthy we exclude ourselves from many of the good things of life. We may press our nose against the window of happiness but never really enter the room. We may put ourselves at the heart of success, but feel we don't belong there; we feel we will be found out and thrown out as a fraud. Lack of belief in our worthiness can act as a closed door and can actively repel so many gifts that Life is waiting for us to receive. The internal alarm systems are activated. Intruders are detected: our defences are threatened. Unconsciously we are pushing away the very things that we want to come to us. Love extends itself without conditions. Our ego sets up all sorts of dramas and beliefs that we are bad and unworthy, but with only one purpose – to blind us to our true spiritual power and nature.

Our ego will always have us believe that unworthiness will buy us something, that it somehow makes us nobler, more acceptable. But it can only close our heart, not open it to grace.

A prayer for worthiness

I am willing to drop my belief in my unworthiness

I am willing to embrace my worthiness

I have the courage to accept I am OK

I open my heart to receive all that is good

I am willing to surrender my self-judgement, and accept love's judgement of me

I am a willing visitor at Heaven's banquet

HOW DO WE PRAY?

I love these words of a young child: 'Sudden prayers make God jump!' Perhaps the one and only rule for prayer is that it should not be too sudden! Other than that there are no rules. We can easily get caught up in worrying whether we are saying the right words, whether we are getting it wrong. With a true intention, there is no right or wrong. The words we use are much less important than our motivation to pray, and the intention behind our words. Some people say that prayer is how we talk to God; others say it is how we set things in motion. There is a common theme, which is the natural human wish to open our hearts and communicate with the sacred principle, a higher power or divine source. Whatever language we use, prayer is the common language of the soul.

The true purpose of prayer is not a desire to express our remorse or to apologize and flagellate ourselves, but to ask to be uplifted in mind and spirit. We needn't pray with guilt, but we can pray for our guilt to be undone. We needn't pray to profess our unworthiness, but to claim our worthiness. We don't pray to create distance but to dissolve it. Prayer is the soul's sincere, deep and inmost desire, uttered without even the need for words. We can be overly concerned with thinking that we can upset God by using the wrong words, or by asking for too much, or for the wrong thing. Mahatma Gandhi said, 'It is better in prayer to have a heart without words than words without heart.' What is vital in prayer is not any particular religious belief or background, but love. A prayer from any religion, with the right intention, is powerful. Love, not belief or technique, is what gives prayer power.

PRAYER IS THE MEDIUM OF MIRACLES

A Course in Miracles teaches us that miracles are not exceptional but are *natural*.

Prayer is a stepping aside, a letting go, a quiet time of listening and loving. It should not be confused with supplication of any kind, because it is a way of remembering your holiness. Why should holiness entreat, being fully entitled to everything Love has to offer? And it is to Love you go in prayer. Prayer is an offering; a giving up of yourself to be at one with Love. There is nothing to ask because there is nothing left to want. That nothingness becomes the altar of God. It disappears in Him.

In the state of love, miracles unfold naturally, but within the realm of fear and guilt we can block miracles and hold them back, but not eradicate them. Miracles occur when time and space are laid to one side and eternal love can shine through. A miracle is *a shift in perception from fear to love.* A miracle is firstly a change of mind, and in that change of mind from fear to love the way we see the world alters. Prayer is not just a tool or a practice; it is an art, even a way of being, a way of keeping our mind linked with the infinite power of the universe. Prayer is not a formula, but an attitude; not an obligation but an opportunity.

When we pray truly we are asking for the realization that *our prayers have already been answered.* In the Bible we are taught that whatever you ask for in prayer, believe that you have received it, and it will be yours. Release is already within us. We have fallen prey to the hypnotic dream that there is something out there that can offer us more than we already *have*, and *are*. Prayer helps us remember that the kingdom is already within us, has always been, and always will be. It reminds us that we are on a glorious journey home, only for us to discover that we have carried 'home' with us all the while. We had it all the time.

WORDS ARE LESS IMPORTANT THAN INTENTION

A friend of mine, Julie, was in a computing job that she really didn't enjoy, and her constant mantra to herself and anyone who would listen was 'Get me out of this job, get me out of this job.' She had an attitude of boredom and frustration, and it was obvious to all that she was not committed to being there. One Monday morning she went into work and was called into her boss's office and made redundant. She was outraged! How could they do this to her? She was furious. She felt powerless. It reminded me of Woody Allen's words: 'Life is terrible, full of pain and suffering and over far too soon!' Julie felt really victimized, even though she got exactly what she prayed for. Alan Cohen calls these 'in your face productions', which is how resistance shows up in our life. When we don't listen to our intuitions and inner guidance the calls get louder and louder until we can't miss them. They are not punishments from a cruel universe, but loving wake-up calls to sleeping souls. Even illnesses and accidents are simply wake-up calls that we haven't heard yet. We try, unsuccessfully, to silence the very parts of us that want to help us most. The real issue for Julie was that she was praying for what she *didn't* want, not what she *did* want. What she really wanted was to find her own gifts and talents and a way of utilizing them for the fulfilment of herself and others. It took her ages to realize that she had exercised her own power, and got exactly what she wanted.

EXERCISE

* *Do you pray?*
* *When? As a first or last resort?*
* *What do you pray for most?*
* *Do you pray for what you* don't *want?*

Alan Cohen suggests that there are two ways of dealing with 'in your face productions'. The first is to get better at listening to those inner promptings, the intuitions that are always being offered to us but that we are unwilling to acknowledge, accept and act on. Then we can avoid crises. The red light on the dashboard warns us of impending problems so that we can take preventive action. Too often we push ourselves harder, trying to control ourselves or our emotions even more, or overriding them, disconnecting the red light rather than aligning ourselves with our spiritual power. The second way to lighten the burden of wake-up calls is to bless them when they turn up. Instead of feeling like a victim, know that they are a huge gift, even if you can't see the gift. Believe that the universe wants to free you, not conspire against you. Acceptance and appreciation soften us and open us to the possibility of transformation and emergence. We don't have to live through crisis and emergency; we can glide through life by listening to the voice for love within us.

PRAYER TRANSFORMS OUR SENSE OF IDENTITY

One major purpose of prayer is to dissolve our sense of separateness, to melt distance, to open our awareness to a greater sense of who we are. Prayer can bridge the distance between who we think we are and who we truly are. Love's spiritual purpose is to burn up our sense of otherness, from each other and from our creator. We don't know who we really are at all. We may have created a sense of identity that is based on fear, guilt and separation, and to know our true self we must take a leap of faith into what seems to be the unknown. Generally we are very reluctant to make that leap, clinging to our existing sense of identity, however uncomfortable that may be. We can label ourselves in many ways: workaholic, loser, successful, dysfunctional, abused, victim, writer, tough, hard worker, criminal, bad, good. But our true identity is much more than this, and life will always challenge us to realize that it cannot be tied to any label.

Painful as our problems may be, we are often reluctant to let them go because *we don't know who we would be without them.* Logic suggests that we should avoid pain and embrace happiness, but we often cling to pain. Although we consciously want to step into greater love, abundance, creativity and joy, there are parts of our unconscious mind that want to stay just as they are. Parts of us are terrified to give up our stories, give up our interpretation of our past. We have become so identified with our past we are terrified that without it we might be nothing; perhaps, we fear, we are nobody at all.

. . . we get down to what Buddha said was the job we have been born for, knowing that letting go of our suffering is the hardest work we will ever do.

STEPHEN LEVINE, Buddhist teacher and author

EXERCISE

* What pain or story are you being called to give up now?
* What sense of your identity no longer serves you?
* What problem are you most scared *not* to have any more?

Love knows our true identity

I don't know who I am
But I am willing to discover
I trust that I can let go, face my fear
And emerge into the light
I know you know the truth
I am willing to accept that truth
However wonderful that may be

THE JOURNEY FROM OUTER TO INNER IDENTITY

Jim had taken two years out from his corporate career, rented out his flat and spent much of that time travelling around the world. He explained to me, 'When I left, so much of my identity was tied up in my work success, the outer approval and recognition and the money. Now, having been without those things for a while, I have such a strong sense of myself that is independent of any work achievements. I feel I am a different person.' Our sense of identity shifts throughout our life, which is natural. The more our sense of self is defined by outer factors, the more we are likely to have a sense of anxiety, while the more we have an inner sense of self, the more at peace we can be.

Although I have written three books now and the first has been in print for several years, it is only fairly recently that I have begun to say to myself and others 'I am a writer'. It may sound strange, but to move from 'I wrote a book' to 'I am a writer' has taken a couple of years and has been a fascinating inner journey. Our sense of identity is a large component of the 'ground' that we think we stand on. How do we define ourselves? By the outer aspects of ourselves, or by an inner knowing and experience of ourselves? One of the major ways is by recognizing what we feel most comfortable saying 'I am' to and discovering whether this sense of identity is more linked to our ego or our spiritual sense of being. One of the most crippling of prisons is that of reduced and diminished identity.

EXERCISE

* *What sense of identity is slipping away from you right now?*
* *What new sense of identity is emerging within you?*

Dying to our illusionary ideas is a part of our spiritual path, and the way to our true power. In Buddhism, death is not seen as a terrifying event that happens at the end of our life, but as a metaphor for letting go and being reborn on a moment by moment basis. Buddhist monks' goal then is to *die before they die, to be free within life*. We can die to our past ideas about ourself in each moment. Every time we die to fear, love is reborn; every time we die to guilt, freedom is reborn; when we die to our judgements, innocence is reborn. When we begin to realize within us a sense of identity that goes beyond anything of this world, death becomes less frightening. It is no longer an end, but a new beginning. Although we fear the destruction of the self we think we are, we begin to know that it is only ever the unreal that dies.

PRAY AND FOLLOW THROUGH WITH ACTION

You have probably heard this joke about John who prayed every week to win the lottery, and every week he moaned because he didn't win, complaining that his prayer had not been answered. After months of disappointment, John went to a church and angrily shook his fist at God and said, 'If you are such a great God, why haven't I won the lottery? Where is my money? If I don't win soon, I am going to become an atheist.' As he was storming out, a voice suddenly boomed out from above, 'The least you could do, John, is to buy a ticket!' John was doing his bit in prayer, but wasn't taking responsibility for acting on his own prayers. When we take steps in the direction of our visions, we demonstrate that we are serious, and that we are truly willing to do what it takes to manifest our dreams. Miracles occur as the universe moves to orchestrate the people, situations and events in ways that we could never have planned. We also need the eyes to see the miracles turning up in our life.

True prayer is active, not passive, but prayer without action lends itself to passivity. Prayer fortifies our action in this world, and is the fuel that propels us in our life; it's not an excuse to withdraw: it gives a new energy and quality to our action, a new consciousness from which to act. In the movie *Jerry Maguire*, Tom Cruise plays a sports agent, who pleads with his client, played by Cuba Gooding Jnr, 'Help me to help you.' We need to be willing to be helped. I love the idea that we pray as if all depends on God and act as if all depends on us. We grow our spiritual muscles by participating in the adventure of life, not by sitting on the sidelines. We grow through inner transformation and outer action. Most spiritual traditions encourage us to take our spirituality into our work, our relationships and our life.

Our life is not about gifts being dropped into our laps: we must claim our power as co-creators with love. Love will give our dreams and ambitions wings, for as we become responsible for our own success we become masterful. To access and experience the real power of prayer, we are called to take a leap of faith, and usually leap after leap of faith. I find that I tend to take lurches of faith rather than leaps! I move forward with doubt and fear often, with a sense of inspiration but not necessarily certainty. I hesitate on the brink of the unknown, knowing the past is no longer true, and feel the push to risk entering new territory. I often wonder if I am inspired or just crazy!

We must step forward and trust the unseen. If we wait until we are sure, we could die waiting. The whole point is to build up faith in our unseen power, not the visible props. If we knew how to accomplish our purpose, faith wouldn't be necessary. We grow in this faith and trust by acting in faith and trust, not just by sitting quietly. This is where we are called to courage, trusting that our leap of faith will land us on higher ground, that we won't plummet downwards. Through practical experience we get to know the existence of a higher power. We know that it is something practical and bankable, not just a vague idea. Powerful people who change the world, their own lives and raise consciousness *pray* and they *do*. They predict the future by choosing to create it. With all the uncertainty in the world now, we must dig into the deepest places within ourselves, and act from faith and love rather than adding to the fear on the planet. We are called to step into darkness so we can illuminate. We are all here to draw forth our true spiritual power and bring the world to a higher level of love.

TRANSFORMING OUR GUILT

Guilt is the feeling you have when you try to imagine you are a separate isolated being, apart from God, apart from your brothers and sisters, and the rest of the universe . . . as long as you try to maintain that illusion, that you are separate, you must stay in conflict.

BRENT HASKELL, author of *Journey Beyond Words*

One of the biggest blocks to love and spiritual prosperity is guilt. In the kingdom of love and holiness, guilt is unknown. All our guilt is created by our ego and projected onto God. Our purpose is not to ask God to release us from the guilt in which we think we are held, but to release ourselves from the guilt in which we are holding ourselves.

The ego is built on guilt. With the belief that we could ever be separate from God came guilt. Prayer is a powerful force to undo the illusion of guilt. We feel a deep guilt that we have killed or usurped God. Underneath the surface is often guilt, and guilt is one of the ways that we can most manipulate and be manipulated by other people. It's not a nice thing to acknowledge, but is true. Someone once said that guilt is the most expensive emotion of all – so much of what we do and things we buy can be motivated by a sense of guilt.

EXERCISE

* *How much of your life is motivated by a feeling of guilt? In any particular relationship, e.g. with your partner, children, boss or employees?*
* *How much do you feel stuck because of guilt in your life?*
* *How do you try to pay off guilt in your life, e.g. by being nice, by working hard, by buying presents or sacrificing yourself?*

When we are motivated by guilt, we compensate and respond out of a sense of duty; we aren't our authentic self.

Guilt is disempowering. It binds us to our past, to mistakes that we made or believed we made. Feeling robbed of our true power, we may be pushed into compensating for the guilt we feel, or defending against the guilt we fear feeling. Wherever we feel guilt, we withdraw from life and create distance. It is an invisible wall between us and others, and often makes us take on roles. We feel bad, and act good. Sometimes we move to another country to try to escape our guilt, but the trouble is we carry it with us wherever we go. Physical distance only provides temporary relief. Real release comes from undoing the guilt.

Below is a poem I wrote when I recognized how guilt had blocked me in my life.

But my guilt got in the way

I was going to tell you how much I love you, but my guilt got in the way
I would have let you really love me, but my guilt got in the way
I was going to visit you when you were dying, but my guilt got in the way
I was going to be light in the world, but my guilt got in the way
I would have found the work I loved, but my guilt got in the way

I could have inspired millions, but my guilt got in the way
I would have known how much God loved me, but my guilt got
in the way
I would have found my true love, but my guilt got in the way
I would have been successful, but my guilt got in the way
I could have made a lot of money, but my guilt got in the way
I would have helped you, but my guilt got in the way
I was going to be happy, but my guilt got in the way

THE WAY THROUGH GUILT

We need to see the price we are paying for our negative judgements. We need to acknowledge how much we have hurt ourselves and to see that those we have judged as enemies are in fact our teachers. *A Course in Miracles* tells us,

Guilt must be given up, and not concealed. Nor can this be done without some pain, and a glimpse of the merciful nature of this step may for some time be followed by a deep retreat into fear . . . Stand still an instant, now, and think what you have done. Do not forget that it is you who did it, and who can therefore let it go. Hold out your hand. This enemy has come to bless you. Take his blessing, and feel how your heart is lifted and your fear released. Do not hold onto it, nor onto him. He is a Son of God, along with you. He is no jailer, but a messenger of Christ. Be this to him, that you may see him thus.

This is forgiveness.

RECLAIMING OUR INNOCENCE

About 20 years ago I went to see a play by Henry Farrell in the West End of London called *Whose Life is it Anyway?* about a hospitalized and bedridden man with a debilitating disease who was fighting for his autonomy and power to make decisions about his own health, life and death. Tom Conti played the character, and in one scene a cleaner comes into his room to chat and pass some time. When the cleaner leaves, the character says, 'I love that guy, he is the only one who is natural around me. He relates to me as a human being, not an illness, and he is the only one who doesn't feel guilty about my condition.'

When we know our innocence, we don't attack ourselves or others, and we are more available to life. We are open to give, receive and share. Our invisible walls of unworthiness have melted and we are truly able to connect with the people around us. We don't need defences. Our innocence – our freedom from guilt – is one of our great gifts to life. Again, it's probably one reason why we love children so much. They haven't learned to feel guilty yet. Indeed, the biggest barrier to love is not fear, but guilt. Many of us feel guilty to some degree. Guilt is such a horrible feeling, though, that we often try to pass it on to someone else. We use scapegoats for our bad feelings of guilt – children, colleagues, partners, bosses and enemies – but there comes a time when we have to face and dissolve any guilt we carry.

There is *ego innocence* and *spiritual innocence*. Ego innocence is often a defence against guilt; it claims innocence yet feels guilt, which is the core of the ego. Rather like a naughty child who takes a sweet that he was told he shouldn't, and then claims 'It wasn't me!' we act in ways that we feel guilty about and then claim: it wasn't me, I had no choice, it was their fault – anything not to have to feel our own guilt. When we feel guilt, we think we deserve punishment. Innocence doesn't see the need for punishment but for correction and for help and love. Through innocence we are open to give, receive, feel, play and enjoy. We know the beauty and abundance of life. We are asked to see ourselves through love's eyes. We need to surround ourselves with people who support our innocence, not reinforce our guilt, who are not interested in condemning or judging us, but accept us. True innocence frees us, and those around us.

A PRAYER FOR HEALING SELF-ATTACK

Love:

I have judged and attacked myself very harshly.

I somehow thought this was required, that somehow this would buy me something.

I thought that my suffering would buy me release.

Help me gently realize I have been mistaken.

Help me see that attacking myself has no purpose.

With the gentlest of hands, help me forgive myself for my mistaken thinking.

Help me undo the pain that I have caused myself, without beating myself up even more.

Help me awaken from this bad dream of pain and suffering, and into the truth that I am loved

Help me understand that the universe is waiting for me to change my thinking

That tender divine hands are waiting to take the shards from my heart.

Give me the courage to know that it is safer to love than attack, that the rewards are so beautiful.

Help me want the rewards more than the pain.

Thank you

The Universe does not consist of spare parts and fragments that do not fit together; similarly, we are whole beings and we have been born with a unique purpose. We must remember that it is within our power to live our lives fully – and the evolution of our own purpose is our life's work.

8

OUR POWER TO LIVE THE WORK
WE WERE BORN TO DO

You are born with a character. It is given, a gift, as the old stories say, from the guardians upon your birth.

JAMES HILLMAN, author of *The Soul's Code*

I need to be up front here and express a great bias. I have been running my own business for 13 years now, and it has been one of the greatest joys and challenges of my life. I love it because it has liberated me to do my best work and allowed me the fullest expression of myself and my abilities. The great joy is that it has allowed me to be myself, and allowed me freedom. It's not just freedom from rules and restrictions, but freedom to create and express, discover and risk, adventure and learn, succeed and make mistakes. Because I love my work, I am motivated: my work is its own reward. It allows me to converse with and interact with my soul's values. I don't need anyone else outside with a stick to make me be motivated, it bubbles up from my own soul. I get energy from the community I am part of, connected to and interact with. I have experienced a flow and a personal evolution I had hardly dreamed was possible.

How can we *not* do what we love? For me my work has become the way that I share all I have and all I know. I write this chapter with trepidation, even a little guilt, as I am explaining and sharing some of the benefits that I and thousands of others have experienced through being self-employed. I know that many people don't believe they can be self-employed, they feel trapped by the need to earn a certain amount of money, meet financial commitments and have to work for someone else. I don't think the two need to be exclusive. I think we can be responsible to our soul, and responsible to our financial commitments. For me the important thing is not that I have been self-employed, but that running my own business has been the perfect vehicle for me to find and follow my calling, to find and express my gifts.

Over these years I have been continually discovering the work I was born to do, and inspiring people to be creative, purposeful and passionate about their life and their work. And I don't think that *the work we were born to do* necessarily means being self-employed. I have met many people in business, government, teaching, law, health care and the ministry who are living their life purpose, being passionate and serving. As I have helped other people find the work they were born to do, it has been a natural progression for many of them to leave either their corporate careers or some other form of employment in order to create their own business. They have decided that being their own boss offers them the best chance to find and create the work and life they want, and it surely can.

We often make the mistake, however, of thinking that getting away from the strictures of organizational life automatically means that we are free. Getting away from the perceived problem is only half the equation. We can escape office politics, lack of control over our own work, and feeling unappreciated, but to create our own freedom and to love and be in charge are different matters. The biggest blocks to our freedom are not outside at all, but are within our mind. We can leave a constricting employment situation only to find ourselves a prisoner of our own thinking and attitudes. And if we leave employment only with the goal of making loads of money, we are missing the inner joys and pleasures available.

I believe that each of us is here for a unique adventure in awakening to our spirituality in the midst of our lives right here, right now. Never in human history has there been so much spiritual information on the planet and never before have there been so many opportunities to share ideas, information and our spiritual gifts. Transformation is not being led by governments, or organizations, but exists in the millions of everyday interactions that we all participate in.

The most important thing you can do is fall in love with what you are going to do for a living.
GEORGE BURNS, comedian

Being self-employed does not suit everyone. For some people it would be stressful: not everyone is ready to cope with this level of responsibility and accountability. But I have found running my own business to be an incredible experience of learning, sharing, growth and self-discovery. The rewards have been vast and my life has felt blessed in ways that I didn't know were possible. It is a great way to begin to satisfy our curiosity about what we can become. We get to learn so much about ourselves, our creative abilities, limitations, hopes, fears, strengths and weaknesses, our gifts and our shadow. We learn so much about other people, what makes their lives work, how we hold ourselves back, how amazing people can be, how awful they can be. It has been, and I imagine will continue to be for the rest of my life, my vehicle for making a difference in the world, and for my continued growth and development. Indeed, running my own business has been one of the best workshops on the planet! Everything I have learned in theory about growth and spirituality I have had the opportunity to, and have sometimes been forced to, apply to my own life.

My freedom is not simply something I claimed through composing and signing my letter of resignation in 1989; that was really only the beginning. Freedom is something I claim on a daily and hourly basis *within my own heart and mind, within my own thinking and feeling*. I have chosen to make my life a conscious inner and outer journey and to bring what is in me out into the world. I strive to have the courage to be transparent, and to hide as little as possible.

RUNNING AN INSPIRED BUSINESS AS THE FULLEST EXPRESSION OF OURSELVES

Being an entrepreneur can give us the ability to infuse our work with our creative voice, our own unique expression of love. We can be ourselves and express our own soul in the world. As we discover more of ourselves, our business becomes a greater expression of ourselves. For me, being self-employed isn't just about money, it's more about continuing to find my own spirituality, soul and creativity. Most workplaces are not yet built around the principle of people finding the fullest expression of themselves and more and more are beginning to realize this.

A DEEP FULFILMENT

Deep meaning and fulfilment *are* possible. To some people this may sound selfish, yet our fullest spiritual expression is why we are here, and it is our gift to the world. It refreshes and replenishes the world. One of the best expressions of this comes from author and teacher Gary Zukav, who says, 'When the deepest part of you becomes engaged in what you are doing, when your activities and actions become gratifying and purposeful, when what you do serves both yourself and others, when you do not tire within but seek the sweet satisfaction of your life and your work, you are doing what you were meant to be doing.' Our business can be the way we *find ourself* not lose ourselves. It is important to remember that we are not our work, we are bigger than any work we will ever do. But our work can allow us to express our love and spirit in the world.

EXPANDING OUR DEFINITIONS OF SUCCESS

One of the joys of running your own show is that you can broaden the criteria and possibilities for what it means to be successful. Whilst the major rewards of much employed work are often financial and material, self-employment offers the potential for many other rewards. These come from within and are just as tangible.

Jane and Mary were five months into running their own business together, having both left corporate jobs. They'd had some quick and easy successes through existing contacts, and were now in a fallow time. Their business was about helping organizations to be more creative in their thinking. They were taking stock of their first few months, and invited me to help them with their thinking and strategy. 'We are a bit concerned that we don't have much work lined up, although we would not have swapped the experience of the last five months for anything. We have learned so much about ourselves, about business, about our relationship. It has been one of the richest times in our lives,' Mary said. As we talked, Jane thought she'd send out an e-mail to some contacts she'd made but hadn't yet met. She put together a creative e-mail, much more creative than anything she had ever done when she was employed.

She sent it out to 20 people and it generated three meetings. One meeting led to an immediate contract. 'Teaching creativity, we sometimes forget that *we* are our first client!' Jane remarked. 'We realized we needed to keep ourselves in our own creative flow, and continually push back the limits of our own thinking.'

OUR POWER OF PERSONAL EVOLUTION

When we commit to following our heart and inspiration, we find ourselves being pulled forward by invisible forces that take us to a true and safe path. This is a remarkable experience; we find our life shaped by forces other than our own mind. It is as if we are following a curriculum but don't have a timetable and the lessons and opportunities turn up with divine timing.

In the Buddhist tradition, there is a concept of *right livelihood*, which is a way of working that enhances ourselves and our environment, making us richer rather than poorer, fuller rather than diminished. In right livelihood, we are on a lifelong journey of being challenged by being supported through and developing a deeper relationship with our work. This doesn't mean that it will always be easy, and part of the purpose of right livelihood is to help us see the places where we are stuck so we can grow, see our shadow and deal with it.

I find my greatest successes and evolution less often come through the route that I had planned and more often through something shifting *within* me as I become receptive to the whisperings of my own soul and heal some of my inner blocks. I do think it is crucial to have a plan and a sense of direction when we start, to research and prepare for the journey. We need to know how to start our journey, and what direction to move in. But often we reach our goals through ways and paths that we *hadn't* anticipated. As we dissolve our blocks, success find us, our outer world changes, opportunities wash up on our shores, meetings and opportunities suddenly appear. We get into the flow more. It happens through a shift from trying to *force* things to happen, to being willing to have things happen. In short, it's about creating the inner space for opportunity. We need to become receptive.

THE POWER OF BEING LESS ATTACHED

A friend of mine recently became a published author for the first time. At first he tried to convince himself that he wasn't concerned whether his book was successful or not. Little by little, it became obvious to me that he *did* care, and understandably so. He was in fact *very* attached to its being successful, but had tried to hide and deny that to himself. For several months he went into bookshops asking if they had it in stock and, if it wasn't there, suggesting they stock it. He gave as many talks as he could, wrote articles and tried to get publicity, with some success. Then he began to feel a lot of pain. He felt he was pushing the river uphill, until one day he just decided to let go of it and become more trusting. Within days he had a call from a major book chain saying they had put his book on their core stock list, and several other breaks soon followed. All at once everything began to flow more easily. The same actions can be more powerful when we are able to be a little less attached.

He was experiencing a common phenomenon. Our neediness actually pushes away the very thing we *think* we want. Paradoxically, the less attached we are, the more we can have. We can't deny our neediness, but we can make friends with it, and move to a different place within us. When we are holding on too tightly, we are trying to control too much and we block out the capacity of the natural intelligence of the universe to be involved.

I read an interview with Ivan Dragicivic who is director of Medjugorje, a shrine in Bosnia-Herzegovina where the Virgin Mary has been appearing since 1981, and which millions of people visit each year. He explained that after many years of observing people coming to the shrine to pray for miracles in their lives, he has seen a pattern emerge. Those who come with open hearts and minds are much more likely to experience peace, grace and even miracles than those who appear demanding and desperate. The great paradox is that *what we are not really attached to and don't really need, we can have as much of as we need, and what we desperately need and are too attached to, we often can't have.* What is required is a shift in motivation and awareness, from ego to spirit, from fear to love, from lack to wholeness. This is what makes all the difference. We shift from being desperate to being attractive. As we find the kingdom within, all else is added. Most of us want the material first, thinking that will give us the kingdom.

MARKETING CAN BE FUN AND CREATIVE TOO

Find ways of marketing that are in harmony with your soul.
BARBARA WINTER, author of *Making a Living without a Job*

For centuries we have been educated to believe that we must separate the way we earn our living from any inner or spiritual life we may have. We are taught that they are different domains and rarely meet comfortably; many people believe they shouldn't meet at all. A great challenge is to integrate our inner and outer lives in order to live more fully and authentically.

Most of us who set up in business on our own do so because we are passionate about our work and want to experience greater fulfilment. Yet to make our business succeed, we have to let people know we exist, and who we are, and what we have to offer. In short, we need to learn how to sell and market our goods and services. This is where many people's hearts drop or get heavy. They don't want to sell or market themselves, they just want to do what they love. One big mistake we make is to try and sell our personal service in a non-personal way. We create a distance between us and what we do. If we squeeze our work into conventional moulds we may lose some of the essence of what we are truly about. What we usually offer is some product or service that is an expression of *us*, and then we try and market it through means that are really *not us*.

Jo was looking at how to develop her business as a coach. She was a classic example of someone who loved what she did but loathed marketing it. She was looking at clever ways of marketing herself, and creating opportunities, and I suggested, 'Why don't you create business for coaching, by *doing* coaching? You could offer to coach people for a half-hour for free, then write about coaching and speak to groups about coaching. This will get you into the flow of what you love and your presence and example are going to be the greatest way that people will say yes to you.'

Jo liked this idea. She began dissolving the distinction she had in her mind between doing what she loved and creating the opportunities to do what she loved. Essentially, by doing what we enjoy we *create* the opportunities. It's simple and yet so powerful. Your presence and your demonstration of what you are passionate about will draw people to you. Doing what we love keeps us in the flow, keeps us connected to our inner energy source. It keeps us growing and learning, and engaged with life and people. The adventure is to learn how to have your business be successful *as an extension of you*: to do all the things we need to do, but without selling out on integrity and while maintaining the essence of what we are about.

THINKING ENTREPRENEURIALLY – OUR POWER TO SERVE

You come in with nothing, and you leave with nothing, so your life isn't about what you get – it's about what you give away. The measure of your life is what you give away. As you focus on serving, you'll discover that the stuff you used to chase after begins to arrive in your life in amounts more than sufficient for your needs.

DR WAYNE DYER, spiritual author and teacher

A true entrepreneur is someone who sees endless opportunities to serve the human family and is willing to receive remuneration for doing it. Serving and helping people is a great joy, and this need not mean we become righteous do-gooders. Through running my own business, I have learned the power of service and sharing. I feed a flame in me by sharing what I have. I get energized by the love that I give and the love that I receive. We can all discover how to tap into our own energy source, from within and from the people we serve and deal with. The love becomes the love we receive, until it becomes a cycle and we cannot tell the difference between giving and receiving: there is only the flow and exchange of energy. When I became committed to teaching I found I was given more to share, and more continued to pour in.

Developing an entrepreneurial mind may be a natural part of our personal development. As we discover the pleasure of service, it is inevitable that we start to feel overwhelmed by the needs of others. A major part of our development is finding how to balance our own needs with those of others, and to support ourselves as much as we support others.

Do you ever feel that you give so much out, but don't get as much in return? Do you ever get burned out? Do you ever feel resentful, as if you are being asked to sacrifice too much to those you're helping and supporting? Many of us have had a thorough training in sacrifice, having been asked to follow role models who are adept at behaving this way. We are told sacrifice is good and that the opposite is selfishness, which is bad. We are told that sacrifice will buy us love and appreciation, and perhaps even a place in Heaven.

But doing something we love, without sacrifice, doesn't have to be in conflict with doing something meaningful. We all need to express what is within us, to follow the calling of our soul. It is our love and energy that make it meaningful and our gift to the world. When we do something that is meaningful for us, our capacity to shine is much greater than if we are doing things that are routine and that don't engage or inspire us. And when we shine we bring light and inspiration to others. Remember this isn't about self-indulgence, it's about self-care that will enable us to serve the human family.

THE JOY OF BECOMING A LIFELONG LEARNER

To learn, discover, expand our awareness – what amazing gifts these are! We can, of course, do this from a fearful place, believing we must always try to keep our competitive edge or we'll be left behind. Or we can recognize that perpetual learning and discovery is one of life's joys, and can actually be a major contributor to a long and happy life. A study of nuns was carried out by Dr David Snowdon, Professor of Neurology at the University of Kentucky's College of Medicine, and written up in his book *Aging with Grace*. He studied 678 nuns, many over the age of 90, and six aged over 100. They attracted attention because so many of them reached old age seemingly without losing their mental faculties and without developing Alzheimer's disease.

Whilst the nuns obviously enjoyed the benefits of healthy living – none of them smoked or drank, and they were physically active – researchers felt this alone wasn't the whole picture. What they thought was a major contributing factor was that they all loved learning and most were teachers, so they were constantly reading, discovering and exposing themselves to new and stimulating ideas and subjects. As part of the study, the nuns had agreed to donate their brains to science after their death, because study of the brain is the only way that Alzheimer's can be confirmed. When some of their brains were analysed, half were found to have advanced, fully blown Alzheimer's disease. Yet they had never shown any symptoms. So being a lifelong learner will not only make us more interesting people, it may hold the key to a long and healthier life too.

EXERCISE

* *Where are you on the pathway to self-discovery and learning?*
* *Do you encourage yourself to learn, or do you berate yourself for not already knowing enough?*
* *Do you think you should be perfect and think you should already know everything?*

LEARNING TO VALIDATE OURSELVES

To successfully run your own business actually doing the work you were born to do, you must fall in love with learning, growth and discovery. But let's remember there is no-one standing there with a clipboard to evaluate your progress, no-one putting ticks and crosses in various boxes and then deciding whether you have passed or not. Often this is a learning that is quite different, and only known *to you*. Only you know what has scared you, baffled you and confused you, or stumped you, and only you know what you have had to overcome and have mastered, where you have inspired and astonished yourself, how much courage you have had to draw on. You will not necessarily end up with a wall full of certificates telling the world how much you have learned, but *you* will know. You may not even end up with more money, but you will have an inner bank account of rich experiences. No boss could ever have given you those. You created them for yourself, and they are yours to celebrate and enjoy, allowing you to sleep at night with a feeling of contentment, knowing that there is nothing else you'd rather be doing, and knowing that your talents are being fully utilized for your own benefit and the love of others.

Part of this journey will take you from external to internal recognition, and in recognizing ourselves we learn how we have grown. Sara Ban Breathnach states beautifully in *Simple Abundance*,

> When you were a child, you got report cards filled by teachers to tell you how you were doing in school. It's difficult to make the transition from external judgement to internal acceptance, but it's a journey we all must make to reach our essential selves as adults . . . Authentic success is internal. Often other people aren't even aware at first that you've reached it. The moment of success is the aware-ness that 'I can do it' or 'I have done it'. And it's comforting to know that this can't be taken away from you by an external event. Not by someone divorcing you, not by someone firing you.

My friend Nancy Rosanoff taught me a big lesson about the power of self-care. She is an author, teacher of intuition and TV presenter. She explained to me, 'When we are running our own business, and teaching things that can seem very intangible, we *are* our product to a large extent, our success is so linked to *us*. We are the one we can invest in, so that we are in a good place to help other people. Being tired, burned out and in sacrifice doesn't help anyone else, especially ourselves!'

ESTABLISHING YOURSELF AND SHARING YOUR LESSONS WITH OTHERS

Many of us draw back from the idea of becoming an expert, believ-ing that we have to be the best, the most knowledgeable, the most successful in our field in order to call ourselves an authority on any subject. In truth, real experts are people who take what they know and what they have learned, and then package that information in various forms and share it with people. They pass on their experience and learning. But if you stop and think about it, you are already an expert on one thing – you! Nobody knows more about you and your life than you do, and it's an important life, full of unique and valuable experiences.

I learned about a man who, having had a major relationship challenge, managed to salvage the situation himself. He then realized that other people might find it valuable to learn what he had learned. So he wrote a short book about it and set up a website called *www.stopyourdivorce.com*. He now makes a regular income from selling the book from his web site. Of course, the quality of advice varies, but there will almost certainly be people who can benefit from some aspect of your life experience.

KNOW WHAT YOU KNOW AND VALUE IT

It might sound strange, but part of being personally powerful is to *know* what we know. Too often we fail to recognize what we know, or tend to dismiss our own knowledge and experience. A friend who ran her own small public relations company suddenly lost her major client whom she had helped grow from near obscurity to extreme success. It really threw her off centre, not only creating money worries, but a small crisis of confidence, too. Some time earlier, she and I had discussed the possibility that she might also run courses for small businesses, teaching them the fundamentals of PR skills to grow their businesses. Her response at the time was, 'But it's so easy, surely everyone knows how to do that.' For me that encapsulated a trap that so many of us fall into. We can't believe that everyone else *doesn't* know how to do what we know how to do effortlessly.

When things come easily or naturally to us, we dismiss them.

To share our knowledge and experience we don't necessarily have to be the best, but we do need to be able to remember what it was like *not* to know, and to have a passion and the skill for sharing our knowledge. We also need to know how to extend our skills so that we can be teachers and educators.

EXERCISE

* *Think for a few moments about all you know.*
* *What skills and experiences do you have?*
* *What do you know how to do?*
* *What have you created?*
* *What have you taught and what could you teach?*
* *What projects have you initiated or been involved in?*
* *What are the most valuable lessons you have learned?*

This is not about exploiting people and squeezing every ounce of income out of your life. It is about sharing and serving people, it is about recognizing that we are blessed with skills and experiences that others don't have and could really benefit from. It is almost arrogant *not* to share our knowledge with others. The truth is, people are probably crying out to know what you know! Among the skills of being an expert is discovering how to 'chunk' and package the information you have. Today there are so many different media, and so many ways you can present your inform-ation – in person, in books, pamphlets, on audio tape or CDs, on web sites, electronically by e-mail.

OUR POWER TO SOLVE PROBLEMS

Running our own business is certainly not an escape from problems and frustrations. Indeed, there may even be more problems at times, as there is no longer anyone else to blame when things go wrong. But we can become creative and skilful at solving problems – our own and those of the people we want to help and serve. We learn new skills that we wouldn't otherwise have had to. We get a new set of problems – but fun ones, that can even be more meaningful to us. Instead of 'How do I deal with office politics?' 'How can I feel more appreciated?' and 'How can I get to be more in charge?' we get problems like 'How do I deal with more people than I can cope with?' 'How can I help more people and make more money with less effort?' and 'How did I earn enough money to pay that much tax and VAT?'

EXERCISE

Think for a few moments about the kind of problems you have right now. List them. Now think about some of the problems you would like to have to deal with, and list them. Have fun with this exercise:

Problems I have:
*
*
*

Problems I would most like to have:
*
*
*

LEARNING TO WORK FOR SOMEONE WE LIKE

There are wonderful bosses as well as less skilful ones, but overall the image of the boss is a negative one – unappreciative, demanding or controlling, and only concerned with money and results. They are the ones we like to blame for all our ills, and dream about getting away from. So what happens when we become the boss? How do we cope with becoming the person we used to blame? Being your own boss can allow you to become creative and it's an excellent opportunity to escape from our traditional thinking about what it means to be *in charge*. I have met many people who feel guilty about escaping corporate life who then push themselves even harder as their own boss than they ever did when they were employed.

When we are our own boss, we are offered opportunity after opportunity to take responsibility for ourselves and others. This means we have to develop our ability to *respond* to ourselves and others. Responsibility is a fascinating word for us when we are running our own show. As Erica Jong wrote, 'Take your life in your hands and what happens? A terrible thing: no-one to blame!' For some it means carrying huge burdens, not delegating or asking for help, and constantly feeling guilty. Indeed, for some it seems success means never asking for help. We can use our business either to escape from or reinforce our old work ethic thinking – that work has to be difficult, a struggle; it should not be enjoyable and we should feel guilt ridden. We need to get over the notion that work is by definition a struggle. Too many people bring prisoner thinking from their old environments to their new business, and miss the opportunities for freedom that setting up your own business can offer.

EXERCISE

✷ *What kind of boss would you like to be to yourself?*

✷ *How do you motivate yourself?*

✷ *How do you reward yourself?*

✷ *What rewards would you like to see and enjoy?*

✷ *Write a contract outlining how you want to treat yourself.*

✷ *How will you support yourself, emotionally and physically?*

✷ *What will and won't you do for, and to, yourself?*

✷ *How would you find inspiration?*

✷ *Who are your inspiring role models for being the boss?*

SELF-EMPLOYMENT AS A VEHICLE FOR SELF-LOVE

Most of us are used to pushing ourselves in our work. We are kind to ourselves when we are successful, but punish ourselves when we fail to match up to our own expectations or make mistakes. Think about the possibility that running your own business could be a major vehicle for learning self-love and being unconditionally kind to yourself. That doesn't mean opting out or being soft on yourself. Our heart and soul are bigger than any success or failure. We can create success through self-love, through supporting, encouraging and celebrating what we do, what we learn, how we serve and who we are.

Graham had been running a creativity business with two other partners and Harry was employed by them. Within a few months, one partner left to return to Germany, another stepped back from active involvement in the business, and suddenly Graham and Harry found themselves running the business together. They wanted me to help them think through a number of things. Although life had thrown them together, they hadn't made a really *conscious* decision to work in partnership. As we talked things through, they realized they *really did* want to reinvent their business, and they decided they really did want to commit to work with each other. 'What actually do you want to commit to?' I asked. They both looked blank. 'It is like you are entering a kind of marriage,' I said. 'How do you want to treat yourselves and each other? What will and won't you do for each other? What are your hopes and fears for yourselves, each other and the business? What are your goals?' Like most of us, they had never given these questions a lot of thought, but were very excited about the possibility of drawing up a 'contract' covering how they wanted to work together and support each other. Obviously this was not legally binding, but as a statement of intention it helped them focus their thoughts. It also provided them with a powerful vision of the future.

FINDING OUR OWN SOUL IN OUR WORK – INTEGRATING THE INNER AND THE OUTER

When we are self-employed we have the opportunity to become more integrated in what we do, to bring our inner and outer worlds together more fully, and to integrate our material and spiritual dimensions. This is not an easy thing for many of us. A few years ago I rediscovered my love of poetry, both that of others and my own ability to write poetry. At first this seemed to create a conflict in me as I thought 'What has poetry got to do with work? It's irrelevant!' But then I realized that my work was really about soul, and how work can be an expression of our soul. Then poetry did have a big part to play.

In the Middle Ages it was thought that each human had a mind, a body and a soul. They were all interrelated and interconnected. It was only with the thinkers of the Enlightenment that the soul was given to the Church for *safe keeping* and the mind and body were given to the domain of science. Science was interested only in perceptible and measurable reality, and because the soul couldn't be touched, weighed or measured, it was not considered worthy of investigation. The soul became the domain of mystics and poets, who were considered to have no real relevance or influence. Through the years the soul has been relegated to the minor leagues and was considered to have only a limited influence in the way we thought or behaved. In an interview with Ruth Lea of the Institute of Directors she said very forcefully, 'People's spiritual lives are nothing to do with the way they earn their living. Their spirituality is a purely private matter.' This split is only a few hundred years old, and now more than ever in history we are called to remember our wholeness.

Running your own business offers no guarantees that you will rediscover your soul or heart, but it may well be that your soul called you to leave a constricting environment and reclaim your physical and spiritual freedom. Reclaiming your soul is daily, hourly work; it is in the choices we make, the things we notice and celebrate, in the parts of ourselves we express in the world. It is the ongoing chance to keep discovering new parts of ourselves and the constant *growing of the territory* on which we are willing to stand, speak, be and express ourselves.

Work can be a conscious spiritual path. This means many things. Here I have identified some things it means to me:

- *Being inspired by, guided and led by my inner voice, not only my ego needs*
- *Living a purposeful life that goes beyond any success or failure I experience*
- *The courage to move from playing safe by roles, to being more of my authentic self*
- *Satisfying my need to serve other people, to make a difference, without sacrificing my own needs in the process*
- *Having to keep facing my fears to play big, to be public and show my soul. I recognize that my fear can be a call to courage*

- *Facing my hidden shadow side, the neglected and lost parts of myself, and striving to integrate them*
- *Going deeper into myself and discovering more of who I am and what I am capable of; what makes me tick, my strengths and weaknesses*
- *Living with seeming uncertainty – not controlling the future but letting it unfold and evolve*
- *Work becomes its own reward*

WORK BECOMES ITS OWN REWARD

Before I set up my own business, I worked largely for the money: it was the major reward. It compensated for the fact that I didn't enjoy the way I spent my time. 'Yes, I'll jump through the hoops for you, because you are paying me to.' Over the years I have made the wonderful discovery that the work itself can be a great reward. I love helping people, I love understanding people, I am intrigued by, and often inspired by, people and their stories. There are times when I feel extremely privileged that someone has shared their innermost dreams with me. I feel honoured that I get to make deep connections with people, and that I am in a position to love and support them. And I completely agree with what the Scottish historian Thomas Carlyle wrote nearly 200 years ago: 'Blessed is he who has found his work; let him ask no other blessedness.'

WORKING JUST FOR THE MONEY

Of course, I have had my fair share of money worries along the way, but I have learned that one of the biggest mistakes I have made, and still at times continue to make, is to focus on how I can make money – treating this as an isolated question that has very little to do with anything else. This way of thinking took me off track and I lost my aim, which is to love and serve. As far as I know, no-one has ever dealt with me because I need their money!

I attract clients because I have skills, ideas and experiences that can help them improve the quality of their lives. When I focus on my needs to the exclusion of meeting other people's, paradoxically it makes me less successful! And it is hard to see beyond ourselves when our own needs are unmet. We need to remind ourselves that we only ever create success when we meet other people's needs, creating win/win situations for all concerned. My prayer now is, 'Give me someone to help and serve – I need their money!'

WORKING FOR LOVE

Work for self, for love and for money, but actually work for the Big Love. Many of our hearts might drop at this stage. We think we will lose our freedom by working for God, but in fact we gain it. Doors open, not close; creativity flourishes, not flounders. We fear that we love writing and speaking, but God wants us to be an accountant or a piano player. But why should God want anything other than our happiness, our love and joy? With so much un-happiness in the world, would love want to create more? I think not. Love wants us to come alive. As Harold Thurman wrote so wonderfully, 'Don't ask yourself what the world needs. Ask yourself what makes you come alive, and then go do that. Because what the world needs is people who have come alive.' Love wants us to be fully *alive*, not suffering and doing something that isn't really us. Working for love does not mean huge sacrifices; it means *giving up* the notion of sacrifice.

When we work for Spirit, we are finally using our gifts for their intended purpose – to do our part in creating Heaven right here on earth. When we hold up our end of the bargain, Spirit will hold up its end of the bargain, which is to support us with everything we need in order to be happy, including money. Spirit does know that love doesn't pay the bills, and that the currency here on earth is cash. We do what we love, because we love it, because there is nothing else we'd rather be doing, because it makes us feel alive like nothing else ever will. And we need money. But we don't do what we love *in order* to earn money. The deal then becomes conditional and skewed.

Heaven knows we need money. When we let go of worrying about that and know it's on its way, we can see if we might be standing in our own way. The question we need to ask ourselves is not 'How do I make the money?' but 'How do I come alive? How do I live in wonder? How can I love and who can I serve?' The answers to these questions send the doors of abundance crashing open. The money turns up, not always immediately, not always in the ways we expect. Sometimes it can take years, and we need to do other work to maintain us while we build our passion. But when we do start to get paid for doing what we love, when we have loved giving, we see the gratitude in people's faces as they pay us. It is a thrilling experience. There are few greater blessings. It is bliss. It is joy. As Enid Bagnold, the English novelist, wrote, 'There may be wonder in money, but, dear God, there is money in wonder.' We may have to wait, but love's delays are not love's denials. A major problem may be that we have a different plan for what we need to be happy.

THE GREATEST REWARDS OF LIFE ARE NOT FINANCIAL

When we work for love we are rewarded in joy. The rewards are phenomenal, and the most important realization is that the greatest rewards of life are not financial. My friend Claire contacted me recently, updating me on the progress of her business as a trainer and consultant: 'It's almost two years since I set up my business and I woke up today for the first time in that period knowing that there was no work booked in, nor any meetings to talk about. But, guess what, I felt so joyful and full of gratitude for my great life! I am so blessed! I feel that because I know I'm doing the right work and I know that I'm giving my gifts and developing my own potential. I've had some great experiences in the last two years, met some fantastic people. I've done some good work, and more work will come, I know. The Universe is looking after me, evidenced by the fact that I'm healthy and happy, have lots of good friends, a great place to live, and I'm not anywhere near the breadline. If, two and a half years ago, I had seen into the future and seen this day when there's no work on the horizon, I might well not have set up my business (who really wants to put themselves into a potentially scary situation?), and that would have been a grave mistake! I also feel that there's a shift happening, that I'm being led to some different work, and that I need to stop doing so much of what I am doing in order to make that transition. A bit like turning a corner, changing direction, you can't do it at speed, you have to slow right down, or, if it's a big change, stop completely momentarily. So watch this space! I might not be busy earning, but I'm having fun.'

SELF-EMPLOYMENT AS A PATH TOWARDS FINDING OUR FREEDOM

Why do you stay in prison, when the door is wide open?
JALALUDDIN RUMI, 12th-century Persian mystic and poet

Freedom is a wonderful word, and a wonderful concept, and means many different things to different people. We can have freedom to do things, and we can have freedom from other people doing things to us. We tend to think of freedom as being an absence of restriction. But our greatest restrictions are not in our circumstances, but in our thinking. It is less about our situation, and much more about our consciousness.

I laugh at myself when I look back and remember how I felt when I discovered that as a self-employed person I needed to register both with the Inland Revenue for income tax and with

Customs and Excise for Value Added Tax. I was terrified as I thought that by having to engage with these authorities, I would completely lose my freedom. But by committing to engage and comply and do what I needed to, I realized that I was then free to run my business *without* interference.

I used to think that freedom was being free from commitments and entanglements. Running away seemed like a good option. I wanted independence because I was scared of being trapped. Little by little I have learned that I can experience freedom *through* commitment, that by committing, doors open, not close, that instead of being trapped, I am released. This is still work in progress for me, from sitting on the sidelines of life to jumping right into the centre, to engage rather than holding back. Running our own show gives us the freedom to structure our own time and can give us freedom to work with our own rhythms and energy. But when we do what we love, the line between work and play is less clear. Sometimes I don't know if I am working or playing. Other times, I love breaks which leave me feeling refreshed and revived, and raring to get back to work.

Our happiness stems from being authentic and making peace with all that we are – not from playing roles. This is what makes us strong and powerful and allows us to open the door to true spiritual partnerships in our life.

9

OUR POWER OF AUTHENTICITY

To be truly authentic persons, we have to allow the aspects of ourselves that we love and accept to coexist with all the aspects that we judge and make wrong.

DEBBIE FORD, author of *The Dark Side of the Light Chasers*

We can't fake authenticity. When we are really ourselves we are defenceless, we flow, we draw people, situations, and events to us. Authenticity is speaking and living our truth in the world. Authenticity is living our life according to our inner voice, marching to our own drum, and is the sum total of all that we are. The more we can drop the masks that conceal what we thought was unacceptable about us, the more we can appreciate ourselves as a unique and creative force in the world. We can stand tall, embracing the world within and the world without. The more we reclaim our lost shadow parts to be more whole and complete, the more authentic we become. Authenticity is all about ceasing to hide our

267

perceived flaws, and being willing to show our gifts and positive qualities to the world. We are authentic when we show our completeness. This is not a one-off exercise that can be completed in a day, but a constant journey, as there are always new levels of authenticity, new depths of understanding and experience to reach.

When we act the opposite way to how we actually think, feel and believe we disempower ourselves hugely. We can easily feel like a fraud, as if we are going to get found out. Authenticity means creating a greater congruence within us. Raj was a successful businessman, very spiritual and devoted to his family, his company and to helping people. He acted very abundantly. 'If I am honest, though, I still feel like I am wearing a mask, there are areas where I still feel a little inauthentic,' he confided in me. 'It may sound funny, but I force myself to act abundantly at times, but there is a part of me that is terrified that there isn't enough to go around. There is a part of me that is really hooked into scarcity and lack, although most people would never see that within me.' We can't just bolt spiritual solutions onto deeper psychic wounds, we need to attend to and begin to heal some of those places where we have unhelpful beliefs and painful feelings in order to be truly congruent.

AUTHENTICITY IS BEING HONEST ABOUT WHERE WE ARE STILL CAUGHT IN FEAR

We all suffer from fear and guilt, but we serve no-one by lying to ourselves or hiding from ourselves. A valuable skill we can develop is to be honest, both to ourselves and to others, without putting ourselves down. To have fearful thinking is a fact, not a judgement. It is an inevitable part of being human. Once we are able to accept this fact, we can ask for help to undo and transform our thinking. When we are caught in judgement, our power is diminished. But it takes great courage to be that vigorously honest with ourselves. It means to be a real spiritual warrior. It is a big challenge to make friends with ourselves.

ACCEPTING AND FACING OUR FEAR

Helen called me for coaching support in some changes she was making to her career. Her first words were, 'But I don't want to have to face my fears.' I was a bit stumped, and then said, 'Perhaps it is time to start facing your fears.' There was a shocked silence, and I had the feeling she wished she was talking to someone else. 'But I have spent so much of my life trying to avoid my fears!' she responded. 'Exactly. You've led a safe life, and now you are telling me that you are bored. Facing your fears will open your heart, bring you alive again, help you find your true motivation, and help you build self-esteem and your power,' I suggested. 'Oh!' Helen replied.

A life spent avoiding our fears is a life only half lived. I am not suggesting that we be reckless and masochistically make ourselves do things we are afraid of and that we don't want to do. In my experience our soul is always calling us to new territory, and our ego mind is always throwing up new fears. So often what scares us calls to us. Fear is often our ego's response to our heart's desires, to our purest intentions. When we begin to understand this, we look at fear differently, seeing it as a signpost to each new gift that our ego is trying to keep out of our reach. Every fear beckons us to greater happiness, deeper fulfilment and abundance.

Helen had recognized her need to move away from what was no longer fulfilling her authentic self. She had resigned from a job in retailing and had taken the first brave steps; now she was being called to a further step, which was to decide and create the life that really she was meant to live.

FRUSTRATION IS A NEW BIRTHING PLACE

Often frustration is a sign of repressed personal power, of a new birth, and of energies we are trying to deny or repress. But we can channel so much energy into holding ourselves back and refusing to acknowledge the calling of our soul. Our soul always wants to break through fear and guilt, and is waiting to free itself from old emotional patterns. I remember having a period when my work wasn't flowing as well as it had and I was feeling quite angry and frustrated. In my view, too few people were coming to my seminars and when I asked myself what was going on the answer came, 'You are playing too small a game. There are lots of ideas, insights and honesty that you are *not* yet sharing with people. You are holding yourself back through fear. Move through the fear, play a bigger game and you'll get back into the flow.' Pretty clear guidance, and something we covered in more detail in Chapter 2.

When I thought about the message I realized that there was a lot that I had written about in my books that I had rarely or never talked about in my seminars. There was a lot of *me* that I wasn't sharing. I suddenly became aware of a whole new area of material that I had to share, and an accompanying new level of fear to clear from my path. I really wanted to talk much more about love and fear, God and spirituality, especially in the corporate world. My ego kept whispering to me *Talk openly about that stuff and you will be persecuted, they'll reject and crucify you! Stay small and you'll be safe.* That was enough to keep me quiet for years! Yet I knew I was resisting this new birth, and that I couldn't be happy unless I dealt with these fears and moved through them. It took me a few weeks to do that, and as I did I gained greater fulfilment. I felt more authenticity, my self-esteem rose because I was being true to myself and new opportunities were opened to me.

EXERCISE

＊　*Where are you feeling most frustrated right now?*

＊　*Ask yourself intuitively 'What am I afraid to be right now?' Listen to the answer and imagine yourself embracing this instead. Be willing to embrace it.*

WHY DO WE BECOME INAUTHENTIC?

What do we do when we are not being authentic? We seek approval, rather than speak our truth; we play politics rather than speak honestly; we say what we think people want to hear rather than what we want to say. There is so much pressure for us to be *inauthentic*. It is not wrong to be inauthentic, but we rob ourselves of a lot. The message is that compensations don't work. They don't make us happy and fulfilled. Roles don't make us happy. We can play the role of the successful person and still feel a failure. Indeed, the roles we play stop us really connecting. Some people don't want our roles, they don't even necessarily want to be impressed; what they want is the real us, what they want is to be inspired by our authenticity. They want our heart, and they want our real feelings. When we live an authentic life we make our soul visible, and that is both powerful and beautiful.

GEORGE HARRISON

On 30 November 2001 I was just getting ready to set off on my first trip to South Africa when the news broke that George Harrison had died in Los Angeles. Like many people, I was very sad. I felt he had been a great light in the world and had the courage to talk about his spirituality and beliefs, often in the face

271

of ridicule. He had inspired me by his openness and his authenticity. What moved me even more was his message to the world as he died. Harrison's family issued a statement saying: 'He left this world as he lived in it, conscious of God, fearless of death, and at peace, surrounded by family and friends. He often said, "Everything else can wait but the search for God cannot wait," and "Love one another."'

I cried, both with sadness and joy. His message was such a gift. The BBC newsreaders, usually talking about wars and suffering, kept repeating George's last words for the next 24 hours and for a day or two it felt as if the world had positively shifted on its axis. We were suddenly hearing and talking about what really mattered – love. The media were being used to share messages of love and inspiration, even in the midst of the sadness of his death. I wished that the media could be used in such ways every day. Something about George Harrison's life and work struck me as being very powerful.

AUTHENTICITY IS CONGRUENCY

Authenticity is about creating congruency between our inner and outer worlds. For many of us, what goes on inside us, and what we show to the world, have a certain incongruence. The less our outer life is connected to our inner life, the more conflict we experience, the weaker we are; the more our outer life is connected to our inner world, the more powerful and at peace we become.

Authentic sharing is what brings us to life, inspires us and gives us hope. It's not just about sharing our pain or problems but also our joy and wonderful experiences. It connects us to other people, it penetrates and melts our defences. In a world so full of sound-bites, platitudes, roles and often lies, real honesty – real authenticity – is like desert rain, precious and potentially life saving.

My friend Kathy was having a difficult time with one of her friends. Kathy had asked her friend to be more honest with her and to share her feelings, and her friend responded, 'But if I told people what I really thought of them I wouldn't have any friends at all.' We often mistake being real with dumping our judgements and unexpressed anger on someone. In fact, this is often what we think a friend is for – someone to blame for how we feel! We need to learn that our feelings are *our* feelings – other people may stimulate them, but they are our feelings. Owning our feelings is crucial on the path of living an authentic life.

A number of people I know are drawn to working in hospices and with the dying, and perhaps this is because in death all the masks come down, and we get really real. I had the honour of being with my partner Helen when her aunt Zena died. Holding her hand and stroking her forehead, telling her we loved her and it was OK for her to go, was a profoundly moving and, in a strange way, a very beautiful experience. I felt as if my heart was ripped wide open, and to help her in her transition was tremendously gratifying. I felt I received a huge gift from Zena in her death. Perhaps our lesson is to learn to be that open and authentic with our feelings in life as well as in death.

AUTHENTIC SELF-EXPRESSION IS THE BASIS OF ALL SUCCESS

Many people want the rewards of spiritual upliftment and inspiration, but by this they do not mean crying their hearts out, or sharing their vulnerability, or grieving over lost love, or whooping with joy. But this is what normal people do. They are in touch with themselves, and spirituality is only an extension of being normal.

DEEPAK CHOPRA, *The Path to Love*

INSIDE OUT

Many people seem to hold their lives together. They've invested a lot of time and money in their appearance, looking good and being seen in all the right places. Inside they may live a different life, one of doubt, fear or guilt. We need to learn to tell our truth. Our ego may convince us that if we tell the truth we will be rejected, when the reverse is often true. When we tell our truth, people feel drawn to us, they resonate with us. And often they actually know that we've built a convincing façade. Façades help us keep secrets safe, keep us apparently safe, hidden and ultimately separated from true fulfilment. Secrets separate and corrode. However dark a secret, once it is in the open, healing and correction can occur, solutions to problems can be found.

THE POWER OF INTEGRITY

Authenticity and integrity are twin traits, but often when we want to live with integrity we feel confused, with conflicting desires and emotions. In my own life my own sense of integrity has been challenged. One time, I had agreed to make a presentation to a group in the west of England. Two weeks before the event, someone else asked me to come and make a presentation to their audience, and offered me five times as much money. My initial reaction was immediate – 'I cannot do it, I am already committed, and cannot change this.' Then I realized that I actually needed the extra money at that time, and was a bit tired of putting other people's needs before my own. I felt torn apart, but sat for a while, and just observed all my thoughts and feelings.

I decided to call Sally, the organizer of the first event, to explain to her what my situation was, to see what the consequence would be if I changed my mind. She said it would be inconvenient to change the event, but it would not be impossible, although obviously she'd rather I didn't. I asked myself, 'What is my own truth? What do I really want?' My answer was to take the new engagement and rearrange the first one. I felt awful. Although it was what I really wanted I felt very guilty at the inconvenience I would cause. I was torn between being authentic and playing the role of being *good*.

I said a prayer, then called Sally back and told her that I was going to go for the new engagement, expecting her to be angry with me. She listened and said it would be a problem, but she really appreciated my honesty, and that I hadn't lied to her or made excuses. I felt a great relief because I was being authentic, and at the end of the conversation Sally said to me, 'Well done for honouring your truth.' I was stunned. There I was causing her inconvenience, and she was telling me *well done!* Within a few hours she had called me back and we had fixed a new date for the event, and we were back on again. I had never done anything like that before, and have not done so since, but it taught me a lot about the power of being authentic.

AUTHENTIC INTENTIONS

It all comes down to intention. As William Blake once said, 'A truth that's told with bad intent beats all the lies you can invent.' Buddhists suggest that before any communication we should ask ourselves, 'Is it true? Is it kind? Is it necessary?' When we want to be authentic with the intention, not of blaming, but of joining with other people, solving problems, or creating flow, we have good intention. Too often we only communicate when we are angry and when we want to blame.

We often equate authenticity with anger. We can spend much of our time being compliant, not upsetting bosses or partners, or pleasing people, and then there comes a time when we have had enough and we switch. All that we've been storing up comes flooding out. And whilst this is one form of authenticity, true authenticity goes deeper. Authenticity is concerned with our *true* feelings in their many hues and colours: joy, beauty, love, happiness, sadness, anger, grief, depression, tenderness, empathy. In fact, in the dictionary there are over 3,000 different words that describe the various emotional states that we can experience.

When someone is authentic, it often disarms us, we don't know how to respond. An Argentinian friend of mine told me a story of an event in her own country. The military had long been suspected of assassinating people and orchestrating many disappearances. Under increasing pressure, the leadership made an announcement and an apology. Yes, they had killed people; yes, they had tortured. They acknowledged this, and publicly apologized. This threw the country into confusion. Many wanted revenge, others applauded their honesty and thought these people could now be trusted.

AUTHENTICALLY POWERFUL PEOPLE ARE WILLING

Being willing could be called the one true act of 'being'. It calls forth who you are in your heart and transcends the chattering of your Monkey Mind. Being willing is your ticket to a life of creativity, power and fulfilment. It will change the course of your life.

MARIA NEMETH, author of *The Energy of Money*

Being willing is simply the power to say 'Yes' in a growing variety of situations, when things go well, but also in the midst of doubts, crises, worries, fear, dislikes, objections and every other obstacle that our ego mind is likely to throw up. Yet we may be proud of our ability to say 'No!', and see it as the source of our greatest power. Developmental psychologists observe that 'No' is one of the first words that we use at two years old to differentiate ourselves from our parents, and some of us pride ourselves on being able to continue saying 'No' for the rest of our lives. Being willing is our choice of 'Yes', of growth, of joy, to open all life's opportunities and experiences. To be able to say 'Yes' to whatever is in front of us, whatever is on our plate, and to recognize that *everything* is a wake-up call, is a truly powerful state of being. To resist nothing is the path to power and liberation.

Being willing is not the same as wanting. Often we need to be willing to do what we *don't* want to do. We may want to start our own business, but not want any uncertainty, yet can become willing to live with a degree of uncertainty. We may not want to grieve the loss of a loved one, but we can become willing. A pregnant woman wants to become a mother but doesn't want the pain of childbirth, but she is willing. What determines our success in any area of life is often our willingness to do what we don't want to do in order to have what we do want. This is not necessarily about making sacrifices, but *is* about stretching ourselves through uncomfortable experiences. Authentically powerful people are usually very willing, or at least willing to be willing! Just being willing to face rather than avoid a fear or discomfort can be energizing.

OUR LITTLE WILLINGNESS

Willingness seems intangible: we can't see it, touch or smell it. When we are willing, we call upon something inside us that is much greater than our ego mind; we tap into the core of our being, and this is very empowering. When we collectively adopted the belief that we were separate from our creator we were also given the power to *undo* separation. *A Course in Miracles* talks about the holy instant, which is when we are free from fear about the future, when we are free of guilt from the past; we are simply free and in the present moment. Our mind is unchained from all that has kept it imprisoned. The *Course* also teaches us: 'The holy instant does not come from your little willingness alone. It is always the result of your small willingness combined with the unlimited power of God's Will.' Our willingness has a multiplier effect. When we are willing, all power is added to our willingness, but our willingness must come from us first. Willingness to be free, willingness to surrender, willingness to no longer need to be right, willingness to forgive, willingness to give up the perceived benefits of separation and independence.

What makes willingness seem so challenging is that it means surrendering, little by little, the idea that we have a separate will and accepting the existence of a greater will, which isn't separate from us. That idea itself often engenders fear in us, as our ego doesn't want to give up its power. We think we will lose ourselves, when it in fact means that we will find our true self. The more we tap into and trust that core power, the more conscious we become and the more we can transform our life.

OUR POWER TO BE WILLING TO DO WHAT WE DON'T WANT TO DO

We have all witnessed or heard inspiring stories about people who have been willing to do what they didn't want to do. We have probably all inspired ourselves by doing something we didn't want to, and we have the capacity to make those choices every day. Vanessa had just been made redundant from a company she founded and which was taken over. She had been to an interview for a new position, but partly because she was still in shock from her redundancy she overlooked some important questions at the interview. 'I feel so stupid – I can't go back and look an idiot because I forgot to ask some basic questions,' she told me. 'Why not?' I asked. 'Oh!' she responded. She realized that she was interested in the job and the company, but needed to find out more before she could make a decision. It took her four days of hell and procrastination before she could muster the willingness to go back and ask for another meeting, to talk in more detail. When she was willing to ask, they were willing to meet her again.

Successful people are willing. They look at important questions, confront areas in which they have been unaware and challenge themselves to know and live their values. They may be afraid to look, and may not know what they will find, but they do it anyway. They may not always want to, but they know the pain involved in living out of integrity with themselves. To *be* willing is drawing on a part of who we are, a strength that comes from our centre, our core.

If we are willing we have the power to bypass our ego mind, and act anyway. We can say, 'I am afraid, I am doubting, I am unclear, I feel unworthy, and I am going to do it anyway.' Being willing is a great affront to our ego, because it loses control. In some Buddhist teachings they call the ego our *Monkey Mind*. It throws up all the questions, and all the disempowering thoughts. Being willing allows us to be powerful at any point in our life, as it draws on our core nature, which is always constant and never diminished. The difference between a psychological and more spiritual approach is that psychology suggests analysing and probing our thoughts and feelings, while a more spiritual approach suggests that *observing* rather than analysing has great power. We can become more of a witness to them. We can notice *without* analysing and being hooked. We can say, 'Ah look, there's fear, hello fear, I am going to speak anyway,' or 'Hello doubt, welcome back, but I think I'll make this decision anyway.' Both analysing and observing have power and their place, and there are times when we have over-analysed something, and need to be willing to change anyway. Sometimes we can become so distracted by our own psychology that we never take authentic action. Without awareness we have no choice; with awareness, a whole new world of choice opens up to us.

WHERE ARE YOU UNWILLING?

EXERCISE

* *In what areas of your life can you notice unwillingness right now? Around relationships? Change? Money? Health?*
* *Write a list of what you know you don't want to do. Then, next to each one, write a yes or no to whether you would be willing to do this, even though you don't want to.*

We cannot go on our own heroic journey because we are forced to, but only because we have chosen to, and are willing to. Being willing is a never-ending opportunity; each moment offers us chances to be willing and unwilling.

Forgiveness is an authentic action for the courageous heart to engage in. It comes when we realize the price that we pay for our resentment, our anger and our judgements. Every unforgiven place within us hides the love in us and from us, and every forgiven place lets us know who we really are in our heart.

AUTHENTICITY CREATES TRUST

When someone is honest and authentic with us, even in difficult times, we begin to build up a trust in them. Julia McCutchen was my publisher at Element Books, and my commissioning editor when I was in the process of becoming a published author for the first time. She was the one who saw the potential in my writing and offered me my first publishing deal. I had enjoyed working with her, and there seemed a real resonance between us. I was looking forward to a long, fruitful and mutually beneficial relationship and was obviously very upset when she was badly hurt by a falling lighting gantry at a sales conference in Cyprus. She was off work for nearly a year after that, and I didn't have much contact with her.

Our next real contact was when she rang me to let me know that Element was having major financial problems and was looking either for finance or a buyer to take them over. I was concerned but trusted that everything would work out OK. I went off to run a course at the Skyros centre in Greece, and in the next conversation we had Julia informed me that the company had been unable to secure a buyer or to secure any further finance, and Element was going into receivership. I had a long conversation with her on my mobile phone at my B&B in Skyros town, and then, feeling devastated by the news, returned to my room and cried my eyes out. My book that was doing so well would no longer be available for sale.

Yes, I was upset but also grateful for the way that Julia handled the situation. She was losing her own job, the company she had built up over 13 years, and was having similar conversations with many other authors, but she still found the time to talk to me, to explain the situation and to express her feelings of sadness and guilt at the inconvenience all this was causing. Although what she told me shocked me, it also served me. She never once lied to me, she never withheld information, and she never tried to gloss over any of the problems. Julia explained how receivership worked, to the best of her knowledge, and made herself available whenever I wanted to speak to her. I was grateful for her willingness to stay engaged with me, share the journey, share the pain and most importantly to be honest and authentic. I really admired her integrity in handling such a difficult situation. And I knew I could trust her.

Over the following months, we met up several times to share notes and swap stories, and hear each other's progress. Luckily my book came back into print within six months, with HarperCollins, not the 12–18 months I had been told it would take. As her health improved, Julia resumed her career, and went to work as a publishing consultant for another major publisher. After a year she felt strongly that it was time to move on and set up her own business. We began to throw a few ideas around. I had a regular flow of people asking me to guide them in their publishing process, and Julia and I often discussed the needs of would-be and already published authors, and how much inspiration, support, information and encouragement they need.

Julia knew how much valuable experience and knowledge she had of UK non-fiction publishing, so she started FireFly Media, a publishing and communications business offering skills and consultancy to publishers and authors. She and I also started to develop some ideas for running events to inspire authors to write and present their creativity to publishers.

Initially through Alternatives, and now through other avenues too, we are developing a programme called 'The Book We Were Born To Write' to support authors. We enjoy working together, and part of what makes our relationship strong is that I know I can trust Julia to be authentic and honest with me, and she knows she can be sure of me. This makes our relationship precious and strong. We have been through the fire together and we have survived, and, more than that, flourished.

THE POWER OF 'I' OPENS THE DOOR TO OUR AUTHENTIC NEEDS AND WANTS

An element of authenticity is knowing what we really want so that we stop trying to fool ourselves and be honest with ourselves. Mari had spent 25 years as a nurse, working hard, treating herself to nice holidays every year, following a path of her own personal and spiritual growth. Otherwise she seemed to deny herself many pleasures, and put her energy into the accident unit where she worked. She seemed a bit of a loner.

When I met Mari she seemed quite serious, even depressed. 'It's just what you are supposed to do,' she explained. 'Life is tough and you just have to work hard, that is how it is. I have a huge fear of my money running out.' She seemed to be quite driven by a sense of duty and obligation and even fear, and not that aware of what *she* wanted. As we talked I began to see that there was a whole other side to Mari. She had a number of women friends who were successful entrepreneurs, and she enjoyed a gamble. She had also just inherited some money, and was beginning to play with the possibility of buying a property to rent out. She had trained in health and beauty and as she talked about these things her energy lifted and she started smiling for the first time. I offered her an exercise. 'Why don't you make a list of what you would really and truly love, and start each with either "I want to" or "I would love to".' A light went on inside her. She started off:

- *I want to finish nursing*
- *I would love to buy a flat, do it up beautifully and rent it out*
- *I would love to have a number of properties that I own and rent out*
- *I want to move to the north of England to be near my family*
- *I want to become more entrepreneurial*
- *I'd love to train as a manicurist, and give beauty treatments*
- *I would love to buy myself a beautiful blue BMW*
- *I want to have fun*
- *I want to help people*
- *I want a lovely man in my life*
- *I want to free myself of my money worries*
- *I want to make a lot more money*
- *I want to have a great life that I am proud of*
- *I want more adventure and excitement in my life*

What she wrote seemed honest and showed that underneath her serious and dutiful side there was a raft of attributes that she'd kept repressed, that she never really let out but that were actually her source of energy. There was an entrepreneurial side to her that she'd hidden. No-one had seemed to encourage these parts. It was almost as if she needed someone to say to her, 'You have suffered and sacrificed enough – now you can enjoy your life.' Mari had a tremendous sense of service. She loved helping people, but had confused service with sacrifice and was suddenly realizing that she could serve people by being happy, and by doing what she loved too. She told me, 'I thought that a life of self-denial was good for me, but am beginning to see that a life of giving myself what I want might be more fun!'

There was tremendous power for Mari in owning her loves, being honest about her desires, rather than denying what she authentically loved and wanted. Over the next few months she really went for it: she put her house on the market, started exploring properties to buy for renting, and even went to a BMW dealership to decide the model she would love. It was such a joy to see her shift into honouring and expressing the neglected parts of her. Her power was in knowing what she wanted, and then in working out how to make it all happen.

There is incredible power in saying 'I'. Whether it is *I want, I am, I feel, I love, I hate*. As children we may have got messages that we were selfish if we talked about 'I' too much, that we should always focus on others. Yet in the spiritual world there is a great tendency to say that the 'I' is an illusion, it is all ego, and ultimately this is true: focusing on ourselves is selfish and only leads to un-happiness. Our focus should be on others. But I don't think we can transcend our ego and personality until we have fully formed it. To recognize our divinity we also have to recognize our humanity in all its fullness.

When we mould and distort ourselves into a shape we think others want us to be we distance ourselves from our internal energy source. Once we begin to tap into our own authenticity, we have connected to an incredible reservoir of energy and creativity. This is the power of our inspiration.

OUR POWER TO MAKE MONEY AUTHENTICALLY

Mastering our personal relationship with money is, in fact, one of the great spiritual challenges of our time.

K. BRADFORD BROWN, co-founder of The Life Training Programme

A major challenge for many spiritual seekers is the area of making money on our spiritual path. We have many confused ideas about what it means to be spiritual and often struggle to take our spirituality beyond our meditation times and live it fully in the remainder of our life. To be authentic is to acknowledge both our material and spiritual needs. Too often we have been taught to deny or repress our spiritual and emotional needs in order to earn our living, or we let our spiritual and creative expression take its full place, but deny our need to live well. We think we have to sacrifice the money for the love, or the love for the money. There is little likelihood that our life will function with true prosperity unless we develop a healthy, positive and creative attitude towards money. We may have the highest intentions, but if we have not resolved our money issues we quickly lose our momentum when the bills and the bank statement arrive.

To be authentic we need to realize a third way, which is to live from the highest place within us, where money is no longer compensation for doing something we don't love, but an *extra* reward for doing what we do love. In this authentic place, no sacrifice is called for or needed. But, as we've seen, God demands no sacrifice – it is we who believe so deeply and passionately in sacrifice. On our journey of authenticity around money, we may well be confronted with and called to heal this thinking that demands sacrifice and that is deeply engrained within us. To be authentically successful and powerful demands *giving up* sacrifice.

OUR POWER OF INSPIRATION

We are no longer ambitious for ourselves, but rather are inspired by the vision of a healed world. Inspiration rearranges our energies. It sources within us a new power and direction. We no longer feel like we're trying to carry the ball to the finishing line, clutching it to our chest and surrounded by hostile forces. We feel instead as though angels are pushing us from behind and making straight our path as we go.

MARIANNE WILLIAMSON, author of *A Return to Love*

Inspiration is electricity that is always available to anyone who understands how to flick the switch. It is the power that transports us from the mire of struggle and sacrifice to the higher ground of ease and grace. To be authentic is to be inspiring and to be inspiring is to be authentic. I like to use the word 'inspired' to describe people who listen to their hearts, or to their inner longings, and live an impassioned life from that place inside themselves. In doing so they create inner fulfilment, and send out ripples of resonance to the hearts of others.

Inspiration can also describe moments of beauty such as a sunset, the rapture of a piece of music, or the connection with a friend or loved one, or helping someone grow or develop. Inspiration touches something of value in us, that goes beyond material gratification. It is concerned with our soul: it is a deep quality that goes beneath the surface of what we do, but is visible in what we do. Inspiration reaches to the core of our existence. Where there is inspiration there is affirmation and encouragement of the evolution of life. Inspiration both creates and sustains life.

The wonderful thing about being inspired is that it doesn't need to be forced. When we are playing roles we often need to force ourselves to be a particular way, or to do things that we would rather not be doing. We go *against* our true nature. When we are inspired we are *coming from* our true nature. We access a reservoir of energy and motivation that is truly limitless – the divine energy and creativity within us. Inspiration fills us up, and we can easily become less needy; consequently we have more time to help others. It takes us beyond ourselves. We have more energy available for satisfaction, not just survival. Inspiration reaches to that deepest desire in us to mean something to the people and world around us. We radiate a different kind of energy to people who are not inspired. We have room to inspire others too.

ROLE MODELS FOR INSPIRATION

Are you surrounded by people that inspire you? Do you have many or any people in your life that inspire you?

EXERCISE

* *Who has inspired me in my life so far?*
* *What aspects of them inspired me?*
* *Who is inspiring you now in your life?*
* *Who inspires you as a manager? Teacher? Parent? Friend? Small business owner? Lover?*
* *Who inspires you in your organization?*

If you struggle with answers, create a project to find some: you will find them if you look. We also have to be vigorously honest with ourselves sometimes and acknowledge that we may be more comfortable with cynicism and criticism. If so, are you willing to give it up to find your creativity?

While great leaders may be competent, technically efficient, talented and high achievers, their most admirable qualities – like openness, honesty, love, courage, integrity, trust and authenticity – have more to do with who they are than with what they do as professionals. What we do is transient: who we are in essence never slips away.

INSPIRATION IS RELATIONAL AND NOT ABSOLUTE

We all find different people and circumstances inspiring. There is probably very little that we *all* find inspiring. Even if we take Nelson Mandela, whom the majority of people find inspiring, if we asked why, we'd probably discover that our reasons are diverse and manifold. What we see in someone, what they move and stir in us, is subjective and unique to us.

BEING AN UNCONSCIOUSLY INSPIRING PERSON

Most people don't set out to be an inspiring role model; their inspiration comes from being true to themselves, to committing themselves to their own loves and passions, what they truly believe in. Their impact on us may be partly a *by-product* of them living their own authentic life. Through their life, they have touched something in us and brought something intangible to life in us. They have touched our soul in some way.

BRINGING LIGHT TO THE DARK

Inspiration is not just an *up* thing. Some of the most inspiring things in life relate to how people cope with pain and difficulty. Inspiration is not found in the absence of shadows, but in the acceptance of shadows as part of our life. I find facing and acknowledging our shadow inspiring, integrating parts of us that we have judged or neglected. To be inspired does not mean producing painting after painting without effort, or writing six books without a pause. It means having the courage to accept and give expression to that which is in us, and *all* that is within us.

Nilesh inspired me. When he told me his story, I was moved to tears. He was with his wife when she was shot dead by a mugger. Very little could be more horrifying. When I met him it was two years since this happened. In the midst of his grief, he asked himself what gift there might be in the pain he was experiencing, what purpose there might be. Even to ask this question showed incredible courage. The answer came to him: 'To teach people how to deal with grief and write a book about how to deal with grief.' He was talking openly about his experiences, the pain and the healing, and I was inspired by his willingness to be honest and continue with his life. When I met him he had received a book offer to write about his experiences and the wonderful work he is now doing.

SOMETIMES YOU JUST REALIZE

Maureen seemed a bit sheepish. 'I have been in career management for many years, but in the last two weeks I have suddenly realized that this is not really me any more.' 'So what have you come to realize?' I asked. 'It sounds crazy, but I want to help with death and dying. This idea has been bubbling away in my consciousness for nearly five years, but it's suddenly clicked into place. But I keep wondering who am I to think about doing something like this?' When I asked her why she felt called to do this work, she replied, 'I didn't have a good relationship with my father for most of my life. He was a harsh man, and unable to show much affection. But as he was dying of cancer, we began to become friends. I experienced real forgiveness. I realized that love and forgiveness are the only things that really matter, and would love to help other people find the peace that I found.'

Maureen's experience is very familiar. With a sense of purpose is also born a sense of doubt and self-questioning, even self-attack. We try to deny our sense of purpose and pretend just to be human, trying to satisfy ourselves with material things alone when we know that our soul is calling out for more. We feel different, but we try to bury our difference away, rather than valuing it. But our purpose is a promise we made, and we will never be fulfilled until we keep our promise. When we turn around and say yes to our purpose, the doors to creative abundance begin to fly open. The more we start to give, the more we are given to give. We begin to experience the joy of true service. As we awaken compassion within us, we naturally begin to extend ourselves and feel the desire to genuinely serve the world. The energies of our growth, our contribution and our healing all become intertwined.

When we begin to follow our call, inspiration and ideas come to us, a new confidence awakens in us, opportunities wash up on the shore; people take an interest in us and what we are doing. We spy synchronicities and the right book, the right connection gets made. Sometimes even the money follows. As the author Gregg Levoy says, 'Perhaps it's nothing more mysterious than the universe supporting growth, and life loving itself.'

I saw a BBC TV programme called *Correspondent*, which each month makes an in-depth investigation into some social issue. This particular programme was called 'Killers Don't Cry', and was concerned with Mogamat Benjamin and Erefaan Jacobs, two inmates of Poolsmoor prison in South Africa. The two men were leaders of a prison gang, and perpetrators of serious violence which had been the reason for their prison sentences, and had continued their violence within prison.

The programme charted the impact of an intervention by a woman called Joanna Thomas, who worked for Cape Town's

Centre for Conflict Resolution. It took her many days to break down the men's suspicion, and then get them to talk about their families, wives and children. She said, 'The key is to form relationships and build trust, which is not easy in an environment where there is so much fear and suspicion. I was never afraid and I do a lot of self-preparation before I go into the prison to clear myself of negativity and ask God to fill me with compassion.'

The men were due to be released, and everyone was expecting that once this happened they would reoffend, returning to the cycle of violence, and end up back in prison. Joanna offered to help them see if they could begin to renounce violence, and turn themselves around, and return to the outside with another, and more healthy, way of being. The programme was at times breathtaking as it showed the workshops where these men were forced, for the first time ever, to confront themselves and examine the evil that had so blighted them and their lives.

Many people thought Joanna was mad even to attempt to work with them. The men did threaten to kill her, but she was fearless and unperturbed. What I found so moving was that underneath all their toughness, all their defences and all their bluster, these were men in pain, hurting, eaten away by guilt and regret, so ashamed of themselves that they couldn't believe that anyone would believe in them or want to help them. When Joanna got them to talk about their fathers, the floodgates really opened. Neither of them could remember a single act of male affection in their upbringing. At this point it seemed that humanity seeped back into the seemingly dehumanized men. That is what motives Joanna Thomas to come back into this place day after day. 'I am not so naïve as to believe that one series of workshops can change a man who has been in the heart of the gang system for most of his life. But I see a struggle and as long as I see it I am prepared to engage with it. I have no doubt that men like Mogamat and Erefaan can be transformed but it will involve a lot of hard work and a real will on the part of the community and society at large. They have a purpose to fulfil on earth.'

The men felt unlovable and had written themselves off. Many people would say, 'And so they should be, they should be ashamed of themselves, they have done wrong,' but this doesn't solve the problem. All judgement does is simply perpetuate the problem. We feel bad and guilty, so we act bad and guilty to try and rid ourselves of the feelings, but then we create more guilt and self-attack and this only continues the cycle. In the end we can feel we just want to die, that this is the only way out, and all we deserve. Joanna said, 'I've seen dramatic change and that inspires me to continue with the work. My one message is that change begins with me.'

TRUSTING IN THE INVISIBLE

We cannot wait for inspiration, nor can we control it, and for some people this creates an incredible tension. 'You mean you want me to hitch myself to a force that I cannot see or touch, manipulate or control? And then you want me to build the foundations of my life on it?' And I answer, 'Yes!' To live through and by inspiration, we do need to develop a new relationship with the invisible world around us and within us. We can cultivate inspiration, we can initiate it. An artist I met on a trip to South Africa told me, 'I don't always get inspired to do my art, but often when I start doing my art, I get inspired.' She had found her way of living with that mystery and forging an inner connection to her own soul. She had become a willing partner and host to inspiration.

TRUST IS INSPIRING

I was amazed to hear recently that in Hatton Garden, the gold and jewellery centre of London, the majority of business is still done completely on trust. When two people agree a price for diamonds, they shake hands, but no contract is drawn up, and initially no money changes hands. They simply trust each other. That trust is not naïve, it has been built up over years and through establishing a reputation for integrity. Without that, the traders simply couldn't do business any more. The trust that their integrity has built up is the core of their ability to do business. I was very touched by this. In these days of corporate scandals, greed and selfishness, it is wonderful to hear of a whole industry operating on trust.

EXERCISE

* *What are some of the most inspiring examples of trust you have witnessed in your life?*
* *Who do you most trust?*
* *When have you most trusted yourself?*
* *Where are you being called to trust more? In what?*

To trust is our choice. The greatest trust is not in anything outside of us, but in the deepest part of our own nature, the love and divinity at the heart of us. Trust is like love – if it's not unconditional, it's not really trust. Most people are worthy of our trust. If we start by thinking this, our life will be much stronger. Sure, not everyone can deal with being trusted. There will be people who lie and take advantage of good will, but this behaviour damages them spiritually as much as it does you materially.

Our trust in others creates trust in us. We can make people feel so trusted and valued that they respond in that way. I heard the story of a woman whose great fear was to be caught alone in the underground at night. She feared being attacked or assaulted. One night travelling home, that very thing happened: she was alone in a carriage when some guys got on who looked as if they might attack her. Suddenly she had an intuition, and approached the men. She said, 'I am a woman alone, and am afraid that I might be attacked. Would you look after me?' The guys looked a little stunned but were actually flattered to be asked and did a wonderful job of looking after, not attacking, her. She placed her trust in them, and they responded.

CONCLUSION

The spiritual path is a journey without distance, to a place we never left.

Anon.

The journey of recovering our personal and spiritual power is the journey back to our very being, to the home that is and always has been within us. It is exciting and full of adventures. It is the journey of remembering that this world holds nothing that we truly want and nothing of value. It is remembering that everything we want and everything we are is already inside us, now and eternally. It is learning to see this world with new eyes, the eyes of love and forgiveness, not judgement and condemnation. It is realizing that there is nothing really to do and everything to be. It is the journey to the joy that lies within your very heart. I wish you every success: you cannot fail to succeed in your journey home. The whole universe is behind you.

BIBLIOGRAPHY

I can personally recommend all the books and tapes below to inspire and uplift you on your journey of unconditional success.

A Course in Miracles, Penguin Arkana, 1975

Allen, James, *As a Man Thinketh*, De Vorss and Co., 1977

Autry, James and Mitchell, Stephen, *Real Power,* Nicholas Brealey, 1998

Ban Breathnach, Sarah, *Simple Abundance*, Bantam, 1997

Barks, Coleman, *The Essential Rumi*, HarperCollins, 1995

Berke, Diane, *Love Always Answers*, Crossroads, 1994

Britten, Rhonda, *Fearless Living*, Hodder and Stoughton, 2002

Cameron, Julia, *The Artist's Way*, Pan Books, 1994

Cameron, Julia, *Walking in the World*, Rider, 2002

Campbell, Joseph and Moyars, Bill, *The Power of Myth*, Bantam, 1988

Caplan, Mariana, *The Way of Failure – Winning through Losing*, Hohm Press, 2001

Carpenter, Tom, *Dialogue on Awakening*, Carpenter Press, 1992

Chopra, Deepak, *The Seven Spiritual Laws of Success*, New World Library, 1994

Chopra, Deepak, *The Path to Love*, Random House, 1998

Cohen, Alan, *Handle with Prayer*, Hay House, 1999

Dass, Ram, *Still Here*, Little Brown, 2002

Dossy, Dr Larry, *Prayer is Good Medicine*, HarperCollins, 1997

Eichman, William Carl, *Meeting Darkness on the Path*, Gnosis, 1990

Ford, Debbie, *The Dark Side of the Light Chasers*, Hodder Mobius, 2001

Gallwey, Timothy, *The Inner Game of Work*, Texere Publishing, 2002

Gladwell, Malcolm, *The Tipping Point*, Abacus, 2000

Haskell, Brent, *Journey beyond Words*, De Vorss, 1994

Haskell, Brent, *The Other Voice*, De Vorss, 1997

Hendricks, Gay, and Luderman, Kate, *The Corporate Mystic*, Bantam Books, 1996

Hillman, James, *The Soul's Code*, Bantam, 1997

Holden, Miranda, *Boundless Love*, Rider, 2002

Holden, Robert, *Happiness NOW!* Hodder and Stoughton, 1998

Holden, Robert, *Shift Happens*, Hodder and Stoughton, 2000

Housden, Maria, *Hannah's Gift*, HarperCollins, 2002

Jampolsky, Gerald, *Love is Letting Go of Fear*, Celestial Arts, 1979

Jampolsky, Gerald, and Cirincione, Diane, *Wake up Calls*, Hay House, 1992

Katie, Byron, *Loving What Is*, Rider, 2002

Kopp, Sheldon, *If You Meet the Buddha on the Road, Kill Him*, Sheldon Press, 1973

Levoy, Gregg, *Callings*, HarperCollins, 1997

Matthews, Andrew, *Follow Your Heart*, Seashell Publishing, 1997

Murphy, Joseph, *The Power of Your Subconscious Mind*, Bantam, 1963

Nemeth, Maria, *The Energy of Money*, Ballantine, 2000

Nobel, Steve, *Freeing the Spirit*, Rider, 2000

O'Donohue, John, *Eternal Echoes*, Bantam, 2000

Ornish, Dr Dean, *Love and Survival*, HarperCollins, 1999

Peck, M. Scott, *The Road Less Travelled*, Arrow, 1990

Prabuphad, Sri, *Your Eternal Well Wisher*,

Price, John Randolph, *The Abundance Book*, Hay House, 1987

Renshaw, Ben, *Successful But Something Missing*, Rider, 2000

Renshaw, Ben, *The Secrets*, Rider, 2002

Rinpoche, Sogyal, *The Tibetan Book of Living and Dying*, Rider, 2002

Russell, Peter, *From Science to God*, New World Library, 2000

Sanders, Tim, *Love is the Killer App*, Hodder Mobius, 2002

Siegel, Bernie, *Love, Medicine and Miracles*, Rider, 1986

Snowdon, Dr David, *Aging with Grace*, Bantam Doubleday, 2001

Spezzano, Chuck, *If It Hurts, It Isn't Love*, Hodder and Stoughton, 1999

Spezzano, Chuck, *50 Ways to Change Your Mind, Change the World*, Hodder Mobius, 2002

Tolle, Eckhart, *The Power of Now*, Hodder and Stoughton, 1999

Walsch, Neale Donald, *Conversations with God*, Hodder Mobius, 1997

Wheatley, Margaret, *Leadership and the New Science*, Berrett-Koehler, 2001

Whyte, David, *The Heart Aroused*, The Industrial Society, 1999

Whyte, David, *Crossing the Unknown Sea*, Penguin, 2001

Williams, Nick, *The Work We Were Born to Do*, Element, 1999

Williams, Nick, *The 12 Principles of the Work We Were Born to Do*, Element, 2002

Williams, Nick, *Unconditional Success*, Bantam, 2002

Williamson, Marianne, *A Return to Love*, HarperCollins, 1992

Williamson, Marianne, *Illuminata*, Rider, 1994

Williamson, Marianne, *Enchanted Love*, Rider, 1999

Williamson, Marianne, *Everyday Grace*, Bantam, 2002

Winter, Barbara, *Making a Living without a Job*, Bantam Doubleday Books, 1994

Wright, Joel, *The Mirror on Still Water*, Mind and Miracles, 1997

Zukav, Gary, *The Heart of the Soul*, Simon and Schuster, 2002

USEFUL CONTACTS AND PARTNER ORGANIZATIONS

UK

Nick Williams

The Heart at Work

PO Box 2236

London W1A 5UA

07000 781922

www.heartatwork.net

e-mail *success@heartatwork.net*

Heart at Work support products and services

Heart at Work, founded by Nick Williams, aims to serve the needs of three key groups:

1. Individuals seeking career inspiration and guidance.
2. Individuals considering or already running their own small businesses, based on their passions.
3. Organizations in the public, private and voluntary sector who want to

release the talent within their staff and inspire the best from their staff.

- Heart at Work runs regular events around the UK, and we'll happily send you a programme. Or you can look at our web site.
- One-to-one coaching with Nick Williams or a skilled colleague.
- We offer a free monthly e-newsletter with inspiration and ideas.
- Contact us for full information on how we can work with your company or conference, from a 60-minute presentation, to a year-long programme.

- **Continual learning and growth on line, wherever you are in the world.**

We offer several on-line e-mail coaching programmes. Every week for 52 weeks you will receive e-mail coaching direct from Nick Williams and Barbara Winter. There are three programmes:
The Work We Were Born To Do – 52 weeks for £35
Money and the Work We Were Born To Do: Making Our Vocation Pay – 22 weeks for £22
Dreambuilders – *unleashing your entrepreneurial spirit* (with Barbara Winter) – 52 weeks for £35
We are also continually developing new programmes.
Subscribe now at *www.emailcoaching.net*

OTHER ORGANIZATIONS MENTIONED IN THE BOOK

Alternatives
St James's Church
197 Piccadilly
London W1J 9FF
020 7287 6711
post@alternatives.org.uk
www.alternatives.org.uk

Weekly talks and workshops in the heart of London. Nick was director of Alternatives for many years.

BBC *Correspondent* programme
The stories about Joanna Thomas and the men in Poolsmore prison in South Africa can be found at: *www.bbc.co.uk/correspondent*

Brian Mills
Ark Angel
Taggs Island
Hampton
Middlesex
TW12 2HA
020 8979 9999
angelsontaggs:@yahoo.co.uk

Chantal Cook
Passion for the Planet radio station
www.passionfortheplanet.com
mail@passionfortheplanet.com

The Findhorn Foundation
The Park
Findhorn
Scotland IV36 3TZ
01309 690311
reception@findhorn.org
www.findhorn.org

Happiness Project
Elms Court
Chapel Way
Botley
Oxford OX2 9LP

01865 244414

hello@happiness.co.uk

www.happiness.co.uk

Runs the work of Nick's friends Robert Holden and Ben Renshaw

The Interfaith Seminary Office

Elms Court

Chapel Way

Botley

Oxford OX2 9LP

01865 244835

newseminary@community.org.uk

www.newseminary.org.uk

Runs the work of Nick's friend Miranda Holden

The Mankind Project

07800 133 045

www.mkp.org.uk

centredirector@mkp.org.uk

Runs spiritual warrior training courses for men. Their mission is to 'heal the world, one man at a time'. They also run courses for women.

The Miracle Network

12a Barness Court

6–8 Westbourne Terrace

London W2 3UW

020 7262 0209

info@miracles.org.uk

www.miracles.org.uk

Supports students of *A Course of Miracles*

Psychology of Vision
France Farm
Pewsey
Wiltshire SN9 6DR
01980 635199
www.psychology-of-vision.com
Supports the work of Chuck and Lency Spezzano and Jeff Allen

PARTNER ORGANIZATIONS AROUND THE GLOBE

USA

Barbara Winter
Winning Ways
PO Box 390412
Minneapolis
MN 55439
babswinter@yahoo.com
001 952 835 5647

SOUTH AFRICA

Carl Morgan
Promotor & Publicist
PO Box 51473
Waterfront
8002
Cape Town
021 685 2000
Fax 021 685 2067
journeys@iafrica.com

IRELAND

Michael Daly
The Barnabas Project
152 Willow Park Drive
Glasnevin
Dublin 11
00 353 1 842 0544
barnabas@gofree.indigo.ie

NEW ZEALAND

Liz Constable
Life Coach
12 Hollywood Ave
Titirangi
Auckland
+ 649 817 5189
goddess@planet.gen.nz

AUSTRALIA

Ian Hutchinson
Life by Design
Suite 19, 88 Helen Street
Lane Cove
NSW 2066
00 61 2 9420 8280
Fax: 00 61 2 9418 7747
www.lifebydesign.com.au
info@lifebydesign.com.au

INDEX